'This book is a rare and successful blend of ethnographic thickness and conceptual depth. The fascinating case study of economy and governance in the city of Rome is elevated to a more general discussion of informality and liminality in the economic, political and cultural fields that will be of interest to scholars across a wide range of fields, including sociology, urban studies, economic and political anthropology and Italian studies.'

Bjørn Thomassen, *Roskilde University, Denmark*

Inhabiting Liminal Spaces

This book draws together debates from two burgeoning fields, liminality and informality studies, to analyze how dynamics of rule-bending take shape in Rome today. Adopting a multiscalar and transdisciplinary approach, it unpacks how gaps and contradictions in institutional rulemaking and application force many residents into protracted liminal states marked by intense vulnerability. By merging a political economy lens with ethnographic research in informal housing, illegal moneylending, unauthorized street-vending and waste collection, the author shows that informalities are not marginal or anomalous conditions, but an integral element of the city's governance logics. Multiple actors together construct the local cultural norms, conventions and moral economies through which rule-negotiation occurs. However, these practices are ultimately unable to reconfigure historically rooted power dynamics and hierarchies. In fact, they often aggravate weak urbanites' difficulties in accessing rights and services. A study that challenges assumptions that informalities are predominantly features of developing economies or limited to specific groups and sectors, this volume's critical approach and innovative methodology will appeal to scholars of sociology and anthropology interested in social theory, urban studies and liminality.

Isabella Clough Marinaro is Associate Professor of Italian Studies at John Cabot University, Italy, where she teaches courses in sociology, urban studies, criminology, and social science research methods. She worked for many years on the political and social conditions of Roma communities in Italy and the policy processes affecting them. Her current research focuses on urban development and governance in Rome, particularly in their interconnections with changing forms of illegal and informal practices. She is the co-editor of *Italian Mafias Today: Territory, Business and Politics* and *Global Rome: Changing Faces of the Eternal City.*

Contemporary Liminality

Series editor: Arpad Szakolczai, University College Cork, Ireland.

This series constitutes a forum for works that make use of concepts such as 'imitation', 'trickster' or 'schismogenesis', but which chiefly deploy the notion of 'liminality', as the basis of a new, anthropologically-focused paradigm in social theory. With its versatility and range of possible uses rivalling mainstream concepts such as 'system', 'structure' or 'institution', liminality by now is a new master concept that promises to spark a renewal in social thought.

While charges of Eurocentrism are widely discussed in sociology and anthropology, most theoretical tools in the social sciences continue to rely on approaches developed from within the modern Western intellectual tradition, whilst concepts developed on the basis of extensive anthropological evidence and which challenged commonplaces of modernist thinking, have been either marginalised and ignored, or trivialised. By challenging the taken-for-granted foundations of social theory through incorporating ideas from major thinkers, such as Nietzsche, Dilthey, Weber, Elias, Voegelin, Foucault and Koselleck, as well as perspectives gained through modern social and cultural anthropology and the central concerns of classical philosophical anthropology Contemporary Liminality offers a new direction in social thought.

Titles in this series

15. Post-Truth Society
A Political Anthropology of Trickster Logic
Arpad Szakolczai

16. The Technologisation of the Social
A Political Anthropology of the Digital Machine
Edited by Paul O'Connor and Marius Ion Ben⊠a

17. Inhabiting Liminal Spaces
Informalities in Governance, Housing, and Economic Activity in Contemporary Italy
Isabella Clough Marinaro

For more information about this series, please visit: https://www.routledge.com/Contemporary-Liminality/book-series/ASHSER1435

Inhabiting Liminal Spaces

Informalities in Governance, Housing, and Economic Activity in Contemporary Italy

Routledge
Taylor & Francis Group
LONDON AND NEW YORK

First published 2022
by Routledge
2 Park Square, Milton Park, Abingdon, Oxon OX14 4RN

and by Routledge
605 Third Avenue, New York, NY 10158

Routledge is an imprint of the Taylor & Francis Group, an informa business

British Library Cataloguing-in-Publication Data
A catalogue record for this book is available from the British Library

Library of Congress Cataloging-in-Publication Data
Names: Marinaro, Isabella Clough, author.
Title: Inhabiting liminal spaces : informalities in governance, housing, and economic activity in contemporary Italy / Isabella Clough Marinaro.
Description: Abingdon, Oxon ; New York, NY : Routledge, 2022. |
Series: Contemporary liminality | Includes bibliographical references and index. |
Summary: "This book draws together debates from two burgeoning fields, liminality and informality studies, to analyze how dynamics of rule-bending take shape in Rome today. Adopting a multiscalar and transdisciplinary approach, it unpacks how gaps and contradictions in institutional rulemaking and application force many residents into protracted liminal states marked by intense vulnerability. By merging a political economy lens with ethnographic research in informal housing, illegal moneylending, unauthorized street-vending and waste collection, the author shows that informalities are not marginal or anomalous conditions, but an integral element of the city's governance logics. Multiple actors together construct the local cultural norms, conventions and moral economies through which rule-negotiation occurs. However, these practices are ultimately unable to reconfigure historically rooted power dynamics and hierarchies. In fact, they often aggravate weak urbanites' difficulties in accessing rights and services. A study that challenges assumptions that informalities are predominantly features of developing economies or limited to specific groups and sectors, this volume's critical approach and innovative methodology will appeal to scholars of sociology and anthropology interested in social theory, urban studies and liminality"-- Provided by publisher.
Identifiers: LCCN 2021042137 (print) | LCCN 2021042138 (ebook) |
ISBN 9780367373634 (hbk) | ISBN 9781032185620 (pbk) |
ISBN 9780429353321 (ebk)
Subjects: LCSH: Housing policy–Italy–Rome. | Housing--Italy--Rome. |
Liminality--Italy--Rome.
Classification: LCC HD7341.R65 M37 2022 (print) |
LCC HD7341.R65 (ebook) | DDC 363.5/5610945632–dc23/eng/20211029
LC record available at https://lccn.loc.gov/2021042137
LC ebook record available at https://lccn.loc.gov/2021042138

ISBN: 978-0-367-37363-4 (hbk)
ISBN: 978-1-032-18562-0 (pbk)
ISBN: 978-0-429-35332-1 (ebk)

DOI: 10.4324/9780429353321

Typeset in Times New Roman
by Taylor & Francis Books

In unfading memory of James Walston, my friend and mentor, without whom all the rest would have been impossible.

Contents

Illustrations

Figures

Tables

Acknowledgements

First, I must thank John Cabot University for giving me a one-semester sabbatical to focus exclusively on this project. My deep gratitude also goes to Bjørn Thomassen for his unwavering support and confidence in my work over so many years – I'm not sure he is aware how important his guidance has always been. I also owe a vast debt to the many colleagues, friends, and students who have given me invaluable encouragement and insights during this long journey. In particular, Giovanni Picker, who helped me unblock some important conceptual difficulties, and Ryan Powell and Cristiana Panella, who pointed out overarching patterns in the case-studies. Karen Bermann and Pamela Harris not only read and gave crucial feedback on various chapters but also sustained me through long conversations and endless walks. Paola Castelli was a wonderful research partner and co-author for chapter 6. Her lucid analysis became a crucial compass in the later phases of the book's development. I am also immensely grateful to Arpad Szakolczai for his generosity in accepting this work for the Contemporary Liminality Series, and to Neil Jordan and Alice Salt at Routledge for making the publishing process easy and painless.

A special thank you goes to the many undergraduate research assistants who helped me with numerous aspects of the book, tracking down and synthesizing materials, nudging me to write more clearly and accessibly, and providing me with sharp critiques. Across the years, they formed a great team: Eliza Hunt, Madelaine Mott, Micah Hinnergardt, Maggie Vlaj, Edoardo Guerzoni, Valeriya Barybina, Veronica Rusich, Zulema Alejandra Palacios Jaramillo, Isha Mandal, Janet Kimani, Camilla Silvi Marchini, Camilla Bottiglieri, Irene Crestanello, Giulia Ramundo, Serena Sancataldo, Ignacio Moreno Pinero, Miguel Kleinhens Pinto Basto Avides, Francesco Felici, Katherene Welsh, Maisie Rowley, Victoria Burns. Some of them became much more than just assistants: comrades-in-arms as invested in the project as I was. I have a feeling I learned more from them than they did from me. Last but certainly not least, there aren't enough thank yous to convey how grateful I am to Paolo, Chiara, and my parents for their inexhaustible patience and support.

Introduction

Rome: the informal city

The modernist fantasy that urban life and politics in advanced democracies are primarily ordered through rational, equitable, and codified rules has by now been shattered. Aside from the many aspects of collective life that continue to be organized through unwritten customary logics, when formal rules do exist, they always carry with them elements of malleability. Rules can overlap and contradict each other. Gaps between them offer rich opportunities for interpretation; they can be bent, negotiated, ignored, and selectively executed. Knowing how to effectively play with the rule, how far one can go in doing so, is a matter of social mastery (Herzfeld, 2021). That there is often a disconnect between the letter of the law/rule and its application is, of course, nothing new. However, the last decade has seen an explosion of investigations into the multitude of manifestations that this informality – this weaving through and around regulatory constraints – can take. These studies clearly show that informality is not anarchy; it is not formlessness or lack of systematicity. Rather, it is a patterned collection of behaviours and power dynamics that are emerging as a defining feature of contemporary economic and political relations around the world.

This book takes those discussions forward by focusing on one city – Rome – within which navigations around official rules are historically rooted practices, but also behaviours that shape and reflect social and power relations today. For some residents, moreover, these practices can become inescapable as their circumstances force them to live between formal rules, suspended in a protracted liminal state where clarity of status remains out of reach. Informalities are understood here not as something external to the established order, but an integral part of the city's complex of intensely interdependent relationships, where political and social negotiations unfold across countless networks and layers, and where economic connections span from the very local to the global. I argue that it is at the single urban level that we can most effectively analyze the reciprocal influences and pressures through which rules are built, contested, bent, and reshaped. It is the scale at which we can most clearly map how the lived experiences of individuals, their micro-level agentive choices and tactics, are at once conditioned by larger forces and participate in moulding them. The local level also enables us to focus on how informalities are lived differently by diversely

DOI: 10.4324/9780429353321-1

positioned actors and, in particular, shine light on those for whom prolonged rule-bending is a necessity for survival and simultaneously a source of vulnerability. As scholars have recently stressed (Chen et al., 2020), developing new theoretical understandings of the importance of informalities in social life requires building upwards from close, ethnographic investigation of how these practices are tied to their historical and geographical context as well as their local systems of power and hierarchy: "to really 'see' informality, we must resist generalisation: there are only particular timed and placed informalities" (Pratt, 2019, p. 614).

In taking the capital of one of the world's most advanced economies as its case study, the book destabilizes various assumptions about how informalities work at the urban level. First, it breaks with the idea that they are predominantly features of developing economies and fast-expanding metropolises. Focusing on Rome problematizes the dichotomic lenses that divide the world into Global North and South and that juxtapose urban governance mechanisms accordingly. On the one hand, as the political hub of one of the largest economies in the European Union, Rome is tied to many globalized economic and political trends. On the other, it has become peripheral to many transnational flows of power and capital. Italy's difficulties in competing in various global markets have fostered a quarter-century of economic stagnation. Concurrently, welfare services and labour protections have been eroded, reflecting the neoliberal and austerity politics of recent decades across much of the world. The endemic underemployment and precarity that have resulted from these forces are key factors in the country's enduringly large undeclared economy. At the same time, daily life is often conditioned by the complicated and slow bureaucratic processes that plague many of the country's institutions. These two elements are among the core structural drivers of widespread rule-bending for survival and personal advancement. The consequences of the COVID-19 pandemic have, meanwhile, exacerbated many of these concerns and are prompting new unofficial ways to solve emerging problems.

Second, the book moves beyond discipline-specific approaches that tend to concentrate on informalities in a single – and often spatially visible – sector of urban life. Instead, it views informalities as power-inflected negotiations that traverse multiple spheres, are enacted by an array of differently positioned actors, and are inextricably embedded in local social histories. Rome, in fact, reveals unique patterns of informal behaviour and social organization that have persisted and become layered across decades, centuries even, and continue to shape the lives of its citizens. Many of these have a clear material dimension, visible in the proliferation of entire self-built neighbourhoods, the city's many squats, and the makeshift accommodation that the poorest residents must resort to. They are also evident in Rome's expansive unregulated street trades and in the way public spaces are continuously adapted to serve the needs of their users. Much informal activity, though, is far less tangible, yet equally central to urban life. The city's shadow economies are just as much fuelled by white-collar practices of tax evasion, illegal lending, under-declared employment, and unofficial commercial transactions hidden behind the walls of its formal workplaces. Rules are also bent and negotiated by bureaucrats, institutional officials, and politicians, both in their internal operations and in their dealings with urban actors across assorted domains. As elsewhere in the world, Rome's informalities "from above" thus interlock with and fuel many practices "from below".

The study thus aims to make both a methodological and theoretical contribution to global scholarship on informality. By taking a transdisciplinary approach to informalities within the social and economic context of a single city, it connects the perspectives of those whose livelihoods and homes are unauthorized and precarious to the macro-level forces with which they must contend. In doing so, it responds to the "call for research that bridges analysis at the macro, sectoral and micro levels to bring out the structural drivers of informality and the structural links between the informality of labour, capital and the state" (Chen et al., 2020, p. 258). It shows how the "differentiated structure" (Roy, 2005, p. 153) of informalities plays out in practice, not just in urban planning but in other governance sectors. At the same time, it heeds calls for grounded theory building that centres on the lived experiences of informalized actors. On the basis of their perspectives, it makes policy recommendations that may advance rights and equality more effectively than the current dualistic alternatives of state repression or formalization.

Informalities are not understood here as reified conditions, categories of people, or places, therefore. Some scholars argue that we should abandon the use of the term "informality" altogether because it so easily becomes a tool for abuse, pathologizing what is quite simply the organization of human life around social rules – some written and most not. Herzfeld (2021), in particular, stresses that the term risks essentializing the law, making it appear a neutral entity and thereby concealing the constructed and continuously negotiated nature of all rules, irrespective of their level of formalization. Indeed, our unwritten norms are often much stronger in determining our behaviour than official rules. As Kelling (2021) highlights, laws and regulations only really become relevant when they are put into action. Much of the time they are disregarded until a conflict emerges. But then they start to matter, their interpretability wielded as ammunition to assert the position and interests of those involved.

I argue that it is precisely in the meeting of laws and uncodified social rules that we are offered a crucial opportunity for conjunctural analysis whose value is at once methodological and theoretical. Political and economic context is not secondary; it is not simply a backdrop against which humans build relational logics that are generalizable, easily compared across different cultures and countries. This book's approach to examining informalities as the outcome and enactment of place-specific social relations is a de-naturalizing, de-ontologizing one. It foregrounds that the law is formed through social relations and tactically made use of in myriad localized encounters, on a playing field that is far from even. Official regulatory frameworks carry with them the state's power to repress, and thereby grant some actors greater latitude to interpret the rules than others. Informality foregrounds the reality that state policies and representatives have a distinct role in placing certain people and behaviours outside or between formalized rules and punishing them accordingly. Simultaneously it underlines that those rules are created and applied flexibly; that pliability is embedded in all state action (Haid & Hilbrandt, 2019). So, informality is about both how people creatively navigate rules and how powerful actors exert symbolic violence by selectively labelling some groups of people as "informal" and "illegal". The focus is on how regulations are mobilized and given meaning over time. It highlights that what is defined as legal is often built on and intertwined with practices that defy the rules. The official and the unofficial, the visible and the hidden, the powerful and the disempowered, are thus tightly interdependent (Panella, 2021).[1] The purpose of this book is to explore the archaeology of how these interconnections have become interwoven and layered and how they continue to permeate social relations in the present.

In unpacking how mechanisms of rule negotiation work across various sectors within a single socio-political reality, the study seeks to map whether similar informal power arrangements and behaviours appear across diverse spheres of urban management and whether, together, they form coherent patterns of "grey governance" (Chiodelli & Tzfadia, 2016). It explores whether shared understandings and methods exist for distributing and accessing resources informally and investigates how these dynamics affect relations in the city; whether they serve to crystallize social inequalities or open up avenues for contestation and the reordering of hierarchies. Although the approach is different from most scholarly contributions that tend to compile and compare case studies across highly diverse geographical and social contexts, the analysis draws on core insights from the rich mosaic that those studies have composed. Three guiding notions that emerge from these global debates are particularly crucial here.[2] First, it is now widely recognized that informality is a *mode of action*: a set of relational processes and practices that anybody can engage in, although how and to what extent depends on the context and one's social position within it. Second, that informality often becomes a *mode of rule*: representatives of state institutions, intermediaries, and community authorities use their privileged roles in negotiating and implementing regulations strategically to exert power and discipline. They thereby transform informality into an ordering logic of governance. Third, that we live in an era of rising informalization that weaves across multiple dimensions. The state itself is increasingly unable to regulate the myriad, shifting networks through which political and economic decisions are made (Boudreau, 2017). Its many layers and actors can manipulate rules for reasons of corruption and self-advancement, but also for the public interest (Boudreau & Davis, 2017). Equally, much capitalist enterprise eludes state regulation, with informality increasingly becoming "the organising principle of the globalised economy" (Breman, 2020, p. 32). Deregulation in many sectors and the accompanying weakening of welfare and labour protections are intensifying undocumented and precarious employment globally (Chen & Carré, 2020). With insecure livelihoods come insecure access to housing and the frequent need to forge alternative systems of welfare and solidarity outside the formal structures of the state.

These global studies demonstrate that there is nothing geographically exceptional about informal power and action. Nevertheless, while rule-bending occurs everywhere, the specific forms it takes, its pervasiveness and its degrees of legitimacy vary massively from one environment to the next. We cannot separate such practices from the particular norms and social institutions of which they are product and manifestation. And these norms in the present cannot be isolated from the local political processes through which some have solidified into formal regulations and institutional systems while others have not. Just as practices shift over time, what behaviours are considered licit or illicit – socially justified or not – also fluctuate as power relations change and normative definitions evolve. Whether informal practices are implicitly accepted, punished, or celebrated also depends on who carries them out. Although navigating around the rules occurs at all societal levels, it presents very different risks and opportunities depending on the resources that actors have access to. Rule-bending by state bureaucrats, private sector managers, and other white-collar actors rarely incurs the same penalties as it does when enacted by groups who lack institutional and social protections and the ability to define the terms of engagement. The motivations for informal action are similarly varied. For many, they are a means of self-advancement, for building networks or finding solutions to obstacles that formal processes do not allow. In many other circumstances, though, they are not a choice but an imperative; the only way to make a livelihood or find a home, to access resources or representation, when official possibilities for doing so are closed off. It is also in these situations that actors are most likely to find themselves in the extended liminal position of being "stuck" between rules, unable to conform to multiple bureaucratic requirements. Intermediaries often find fruitful terrain between these different positions, linking those who need regulations to be flexible in order to manage their lives with those able to turn blind eyes or bend the rules. From this perspective, informal practices can be understood as vectors through which people negotiate power and resources.

Mapping power-inflected informalities

The book thus adopts a political economy approach to make sense of how informalities in Rome intertwine at different scales and in different spheres. It focuses on four sectors within which unauthorized activities are particularly widespread in the city: housing, street vending, moneylending, and waste management. Each case-study chapter maps a genealogy of how the relevant field has evolved, building up its formal mechanisms and generating unofficial modalities – "workarounds" – in the process. In cementing certain practices and normative views into regulations and official protocols, these processes have ordered each field to reflect specific ideological perspectives and power relations. They have defined conduct as correct or incorrect, determined which paperwork is indispensable and which is inadequate, and have honed value-based mechanisms for sanctioning people who do not fit the categories thereby constructed. Just as formalization institutionalizes group interests, informalization hinges on the same definitional processes. As some behaviours and statuses have acquired official legitimacy, others have been stigmatized or criminalized. The arrangements of these labels are not static, though. Interests and power positions mutate, and normative definitions shift with them. With time, some informal behaviours have become absorbed into the formal order while others have been legislated against, pushed into illegality. Some official practices have ceased to be accepted, and some unwritten ones have endured as the common-sense ways of "getting things done" (Ledeneva, 2018). Therefore, analyzing the informalities of today requires tracking the ongoing dance of formalization and informalization through which they have been fashioned and continue to evolve.

Informalities are, moreover, a matter of degree. For some people, they are fleeting, momentary practices that can be easily interrupted or avoided if the disincentives become strong enough. For others they are inescapable and lasting, often accompanied by continuous danger of repression or of life-altering upheavals. In these cases, operating outside or between the rules is not only a practice but also a condition that affects multiple aspects of life at once. For example, being unable to work in the official economy can mean lacking the bureaucratic credentials to access registered housing, which then determines the right to residency papers, health care, and other forms of social security. Its effects are carried in people's bodies, in their interactions with materiality, in their daily sociality. The book therefore incorporates an ethnographic focus on some of the groups living in such protracted and interwoven situations of informality: residents of a public housing project who bypass, or are excluded from, official systems of housing allocation; migrants and marginalized minorities who trade informally in street markets when legal employment is inaccessible or exploitative; small business owners who turn to informal credit providers when formal financial institutions do not meet their needs; unofficial waste collectors that build livelihoods in the folds of the official garbage management sector. Having unravelled the systemic forces that produce the legally ambiguous positions within which these actors operate, each case-study chapter explores how they harness the flexibility of rules to try to make a better life for themselves, activating their knowledge and networks to maintain agency and autonomy in the face of high obstacles and risks. The discussion then examines how they negotiate with institutional actors and narrate those experiences, making sense of the regulatory frameworks they encounter and the dynamics they contribute to shaping through them.

This focus on groups in positions of subalternity is in line with debates on informality that have emerged in many post-colonial contexts. At the same time, it takes forward a growing body of ethnographic work centring on the experiences of migrants and disadvantaged minorities in their engagements with institutions in Italy specifically. Since migrants are those most likely to find themselves stuck in the gaps between Italy's complex bureaucratic requirements and processes, rich ethnographies are emerging on the ways many negotiate around the rules in order to meet their most basic needs.

Tuckett (2018), for example, details how migrants navigate the shifting legislation and inconsistent implementation of Italy's immigration regime, paradoxically bending the rules to stay within the rules. Marchetti and Pinelli's (2017) collection on informal inclusion strategies used by recent migrants and asylum seekers, and Peano's (2012) analyses of the ways in which migrant sex workers resist against disciplinary systems, provide important examples of how people employ subjectivities to escape state control. Other scholars have explored the techniques of visibility and invisibility adopted by immigrant vendors in their unauthorized street trades, juggling the dangers of police repression with strategies for expanding commercial and solidarity networks (Piazzoni, 2020; Clough Marinaro & Panella, 2021). The accumulated skills, knowledge and neighbourhood relations that are essential for survival at the collective level are also core to the informal housing solutions through which Roma (Solimene, 2019) and squatters (Grazioli, 2021) create stable homes and communities in the face of precarity. Non-nationals and minorities are not, however, the only actors for whom it is extremely difficult to conform to Italy's official bureaucratic systems or to access employment through official channels. Signorelli's (1983) classic study of young Italians' reliance on clientelism to obtain jobs is emblematic of such dynamics. Pardo's ethnography of entrepreneurs in Naples (2000), Herzfeld's accounts of the difficult choices faced by business people in the Roman neighbourhood of Monti (2009), and Guano's investigation of the financial constraints on flea-market traders (2010) all turn the spotlight on the lived experiences of Italians for whom official statuses and criteria also present major obstacles.

Despite these crucial contributions, ethnographies of informalities in Italy remain rare. It has been predominantly at the macro-level of analysis that studies have investigated how unregulated power relations unfold, focusing on mechanisms of corruption (della Porta & Vannucci, 2017), clientelism in politics (Briquet, 2015), and the "grey area" of relationships between mafias and the white-collar professionals who enact their economic and political interests (Sciarrone, 2019). In contrast, how ordinary citizens operate at the margins of the law, how they may take advantage of institutional corruption or opportunities for personal favours, and how they can use their electoral weight to ensure that some rules remain elastic has escaped close attention. The one exception to this is the sphere of unauthorized housing construction and occupation, whose diverse manifestations and potential enmeshment with politics and crime have been widely dissected (Belotti & Annunziata, 2017; Berruti, 2019; Chiodelli, 2019; Chiodelli & Gentili, 2021; Chiodelli et al., 2020; Coppola, 2018; Esposito & Chiodelli, 2020). Perhaps because housing informalities are so widespread across the country and often so visible in their spatial manifestations, a rich stream of research has highlighted the ways in which institutional actions or inactions foster such practices. Here too, though, a focus on the systemic level predominates, with few ethnographic accounts exploring how people organize their lives within contexts of housing ambiguity, how they narrate their experiences and decision-making processes, and how they engage day to day with the authorities and other residents.

The liminality of informalities

All informal practices are liminal. They are, by definition, positioned outside regulatory clarity, in those indeterminate spaces between what is officially sanctioned by the law and what is definitively beyond it. Their constantly shifting relationship both with formality and illegality causes them to be suspended outside the official order and yet simultaneously deeply intertwined with it. Looking at informalities through the analytical lens of liminality helps us account for the power that regulatory boundaries exert on the people who operate at their margins. It is where the rules are at their most elastic that constraints are made visible and can be problematized. Liminality brings to the fore how living in a condition of uncertainty generates experiences of intense stress, affecting not only individuals but often entire collectivities. In our contemporary era of ever-eroding certainties and continuous flux, how people cope with ambiguity and turmoil in the absence of clear statuses and repertoires of predefined behaviours is a growing topic of investigation (Andrews & Roberts, 2012; Downey et al., 2018; Horváth et al., 2015; Stenner, 2018; Szakolczai, 2000; Thomassen, 2018). In focusing on the power of the in-between, liminality scholarship emphasizes both the danger inherent in such circumstances and the ferment and capacity for social change that spring from situations where nothing is predetermined and everything is negotiable. It is arguably at the margins and on thresholds where the potential for creativity is at its most intense. At the same time, some thinkers – Thomassen (2015) in particular – have underlined the gradational and multi-scalar nature of liminality. A threshold state may be fleeting and quickly resolved as a person transitions from one social status or condition to another, for example when a high school graduate becomes a university student. But in many of the situations of informality explored in this book's case studies, in-between states become protracted and sometimes permanent. Where there is no clear path to resolution – to reintegration into a social order of recognized positions, – the consequences for those dealing with extended informality are profound. Many face conditions of immense vulnerability, exposed to the continuous threat that the rules will be tightened or enforced, that they may lose their homes or their income. At the same time, when situations of indeterminacy are prolonged, people will generate their own ordering mechanisms, forging practices and structures that produce predictability in precarity. Dominant social norms are thereby often upended. What is licit behaviour becomes complicated and redefined as alternative power relations and value systems are established.

This study's emphasis on how situations of liminality come to be and are managed by those who inhabit them has evolved inductively out of a set of separate ethnographic fieldwork projects carried out over five years, between 2015 and 2020. I originally considered each one entirely distinct, although they all shared the same concern with understanding how state actors are able to aggravate the marginalization and precarity of already disadvantaged groups in the process of altering regulations and their implementation. As the projects took shape, though, it became clear that the various urbanites involved – the mostly Italian housing squatters, the middle-class informal borrowers, the migrant street vendors and waste collectors – shared similar patterns of experience despite the many socio-economic and cultural differences between them. First, they were all profoundly affected by the uncertain temporalities of their situations. All my interviewees and research participants articulated the difficulties of managing their lives in the face of ever-changing institutional deadlines and timeframes. Certainly, the protractedness of their liminal conditions was described as wearing and anxiety-generating, but it was particularly the unpredictability of institutional actions that reinforced their sense of powerlessness and the difficulty of exerting agency and control over their lives. Each of these situations was marked by a lack of policies or social mechanisms offering clearly defined routes out of the liminality; a lack of established rites and guides for exiting the condition of ambiguity within which they often felt stuck. Thus, operating between the rules was not in itself the most problematic feature of their situations. It was the *mobility* of the boundaries that made it impossible to strategize and plan for the future. It fostered a sense of being blocked in an extended present of permanent temporariness that not only curtailed the future but also undermined the certainties of what they had built up in the past.

The centrality of time thus emerges in this book as a core dimension of how informalities are produced and made sense of. While some scholars have highlighted how the unpredictable and often drawn-out temporalities of state bureaucracies disempower subaltern groups (e.g. Auyero, 2012), a more extensive investigation is needed to determine how actors across social classes and situations navigate those temporalities in ways that also serve to negotiate institutional power and demand rights. To do so, I take forward the concept of *temporal capital*. This helps to focus on how informal practices, and the knowledge and expertise that accompany them, build up over time and acquire symbolic value, becoming a currency in local social relations and negotiations around rules. The concept is integrated within a broader theoretical emphasis on informal practices as strategies and tactics through which actors channel the resources available to them: the differential levels of social, political, economic, cultural, and symbolic capital with which they construct and contest power relations (Bourdieu, 1986). Informal practices are thus conceptualized as a means to maintain or subvert relations of power, depending on the specific interests and positions of the actors involved. These conceptual debates, outlined in greater depth in chapter 1, lay the foundation for exploring whether there is an identifiable, coherent "organizing logic" (AlSayyad & Roy, 2004, p. 5) in how urban governance sectors in Rome are managed.

The second motif that surfaces through each case study, in fact, is that the informal and liminal situations of my interlocutors are inextricably connected to a chain of informal practices further up the social hierarchy, where rule-bending is less driven by survival needs and more by pragmatic individual or political interests. Indeed, each of the chapters shows that the practices of the research subjects are often directly conditioned by the failure of institutional actors to apply their own regulations – or their partial and discretionary choices about how to implement them. These subjects are all located within a structured system of power which, though malleable and contestable, constrains their spaces for action. How they activate resources to push against or bypass those constraints, to negotiate with intermediaries and to encroach on what is permitted, is fundamental to conceptualizing both the potential for change inherent in situations of protracted liminality and the inescapable inertia that being "stuck" in liminality can equally entail.

The third motif concerns the complex interconnections between informalities and illegality. Although informal negotiations usually engage with the gaps and loopholes of the law, they can overlap with illegal practices, especially when regulations are multi-layered or contradictory. Indeed, they may break regulations at some levels while simultaneously respecting others.[3] Moreover, as rules are introduced or reformulated, the status of activities that were previously unregulated or tolerated may become redefined as illegal. Informal behaviours can be understood as positioned on a sliding scale with full officialization at one end and absolute illegalization at the other, with different degrees of rule-bending intertwining with formal orders along that spectrum. Just as institutional actors can exploit these ambiguities, criminal or extortive figures can also take advantage of them. This is evident in Italy, where crime groups use their illegal proceeds to provide alternative welfare, loans, and employment in their territories, especially in times of crisis such as the COVID-19 pandemic (Coletti, 2020; Saviano, 2020a, 2020b; The Economist, 2020). When such organizations acquire public authority or penetrate political institutions, they may influence regulatory processes in ways that open up new possibilities for informal action. A notable case that has directly concerned Rome is the criminal organization dubbed *Mondo di Mezzo* (Middle Earth) or *Mafia Capitale*, that extended across various municipal departments and urban political networks until 2014. Its members used their institutional embeddedness to ensure that regulations remained widely unenforced and official documentation unchecked for many years, such that parts of "Rome's administrative system in effect operated in an absence of rules" (CPI, 2017, p. 10).[4] Perpetuating a system in which regulations were only selectively monitored and implemented not only produced benefits for the criminal network itself but also generated opportunities for other, unconnected, actors to take advantage of the resulting institutional confusion and inertia. Not all fields discussed in this book were directly affected by these operations. However, each of the case studies brings to light spaces of ambiguity that have furnished possibilities – some more expansive than others – for criminal actors to gain power or profit. Analyzing how these dynamics have evolved helps us to move towards a more nuanced explanation of how informalities interlink with illegality than has been offered so far.

Methodological approaches

The specific sectors presented in the case-study chapters – public housing, street trade, credit relations, and waste management – are ones in which informal practices are particularly prevalent in Rome. They have all been targeted by intensive policies of formalization or repression in recent years, indicating that informal activities were deemed by the relevant authorities to have reached problematic degrees. These sectors are of course by no means exhaustive of urban governance spheres or of the contexts in which informal practices flourish. Indeed, future research will need to investigate the fields of policy-making and urban planning more generally, the decision-making processes of law enforcement agents in equivocal situations, and the management of migrants' ambiguous statuses. The specific spheres studied here nevertheless bring together a wide range of actors in diverse positions of power who participate differentially in informal practices according to the resources available to them.

Every chapter first presents a historical overview of the sector and the regulatory frameworks that structure it, identifying how its political and economic stakes have been shaped over time and how those developments have been influenced by external factors nationally, regionally, and globally. The Roman cases are thus contextualized within the theoretical lenses and empirical findings developed in related spheres internationally. The chapters then map the positions of core actors in the field and their relationships to one another, revealing patterns in their encounters and tracing the ties that connect them both horizontally – the support and solidarity networks among agents at similar levels of the social hierarchy – and vertically: the links that emerge across different layers. Next, the discussion concentrates on the contextual circumstances underpinning institutional decisions to regularize or otherwise eliminate the informalities in the field. It analyzes the factors that have prompted the policy shifts: the temporal pressures influencing decisions and the broader political rationalities driving the choices of repression, toleration, or formalization (Smart & Aguilera, 2020). The methods used to implement the new approaches are investigated to assess how regulatory changes have affected the lives of the interviewees and disturbed the field's established power dynamics. In particular, I question whether new positions have thereby emerged – novel spaces and opportunities for action but also new temporal and material constraints. The focus then turns to how actors at all levels – institutional representatives, intermediaries, and the social groups targeted – mobilize their resources, adapting to the changed circumstances and moulding the new relational configurations to their own ends. Through the subsequent ethnographic discussion, I explore how those most affected by these shifts articulate their experiences, coping strategies, and sense-making as they organize their lives in the gaps between the rules. The analysis emphasizes whether the regulatory changes have resolved situations of liminality for those previously stuck in them, reintegrating them into the formal structured order, or whether new forms of ambiguity have instead been generated. In giving voice and visibility to some of the city's most hidden actors, it reveals how they participate in symbolic struggles over what practices – formal and informal – are defined as legitimate. It probes how in their actions and discourses they influence those of other figures in the field, not simply submitting to regulatory change but actively participating in its logics and micro-politics, at times forcing the institutions to bend to their pressures. Thus, each case study underlines how everyday micro-activities and macro-processes are co-constitutively shaped (Cirolia & Scheba, 2018, p. 5).

Doing ethnography with vulnerable actors who bend or break the law is notoriously difficult, given the fears they may have of exposure to the authorities and the punitive arm of the state. Reticence is further aggravated where there is strong social stigma involved, such as in cases of illegal borrowing or gleaning from dumpsters. Inevitably, my position as an outsider to the communities added a further layer of mistrust. My privileged status as a researcher working with people in multi-sited and varied situations of poverty and precarity meant that I was never able to become a fully integrated participant. Nevertheless, my own ambiguous situation as a foreigner and a woman did partly mitigate the symbolic distance and power differentials between us. Having previously spent two decades doing fieldwork with Roma groups in the capital, I had already built long-standing relations of trust with many of the street vendors and waste traders discussed in chapters 4 and 6.[5] My access to important gatekeepers in the public housing project on which chapter 3 focuses also ensured that my trustworthiness was vouched for, enabling me to hold many informal discussions in the complex, participate in collective events, and carry out life-history interviews, although the marked differences in vulnerability among residents did result in some people declining to talk to me. Of all the groups involved, it was informal borrowers who were most difficult to access. While I did interview three key individuals who had experienced the liminality of protracted debt, I was unable to directly participate in the contexts of informal/illegal lending and had to depend on mediators and representatives to obtain an overview of the different pressures at play. Thus, multiple qualitative research strategies were used for the ethnographic sections, ranging from participant observation and unstructured field conversations to oral-history accounts to semi-structured interviews with grassroots actors, front-line bureaucrats, and NGO workers. A wide range of topics and experiences were covered in these encounters, but here I focus primarily on how subjects recounted the temporal evolution of the informal practices; how and why they embarked on these activities, what external factors influenced the continuation or shifts in practices, what strategies of survival they honed in the process, and what concerns and priorities they expressed for the present and the future.

In addition to the challenges of primary data collection, it is important to note that secondary sources, in the form of institutional data, also pose problems. The issue of "dark numbers" – that is, the impossibility of systematically collecting accurate overviews of informal or illegal activities that escape the gaze of the state – is an issue that pervades any research in this field. I do incorporate official statistics where available to provide quantitative contextualization; however, their lack of reliability and depth is always borne in mind. To compensate for their very partial nature, I also draw on a wide variety of other documentary sources, including media reporting, legal and regulatory texts, non-governmental studies. The research thus seeks to triangulate between the perspectives of grassroots actors and intermediaries and material produced by formal institutions and state agencies.

Chapter 6 then implements a very different and innovative approach to understanding informalities in the city. It analyzes the results of an online survey carried out between September and December 2020 with over 170 city residents across generations, classes, education levels, and employment. The goal is to map whether ordinary Romans perceive rule-bending to be widespread in the public's interactions with formal institutions and their regulations. It explores the extent to which respondents consider state bureaucracies and services to be efficient and fair in their provision of resources. It then questions whether rule-negotiating behaviours are viewed as endemic or group-specific and whether respondents articulate a scale of approval/disapproval depending on what informal practices are being carried out, who the actors are, what their presumed motivations are, and which contexts they occur in. The study thus makes a preliminary step towards understanding how far such practices are considered a normal and inescapable modality of Rome's urban governance.

The conclusion traces the themes and practical interconnections that emerge through the previous chapters. In comparing the four governance fields and the perspectives of the survey respondents, it highlights how institutionally produced regulatory overload, unpredictability, and opacity are the core drivers of all the informalities examined. It identifies how far different actors in the various spheres have been able to exploit the ensuing regulatory grey areas to their tactical or strategic ends, demonstrating that disadvantaged groups are those most systematically constrained in their ability to access services and public spaces through loopholes and manoeuvres. It argues that informal practices are not able to fundamentally redefine social hierarchies and produce real structural change despite the efforts of many of the actors involved. On the contrary, the discussion shows that informalities have become embedded in, and symbiotic with, governance dynamics that uphold the logics of neoliberal inequality.

This conclusion has important implications for public policy at the local and national level. Many of the dynamics analyzed originate in institutional actions which, while often well intentioned, do not yield the outcomes originally anticipated, resulting in wasted funds or an erosion of institutional legitimacy. The analysis therefore points to the challenges but also the possibilities for reform that could, if implemented, produce more equitable, transparent, and trust-based interactions between public institutions and citizens, especially marginalized ones. Particularly, it advances recommendations that target the causes, rather than expressions, of informality. The global implications of this study are equally important. By providing data-rich evidence of how informal negotiations operate across governance spheres and social groups, the discussion offers useful tools for advancing our understandings of informalities beyond the sector-specific approaches that still predominate. Foregrounding how people mobilize – or are constrained by – time and capital, and how they co-produce informality not just from "below" but from "within", will, it is hoped, further refine our analyses of how power works in real-life urban settings.

Notes

1 Panella (2021) provides a useful example of such dynamics in the lives of undocumented agricultural workers whose illegal status in Italy allows them to be exploited in the fields to produce food that is then sold in the legal consumer markets. They are treated as hidden outlaws, while simultaneously publicly legitimized when they visibly protest in city streets against Italy's widespread system of illegal hiring by gangmasters.
2 The conceptual contributions made in this literature are outlined in chapter 1.
3 See, for example, Chiodelli (2019) on how housing construction can respect some building codes but violate other legislation.
4 All translations in this book are by the author unless otherwise specified.
5 The methodological approach and challenges faced in the individual ethnographies are explained in greater depth in each specific chapter.

References

AlSayyad, S., & Roy, A. (2004). Urban informality: Crossing borders. In A. Roy & S. AlSayyad (eds), *Urban informality: Transnational perspectives from the Middle East, Latin America, and South Asia* (pp. 1–6). Lexington Books.

Andrews, H., & Roberts, L. (2012). Introduction: Re-mapping liminality. In H. Andrews & L. Roberts (eds), *Liminal landscapes: Travel, experience and spaces in-between* (pp. 1–17). Routledge. https://doi.org/10.4324/9780203123164-7.

Auyero, J. (2012). *Patients of the state: The politics of waiting in Argentina*. Duke University Press.

Belotti, E., & Annunziata, S. (2017). Governare l'abitare informale. Considerazioni a partire dai casi di Milano e Roma. In Urban@It (ed.), *Rapporto sulle città. Mind the gap, il distacco tra politiche e città*. Il Mulino.

Berruti, G. (2019). *Fuori norma. Percorsi e ragionamenti su urbanistica e informale*. INU Edizioni.

Boudreau, J.-A. (2017). *Global urban politics: Informalization of the state*. Urban Futures.

Boudreau, J.-A., & Davis, D. (2017). Introduction: A processual approach to informalization. *Current Sociology*, 65(2), 151–166. https://doi.org/10.1177%2F0011392116657286.

Bourdieu, P. (1986). The forms of capital. In J. G. Richardso *n* (ed.), *Handbook of theory and research for the sociology of education* (pp. 241–258). Greenwood Press.

Breman, J. (2020). The bane of the labouring poor under globalised capitalism. In M. Chen & F. Carré (eds), *The informal economy revisited: Examining the past, envisioning the future* (1st ed., pp. 31–37). Routledge. https://doi.org/10.4324/9780429200724.

Briquet, J.-L. (2015). Clientelism. In E. G. Parini, A. Mammone, & G. A. Veltri (eds), *The Routledge handbook of contemporary Italy: History, politics, society* (pp. 252–261). Routledge. https://doi.org/10.4324/9781315709970.

Chen, M. A., & Carré, F. (2020). Introduction. In M. A. Chen & F. Carré (eds), *The informal economy revisited: Examining the past, envisioning the future* (pp. 1–27). Routledge. https://doi.org/10.4324/9780429200724-1.

Chen, M. A., Carré, F., & Roever, S. (2020). Conclusion. In M. A. Chen & F. Carré (eds), *The informal economy revisited: Examining the past, envisioning the future* (pp. 257–268). Routledge. https://doi.org/10.4324/9780429200724-46.

Chiodelli, F. (2019). The dark side of urban informality in the Global North: Housing illegality and organized crime in Northern Italy. *International Journal of Urban and Regional Research*, 43(3), 497–516. https://doi.org/10.1111/1468-2427.12745.

Chiodelli, F., Coppola, A., Belotti, E., Berruti, G., Clough Marinaro, I., Curci, F., & Zanfi, F. (2020). The production of informal space: A critical atlas of housing informalities in Italy between public institutions and political strategies. *Progress in Planning*. Advance online publication. https://doi.org/10.1016/j.progress.2020.100495.

Chiodelli, F., & Gentili, M. (2021). The many shades of grey in urban governance: How illegality shapes urban planning, policy and development. *Political Geography*, 84. Advance online publication. https://doi.org/10.1016/j.polgeo.2020.102309.

Chiodelli, F., & Tzfadia, E. (2016). The multifaceted relation between formal institutions and the production of informal urban spaces: An editorial introduction. *Geography Research Forum*, 36, 1–14.

Cirolia, L. R., & Scheba, S. (2018). Towards a multi-scalar reading of informality in Delft, South Africa: Weaving the 'everyday' with wider structural tracings. *Urban Studies*, 56(3), 594–611. https://doi.org/10.1177/0042098017753326.

Clough Marinaro, I., & Panella, C. (2021). Informal economies, illegal subjects: Roma and Senegalese traders in Rome. In W. E. Little & C. Panella (eds), *Norms and illegality: Intimate ethnographies and politics* (pp. 111–136). Lexington Books.

Coletti, A. (2020). The welfare system of Italian mafias. In F. Allum, I. Clough Marinaro, & R. Sciarrone (eds), *Italian mafias today: Territory, business and politics* (pp. 111–124). Edward Elgar Publishing. https://doi.org/10.4337/9781789904147.00016.

Coppola, A. (2018). A very old neo-liberalism: The changing politics and policy of urban informality in the Roman borgate. In L. Caldwell & F. Camilletti (eds), *Rome: Modernity, postmodernity and beyond* (pp. 83–98). Legenda. https://doi.org/10.2307/j.ctv16kkz64.

CPI (Commissione parlamentare d'inchiesta sulle attività illecite connesse al ciclo dei rifiuti e su illeciti ambientali ad esse correlati) (2017). Relazione sul ciclo dei rifiuti di Roma Capitale e fenomeni illeciti nel territorio del Lazio. www.senato.it/service/PDF/PDFServer/BGT/1063695.pdf.

della Porta, D., & Vannucci A. (2017). *Corrupt exchanges: Actors, resources, and mechanisms of political corruption*. Routledge. https://doi.org/10.4324/9781315080284.

Downey, D., Kinane, I., & Parker, E. (2018). *Landscapes of liminality: Between space and place*. Rowman & Littlefield.

Esposito, E., & Chiodelli, F. (2020). Juggling the formal and the informal: The regulatory environment of the illegal access to public housing in Naples. *Geoforum*, 113, 50–59. https://doi.org/10.1016/j.geoforum.2020.05.002.

Grazioli, M. (2021). *Housing, urban commons and the right to the city in post-crisis Rome: Metropoliz, the squatted Città Meticcia*. Palgrave.

Guano. E. (2010). Taxpayers, thieves, and the state: Fiscal citizenship in contemporary Italy. *Ethnos*, 75(4), 377–401. https://doi.org/10.1080/00141844.2010.522246.

Haid, C. G., & Hilbrandt, H. (2019) Urban informality and the state: Geographical translations and conceptual alliances. *International Journal of Urban and Regional Research*, 43(3), 551–562. https://doi.org/10.1111/1468-2427.12700.

Herzfeld, M. (2009). *Evicted from eternity. The restructuring of modern Rome.* Chicago University Press. https://doi.org/10.7208/chicago/9780226329079.001.0001.

Herzfeld, M. (2021). Methodological legalism. In C. Panella & W. E. Little (eds), *Norms and illegality: Intimate ethnographies and politics* (pp. 37–58). Lexington Books.

Horváth, A., Thomassen, B., & Wydra, H. (eds). (2015). *Breaking boundaries: Varieties of liminality.* Berghahn. https://doi.org/10.2307/j.ctt9qcxbg.

Kelling, E. (2021). The role of informality and illegality in London's incremental housing extension practices [Conference presentation]. Houses of Cards: The Rules and Institutions of Housing Illegality/Informality in Western Countries, 19–21 April. University of Cambridge and University of Turin. Online. http://houseofcards.crassh.cam.ac.uk/.

Ledeneva, A. (ed.). (2018). *The global encyclopaedia of informality: Understanding social and cultural complexity (Vols 1&2).* UCL Press. https://doi.org/10.14324/111.9781911307907.

Marchetti, C., & Pinelli, B. (eds). (2017). *Confini d'Europa: modelli di controllo e inclusion informali.* Raffaello Cortina Editore.

Panella, C. (2021). On doing fieldwork, outspokenly: Ethics, money, and antiquities illegal trade. In C. Panella & W. E. Little (eds), *Norms and illegality: Intimate ethnographies and politics* (pp. 59–88). Lexington Books.

Pardo, I. (2000). Credit, entrepreneurship and the repayment of debt. Mismatched conceptions of legitimacy in Italy. *Self, Agency and Society*, 2(2), 51–87.

Peano, I. (2012). Excesses and double standards: Migrant prostitutes, sovereignty and exceptions in contemporary Italy. *Modern Italy*, 17(4), 419–432. doi:10.1080/13532944.2012.706994.

Peano, I. (2013). Opaque loves: Governance and escape in the intimate sphere of Nigerian sex workers. *Etnografia e Ricerca Qualitativa*, 6(3), 359–384. doi:10.3240/75030.

Piazzoni, F. (2020). Visibility as justice: Immigrant street vendors and the right to difference in Rome. *Journal of Planning Education and Research*. Advance online publication. https://doi.org/10.1177/0739456x20956387.

Pratt, A. (2019). Formality as exception. *Urban Studies*, 56(3), 612–615. https://doi.org/10.1177/0042098018810600.

Roy, A. (2005). Urban Informality: Toward an epistemology of planning. *Journal of the American Planning Association*, 71(2), 147–158. https://doi.org/10.1080/01944360508976689.

Saviano, R. (2020a). La mafia del coronavirus: Dalla droga alla sanità, la pandemia aiuta l'economia criminale. *La Repubblica*, 23 March. www.repubblica.it/cronaca/2020/03/23/news/la_mafia_del_virus_dalla_droga_alla_sanita_la_pandemia_aiuta_l_economia_criminale-252023708/.

Saviano, R. (2020b). Il contagio mafioso: così la criminalità sfrutta l'epidemia. *La Repubblica*, 25 August. www.repubblica.it/cronaca/2020/08/25/news/covid_cosi_le_mafie_sfruttano_l_epidemia-265405132/.

Sciarrone, R. (2019). The economic dimension of mafias, social capital and the "grey area". In F. Allum, I. Clough Marinaro, & R. Sciarrone (eds), *Italian mafias today:*

Territory, business and politics (pp. 76–90). Edward Elgar Publishing. https://doi.org/10.4337/9781789904147.00014.

Signorelli, A. (1983). *Chi può e chi aspetta. Giovani e clientelismo in un'area interna del Mezzogiorno*. Liguori.

Smart, A., & Aguilera, T. (2020). Towards a political economy of toleration of illegality: Comparing tolerated squatting in Hong Kong and Paris. In U. Grashoff (ed.), *Comparative approaches to informal housing across the globe* (pp. 39–65). Fringe. https://doi.org/10.2307/j.ctv13xpsrb.10.

Solimene, M. (2019). The (in)formal, the (il)legal and the (il)licit: Roma informal settlements and institutional pragmatics of compromise and compassion in a Roman periphery. *Cities*, 95. Advance online publication. https://doi.org/10.1016/j.cities.2019.05.038.

Stenner, P. (2018). *Liminality and experience: A transdisciplinary approach to the psychosocial*. Palgrave Macmillan. https://doi.org/10.1057/978-1-137-27211-9.

Szakolczai, A. (2000). *Reflexive historical sociology*. Routledge. https://doi.org/10.4324/9780203193617.

The Economist. (2020). Covid nostra. *The Economist*, 435(9194), 49–50.

Thomassen, B. (2015). Thinking with liminality: To the boundaries of an anthropological concept. In A. Horváth, B. Thomassen, & H. Wydra (eds), *Breaking boundaries: Varieties of liminality* (pp. 39–60). Berghahn.

Thomassen, B. (2018). *Liminality and the modern: Living through the in-between*. Routledge. https://doi.org/10.4324/9781315592435.

Tuckett, A. (2018). *Rules, paper, status: Migrants and precarious bureaucracy in contemporary Italy*. Stanford University Press. https://doi.org/10.1515/9781503606500.

1 Tracing informalities across scales and fields

Introduction

Most of our social interactions follow logics and patterns that are not codified in formal regulations. When official rules do exist, we are selective about which ones we follow closely and which we consider negotiable, open to interpretation or circumvention. A wealth of research shows that informal exchanges and ways of manoeuvring around rules are often similar across time and space. The core conceptual advances in this recent global scholarship are outlined in this chapter, highlighting the multidimensional ways in which actors of all types engage in informal problem-solving tactics or strategies to advance their interests. Although many such interactions occur away from the state, between private individuals,[1] my focus here is on how urban governance works in practice: how policy decisions are implemented, and what resources people activate to influence those processes. I concentrate on how state institutions, politicians, street-level bureaucrats, and a wide variety of non-state actors come together to produce local norms and understandings about which official rules may be bent and how. In setting the foundations for analyzing how informal power operates in contemporary Rome, the discussion highlights how informal practices may become integral to the workings of formal institutions, generating unwritten rules or expedients to which many actors then adhere. Non-institutional actors respond to the opportunities and obstacles created, to satisfy their needs or to manipulate and subvert existing hierarchies. Although informal dynamics are co-produced between all these actors, the power relations between them are not equal. The macro-level structures of the legal, economic, and political environment strongly shape how spaces for informal action emerge. The discussion thus underlines the utility of political economy approaches to informality for mapping the power-inflected mechanisms that link actors, their perceptions, and their practices, across multiple scales. In the process, it also conceptualizes the unstable relationships between informality and illegality. It stresses the distinctions between these conditions, but also the potential for actors to move between them and the possibility for criminal groups to benefit from regulatory ambiguities.

DOI: 10.4324/9780429353321-2

While the theoretical advances in informality studies are central to the analysis throughout this book, I argue that they do not go far enough in conceptualizing the positions and relative social weight of actors and their possibilities for advancing or defending their interests through informal practices. They also often lack a detailed analysis of the temporal forces influencing how behaviours develop and how regulations are enacted and experienced. The discussion therefore borrows elements of Bourdieu's theory of practice to tease out how informal negotiations emerge from entrenched patterns of social and political behaviour within a given field of urban life. This focuses attention on how hierarchical positions have evolved over time and delineated subjects' relative options for action, generating shared understandings of power and of what informal behaviours are feasible and legitimate. I concentrate particularly on the various forms of knowledge and capital available to actors and the relative contextual value of those resources. How differently positioned people may mobilize these through informal negotiations to change or perpetuate established power relations is crucial in assessing whether such practices effect social change within and across different fields. These positions are largely place-specific and cannot be assumed to be replicated in other socio-political settings. It is on the basis of this theoretical reasoning that the analyses in this book focus on a single city rather than following the comparative approach typical of informality studies.

Furthermore, in highlighting the innumerable ways in which informal practices occur, scholars have tended to overlook the qualitative differences among types of informalities. Some informal practices are flexible and provisional, their influences in people's lives fleeting. Others are far more pervasive, durable, and dangerous. To grapple with these differences in *degree*, I turn to recent insights from the field of liminality studies. Its focus on how people experience and cope with living in ambiguous positions, creating order and predictability in such situations, as well as routes and rites for exiting them, is particularly helpful when studying protracted, possibly permanent, situations of informality. This lens reveals the potential limitations on agency of finding oneself suspended between the law and illegality, protection and punishment, precarity and stability. The social stigmatization of in-between conditions is of particular importance in mapping their institutional treatment. At the same time, scholars of liminality foreground the transformative capacity inherent in such situations, underlining how hierarchies and ideologies may be overturned and new forms of practice normalized. This attention to the symbolic weight and tumultuous experiences of living in liminal states is fused with a systemic perspective on the power dynamics at play to grasp how such situations are produced and then managed by all the actors involved.

Informality: rules, power and governance

The concept of informality is often criticised for being so broad as to be analytically unhelpful (Herrle & Fokdal, 2011), encompassing, as it does, any aspect of social life that escapes or confounds explicit regulation, ranging from micro-level individual exchanges of favours to "informalization" of states in the context of globalization (Boudreau, 2017). Yet it is arguably the multidimensional and flexible nature of the term that has underpinned its intense revival in recent years, as studies of rising precarization and hidden forms of governance have proliferated across geographical and social space.[2] The multiplicity of cases of life "between" and "beyond" the rules, spanning both hemispheres and all levels of economic development, challenge assumptions that social, political, and economic interactions are predominantly organized around codified rules and procedures and that informality represents a deviation of that order. Indeed, it is often the norm of everyday life, rather than the exception (Ledeneva, 2018; Pratt, 2019). The wealth of ethnographic studies now available make clear that informal practices are by no means restricted to socially vulnerable groups, nor are they necessarily a form of resistance to the state or to oppression. Rather, they are strategies of negotiation within which various actors, with differing roles and resources, participate to their own ends.

Despite this recognition that such practices take shape across multiple spheres of life, scholarship tends to be organized into sector-specific approaches, although cross-fertilization is now growing as the field evolves.[3] The original concentration on unregulated employment in the 1970s has generated ever more sophisticated analyses in recent decades of informal economic practices in both emerging and advanced economies (Boels, 2016; Brown, 2017; Marcelli et al., 2014; Polese et al., 2017b). The attention to unauthorized urban settlements in developing countries that flourished in the 1980s and 1990s has laid the foundation for a slew of studies on informal housing production, use of public space, and urban planning processes also in Europe, North America, and Australia (Durst & Wegmann, 2017; Gurran et al., 2020; Haid, 2017; Jaffe & Koster, 2019; Langegger & Koester, 2017; Lombard, 2019; Mukhija & Loukaitou-Sideris, 2014; Nasreen & Ruming, 2020; Pradel-Miquel, 2017; Verloo, 2017). The debates that have emerged in the 2000s in critical urban studies, coupled with a vast body of work on the transition from socialism in Eastern Europe and the former Soviet Union (Giordano & Hayoz, 2013; Morris & Polese, 2015; Polese et al., 2017a), have contributed essential conceptual advances that transcend those original disciplinary rigidities. Thanks to their focus on transactions and decision-making processes across domains as varied as healthcare and education, as well as high-end housing production, understandings of informality have shifted from foregrounding survival strategies in conditions of poverty to unpacking the integral roles that informal negotiations play in governance dynamics across an array of political contexts. Nevertheless, despite such progress, much research continues to emphasize changes underway in developing countries, reflecting a tendency to avoid analyzing "urban informality as a constituent process of cities beyond [...] the 'non-west'" (Marx & Kelling, 2019, p. 496). In this way, colonial hierarchies are revived (Varley, 2013) and the "West" or "North" continues to be treated as only tangentially touched by such issues (Haid & Hilbrandt, 2019). The rich analytical perspectives that have emerged from these post-colonial and post-socialist contexts now need to be globalized and applied to less explored political and economic environments such as the Italian one.

Negotiating rules: informality as intertwinement

The enduring importance of the informality lens lies in its ability to unveil dynamics through which social life is regulated and ordered. It allows us to question the ideological assumptions upon which rules and policies are built, and the interests that they may advance. It thus exposes the messy processes behind the naturalizing fiction that rules are created and enforced neutrally. Far from being "outside" or in opposition to the state and its regulatory systems, informal negotiations and practices are often intrinsic to how official institutions operate; how regulations are formulated and how they are then executed (Canclini, 2019; Mica et al., 2015). Equivocal wording, overlaps, or gaps between rules can create ample space for subjective interpretation, exploitation of loopholes, and implementation through officials' discretionality or selective blind-eye-turning (Demirtas-Milz, 2013; Rubin, 2018; Smart et al., 2017). Moreover, informality may emerge where policies fail or institutions are absent, becoming complementary to the state, enabling it to function by operating in the gaps where official rules do not exist (Altrock, 2016). Alternatively, it may be supplementary (Altrock, 2016), where extant rules and processes do not work, are not useful (Rubin, 2018), or are not implemented properly. Thus, informal actions may be the only "working solution" for bureaucrats and other actors who must navigate contradictory or inadequate regulations (Morris & Polese, 2015, p. 8), or who need to break the rules to provide services for the public good (Boudreau & Davis, 2017; Naqvi, 2017).

Equally, spheres of life that are not officially regulated often involve practices that borrow organizational mechanisms from formal sectors or that seek, at least in part, to comply with regulations (Grashoff, 2019). Chiodelli and Moroni's (2014) use of the term nomotropism is particularly helpful in conceptualizing the many ways in which people – citizens and officials – act in light of formal rules, without necessarily fully obeying them. The authors underline that most grassroots actors who violate rules do so for lack of alternatives, seeking stability and security of residence or income, in the knowledge that access to other rights and benefits is often contingent on such stability. The need to conform as much as possible to regulatory requirements – if only incrementally over time – reveals the powerful, albeit often indirect, effect that official rules exert over social actions and choices. Indeed, it is by appealing to various levels of the law that people living in conditions of informality may eventually achieve formal recognition of their situation (Van Gelder, 2013). Moreover, informal moulding of formal rules may have a circular influence, resulting in state institutions accepting and accommodating some informal practices into their own regulations and policies. The process of adjustment and compromise is thus often bi-directional (Rubin, 2018, p. 2231). Formality and informality must be understood as deeply intertwined (Acuto et al., 2019; McFarlane & Waibel, 2016), with people acting formally and informally at once or along a continuum of degrees, with many shades of hybridity where they interlock and blur (Altrock, 2016; Mica, 2016). Rather than constituting a particular set of sectors or spheres, formality and informality are "modes of action" (Varriale, 2014, p. 138), mobilized in a wide variety of situations and constantly open to adaptation and change as circumstances and goals evolve.

State-produced informalities

Despite the participation of multiple actors, power differentials are often fundamental to why informal practices exist, how they operate, and how they are treated. As Roy (2009, p. 80) has famously defined it, informality is the sphere of deregulation within "the ever-shifting relationship between what is legal and illegal, legitimate and illegitimate, authorized and unauthorized." It is the state – through the operations of its institutions and representatives – that has the power to "define the informal, determine its conditions of action, and influence its forms and paths of development" (Esposito & Chiodelli, 2020, p. 52). Much empirical research shows that states' categorizations of particular activities, spaces, or groups of people as informal often perpetuate elite interests and thereby (re)produce inequalities (McFarlane & Waibel, 2016; Müller, 2017; Roy, 2009). It is through this power to label and punish that the state demonstrates "its political potency," often criminalizing the rule-breaking of weak social groups while enacting "the (invisible) valorization of elite informalities and illegalities" (Roy, 2018, p. 2243). When state actors exploit flexible and unclear regulations, they create states of exception, determining which actions – including their own – are kept outside the law. In this view, informality is not a haphazard outcome of institutional ineffectiveness, but a device – a mode of rule – whereby the law is strategically left open to interpretation by those in positions of power. Informality does not always exist outside or in spite of the state, therefore, but frequently *because of* selective actions of state officials. This is "a calculated informality" (Roy, 2009, p. 80), which provides "a tactical tool" that can be wielded by institutional actors to achieve specific goals (Demirtas-Milz, 2013, p. 691). Where these actors strategically and systematically weave between formal rules and informal actions, we have mechanisms of "grey governance" Chiodelli and Tzfadia (2016, p. 7).

The distinctions that need to be identified are not between formal and informal, therefore, but between different types of informality and how these are enabled and treated by the state (Roy, 2009). Middle-class, capitalist-driven ones are those most often sanctioned, while those of poor urbanites are frequently repressed. These ambiguities "serve as modes of sovereignty and discipline" (Roy, 2009, p. 83), often resulting in domination over economically and politically vulnerable groups while becoming an instrument of accumulation and power for the groups the state chooses to legitimize. Such dynamics are clearly demonstrated in Yiftachel's studies of how urban policies are used in Israel to force minorities into confined, informal spaces where they are then strategically deprived of citizenship rights in ways that reinforce ethno-religious hierarchies (2009a, 2009b). Marginality is thereby normalized, with subaltern subjects pushed into the precarious limbo of "grey spaces," subject to state actors' decisions about how to govern them. Over time, officials may choose to neglect them and perpetuate the status quo through a politics of "un-recognition" (2009b, p. 91), they may selectively "launder" them through formalizing – or "whitening" – their status, or "blacken" them, exposing their targets to "the 'darkness' of eviction, destruction and death" (Yiftachel, 2009a, p. 243).[4] The people who find themselves subject to practices of "grey spacing" – and the partial exclusion from political and economic participation that this often generates – are not passive, however. They can and often do respond through strategies of self-organization and struggle. Nevertheless, the playing field upon which they act is highly unequal, making it difficult for those designated as "informals" to counter the disparities that are maintained through state-produced informality.

Informalities as resistance and compromise

Notwithstanding the abundant evidence of state involvement in informal practices, informality should not be viewed as an exclusively or inherently oppressive modality. It is a social space within which actors seek power, advantage, or survival. Power may be unequal, but it is rarely unidirectional. This terrain is one in which existing hierarchies may also be contested and subverted. Following Scott's seminal studies of the tactics employed by subaltern peasants to resist elite and institutional power over their lives (1976, 1985, 2009), much scholarship explores the ways in which similar forms of subversion and resistance are used in contemporary environments to effect change by groups that lack formal access to institutional power (Davoli, 2018; Lendaro, 2019). A crucial contribution to this discussion is Bayat's (2004) concept of the "quiet encroachment of the ordinary" which underlines how informal activities of weak groups are often enacted not with a clear or organized intention to resist the state, but through a concrete need to improve conditions and obtain otherwise unavailable social goods and services. It is a means of achieving redistribution and autonomy. In order to be sustainable, it must often be carried out through micro-level incremental actions, invisible enough to evade repressive backlashes but at the same time able to have a cumulative, political impact on the urban landscape and governmental choices.

There is therefore an ebb and flow to many informal practices as actors calculate the need to retreat if the speed or visibility of their encroachments risk generating conflict with the state. Strategic timings are central to any informal activity, revealing the temporal fluidity, rather than linear progression, that marks many such practices. Since "informals" usually need access to state protections and services, a similar seesawing emerges between acts of resistance and at least an outward performance of deference.[5] In many cases, actors must invest in personalized negotiations with local officials in order to access discretionary favours and services. There is a strongly performative dimension to negotiations around rules, with weakly positioned individuals dramatizing compliance when it benefits them, instead using the hidden transcripts (Scott, 2009) of humour, irony, or contestation to unmask the underlying contradictions when appropriate (Clough Marinaro & Solimene, 2020). Nevertheless, in democratic contexts where actors operating in informal ways constitute a large segment of the electorate, they may achieve "bold encroachment" through collective action, making their situations visible and potentially forcing the authorities to formally address their needs (Gillespie, 2017).

The political connotations that informal manoeuvres take on are not limited to micro-tactics of subalterns or to elite- and capitalist-advancing strategies. State actors may be inspired to bend or ignore rules as a means of facilitating access to services and forms of welfare for those officially excluded: "a kind of helpful informality of the state" (Rubin, 2018, p. 2239). Thus, bureaucrats' tacit acceptance of the informal practices of vulnerable groups, despite official discourses of rejection and zero tolerance, may be motivated by compassion (Solimene, 2019) or forbearance (Holland, 2017). In the latter case, this may manifest as an informal distribution of welfare that aims to generate crucial political support, especially in the run-up to election time. Leniency can be modulated for political goals, therefore; life can be made easier for the poor at certain times, but law enforcement may also be selectively tightened when the electoral base to be courted shifts to a middle-class one where legalistic policies and discourses hold greater sway. Forbearance may be redistributive in its outcomes, but its modality is often clientelistic, with the possible result that more stable and transparent forms of welfare provision become difficult to implement in the long term (Holland, 2017). Informal welfare serves to displace grassroots frustrations and defuse dissent, but may also shore up structural inequalities, further entrenching the need for informal solutions. This is the case in areas of Italy, especially in the housing sector in some southern regions, where institutional acceptance of widespread rule violation neutralizes potential conflicts by avoiding major societal upheavals in the short term (Esposito & Chiodelli, 2020). The inherent danger of any system that perpetuates recourse to discretionary decision-making is the impossibility of ensuring that bureaucrats do not abuse it for personal gain. There is no guarantee that flexibility is "exercised with a sense of social responsibility" (Naqvi, 2017, p. 196). Nevertheless, in conditions of very fast change, such as in booming sectors of the Chinese economy, institutional acceptance, or "conceded informality," may be crucial in smoothly adapting to new circumstances (Schoon & Altrock, 2014). Whatever the socio-political context, institutional actors' decisions on how to respond involve implicit cost-benefit calculations of the relative social perils of repressing large-scale informalities or managing them through selective negotiation (Polese et al., 2019).

Political economies of informality

(In)formalities cannot, therefore, be detached from political and economic interests at the macro- and local levels. While the forms of agency discussed above are core to the dynamic and mutual influence of formal and informal behaviours, we cannot ignore the structural circumstances within which they originate and the constraints these exert on their possibilities of operation (Banks et al., 2019). A political economy approach is essential to grasping the role of the law, government policies, and macro-economic arrangements in producing the disadvantages and opportunities to which informal practices are a response. At the same time, it focuses on the fact that the state is not a single, homogeneous body but a set of entities operating at "different scales, with conflicting political interests" and with their own differences in power (Haid & Hilbrandt, 2019, p. 5). It is through a multi-scalar analysis that we can trace the linkages between macro-level pressures and shifts, the spaces that open up for meso-level actors to take advantage of ensuing ambiguities, and the ways in which grassroots actors mobilize their resources to extract what benefits they can or mitigate losses. In recognising the opportunities and limitations to different groups' scope of action, we can identify the relative "winners" and "losers" (Banks et al., 2019) created through stratification processes embedded in both formal and informal social relations. This approach incorporates the multiple actors that participate in and shape informal urban governance, while foregrounding their respective positions of power and the differing resources available to them.

Positioning informalities within macro-level processes inevitably brings to the fore the role played by neoliberal restructuring. Indeed, many scholars view neoliberalization as a fundamental catalyst in the expansion and proliferation of informal practices in housing production, income-generation, and urban governance around the globe (Boudreau, 2017; Graaff & Ha, 2015; Hillenkamp et al., 2013; Joassart-Marcelli, 2019). Policies of welfare retrenchment, deregulation of numerous economic sectors, and the consequent precarization of employment have contributed to rising inequalities globally in recent decades. With these have come the financialization of housing and its associated drives to "cleanse" and "renew" urban centres, mobilized through political rhetorics that criminalize poverty and immigration (Boudreau & Davis, 2017; Lombard, 2019; Wacquant, 2008). Nevertheless, these neoliberal patterns play out very differently in their specific national and urban contexts, taking on hybrid and constantly shifting forms in symbiosis with their economic and political setting (Peck, 2010). Italy has certainly seen an outsourcing of welfare services to the third sector and surveillance and security responsibilities to non-state actors (Ivasiuc, 2015). Public spending cuts have taken their toll on low-cost housing production and healthcare, and urban governance models are increasingly involving private enterprises (Moini, 2015; Moini & d'Albergo, 2015). Yet, the country has also resisted some of the deregulatory pressures seen elsewhere in Europe. We must therefore be careful not to over-determine the relationship between neoliberal processes and informality in ways that risk obscuring patterns of behaviour with roots in longer-term governance mechanisms and social practices.

Any understanding of how informal governance operates must, consequently, take account of all the state and non-state actors involved, especially those meso-level figures – such as private investors, banks, NGOs, experts – who wield significant influence in decision-making and implementation of policy, often with very limited accountability. As Picker (2019) has demonstrated, the authority to manage complex social situations is frequently delegated to (or appropriated by) such actors through mechanisms of "disaggregated governance." When this management is enacted through discretionary exceptions to or suspensions of the law, these agents take up elements of sovereignty that are normally under the purview of the state. This echoes AlSayyad and Roy's argument that contemporary cities are organized through "multiple and competing sovereignties which [...] produce fiefdoms of regulation or zones of 'no-law'" (2006, p. 1) where non-state actors "have emerged as the de facto state" (2006, p. 10). In such clashing, private systems of governance, patronage becomes a central logic of rule, further perpetuating the potential for opacities and inequalities of power. In many cases this means operating as intermediaries between weaker citizens and formal institutions, reducing the space of autonomy and advancement for less powerful actors while enabling the former to protect their continued ability to profit, financially or otherwise, from those inequalities (Banks et al., 2019).

From informalities to illegalities

Given these dynamic relationships between informal practices and regulatory orders, plenty of situations can arise in which informal actions violate codified law. It is because of this potential for informality to blur into illegality, or for the two to co-exist in various ways, that the terms are often used interchangeably (see, for example, Shapland & Ponsaers, 2009). I would argue, though, for maintaining analytical distinctions between the two concepts. As we have seen, many informal activities occur "beyond the law" (Polese et al., 2019), where there is no explicit regulation to transgress. Innumerable others clearly operate *within* the law, exploiting its loopholes or contradictions at different scales, or negotiate *how* the law is implemented. Where they do directly breach regulations, these are often administrative processes – bureaucratic standards, procedures, timeframes – rather than national or local legislation. In such circumstances, informality has nothing to do with illegality. Conversely, what is termed "informal" is often explicitly illegal; for example, when construction contravenes planning or building codes, or when an informal exchange infringes anti-corruption legislation.

Yet it is at times difficult to distinguish between practices that are informal and those that are illegal, partly because the apparent clear-cut opposition of legality and illegality is, in fact, often as entangled as that of in/formality. Legislation is constantly subject to change. As it is scrapped or introduced, amended, or reformed, actions that were previously legal or unregulated may shift into illegality. Vice versa, illegal ones may be legalized or decriminalized. When mapping legal landscapes, the temporal mobilities of law are as important to consider as the disjunctures between different institutional scales and geographical jurisdictions. Where bureaucratic processes are labyrinthine and impracticable, actors may have no alternative but to break the law in order to conform with its requirements, as is the case of migrants in Italy who pay for false employment contracts to be eligible for work permits whose restrictions exclude their real jobs (Calavita, 2005; Tuckett, 2018). The uncertain legal statuses that many migrants face globally – neither fully documented or undocumented, or straddling both, often for extended or repeated periods – force us to recognize the existence of liminal legalities (Menjívar, 2006). These concepts capture the reality that – as with in/formality – il/legality is not an antinomy but a spectrum: a "variety of semi-legal statuses scattered along a multidimensional space between the two poles 'legal–illegal'" (Kubal, 2013, p. 62).

Even when actions clearly violate the law, it is now widely accepted that "not all situations or practices are equally illegal or illegal in similar ways" (Polese et al., 2019, p. 11). Rather, we have gradations of illegality (Chiodelli, 2019; Pizzo & Altavilla, 2018), reflecting not only the typology of regulations being contravened but also the strictness with which they are enforced. Situations may be *de jure* illegal but remain *de facto* unimplemented due to political disinterest, bureaucratic incompetence or overload, or strategic manoeuvres, such as delaying judgement in order to push a crime beyond the statute of limitations. Certain types of law-breaking are therefore actively tolerated or permitted by state bodies or, in the case of repeated amnesties, effectively encouraged. Here too, temporalities are central, as decisions about how and when to enforce the law are often political, motivated by crises, imminent elections, market interests, or other macro pressures of the moment.

In the spaces of regulatory opacity and negotiation over implementation, informal actions can serve to directly facilitate illegal ones. For example, officials can choose not to notice illegal transactions or avoid checking the veracity of people's documented statuses.[6] Such dynamics are useful to a wide variety of actors and are certainly not the exclusive domain of professional criminals (Chiodelli, 2019; Dorn & Meerts, 2009; Pizzo & Altavilla, 2018). Nevertheless, in the opaque and uneven terrain of informal exchanges, actors with clientelistic or corrupt networks that span into the state infrastructure are particularly able to influence institutional behaviours. In Italy, mafia groups have such extensive social capital, especially at local and regional levels.[7] They draw their power from "forms of exchange rooted in reciprocity and complicity; controlling social networks and manipulating cultural codes; exercising functions of political regulation and mediation" (Sciarrone, 2019,

p. 76). Their social capital is underpinned by a two-way exchange. They utilize the skills and resources of non-mafia allies – public officials, politicians, lawyers, and doctors – who enable them to pursue their activities with little legal scrutiny. These professionals, in turn, benefit from the criminals' financial power and tentacular socio-political relations. The concept of a "grey area" has emerged in Italy to characterize this vast sphere of informal ties through which mafias engage with legal actors in pursuit of their long-term illegal goals.

Mafias or other criminal groups may further advance their power through exploiting the vulnerabilities of marginalized actors for whom informal activities are an unavoidable necessity. Living or working in informal or illegal situations may have the multiplier effect of further excluding the latter from legal rights and social protections, pushing them deeper into shadow zones of invisibility from formal institutions. Criminal groups may step in to offer their own alternative services and protections, profiting then from low-cost labour and other hidden resources in their production of illegal goods and services. They may also be brought in temporarily to enforce informal contracts when other strategies for resolving disputes outside formal structures are unsuccessful. There is not, however, an automatic connection between the two. Numerous informal domains in Italy are not penetrated by organized crime. Practices in some spheres may mimic behaviours – such as intimidation – learned from mafia actors, without the latter's direct or continued involvement (Chiodelli, 2019; Esposito & Chiodelli, 2020). Unofficial systems of welfare or power can also emerge entirely independently despite their "dangerous similarities with the mafia organisation" (Pizzo & Altavilla, 2018, p. 173). The mere inaction of the state is not motivation enough to draw mafias into spheres they do not already control. Such choices are determined by members' long-term strategic goals, their interest in accentuating a territorial presence (or not), their social capital, the potential profitability of the sector, among other considerations. What role these forces play can only be evinced empirically from concrete case studies. Each chapter of this book thus examines whether the power dynamics reflected and produced through informal practices create opportunities for criminal actors – mafia-type or otherwise – to expand their influence and exploit inequalities to their own ends. These possible entwinements are viewed as one of the various sets of relations that can be formed along that complex spectrum stretching from the fully formal to the entirely illegal.

In sum, informal practices and negotiations are ways in which actors mobilize their knowledge and capabilities, their financial and symbolic resources, and their social networks to advance or defend their interests in fields where such resources are unevenly distributed, through producing, interpreting, and violating regulations. It is by analyzing these patterned actions that we can bridge macro-structural, "top-down" approaches to power inequalities (Wacquant, 2019b) and the rich "bottom-up" accounts of the day-to-day production of social life by city residents (Simone & Pieterse, 2017). In the social space of informality, people do not merely adapt to or resist formal rules. They test and contest them and, in certain circumstances, manage to push back against them, forcing rules and regulatory practices to be redefined. Informalities are therefore part of the continuous process of constituting a normative order – both codified and unwritten – through relations of power that grow out of and respond to the local context.

Economies of Informal Practices

In moving away from dualistic approaches that position the state against citizens, agency against structure, current discussions of informality implicitly owe much to Pierre Bourdieu's theory of practice. Understandings of informal practices as ways of "knowing" local social life (McFarlane & Waibel 2016), as a currency through which people "structur[e] the social and spatial organisation of the city" (Marx & Kelling, 2019, p. 502), but also a signifier through "which social positions are taken, ascribed, and contested" (Müller, 2017, p. 3), variously echo Bourdieu's approach to mapping an "economy of practices" (1986, p. 16). I argue in this section that features of his interconnected triad – habitus, capital, and field –, alongside some recent critiques and reworkings, can be employed further to address three of the enduring theoretical gaps in how informality is often examined. These concern the importance of a) foregrounding the locally-specific historical genesis and evolution of informal practices and the contexts of their social acceptability and taken-for-grantedness, b) identifying the hierarchies of resources and constraints that bear on actors' opportunities for effective informal action, c) moving beyond sector-specific lenses to trace how actors' accrued competencies and understandings of informality may operate within and across different social environments.

Bourdieu insisted that any analysis of the skills, knowledge, and tactics that actors draw on and reproduce in their daily lives must be contextualized within the broader framework of social structures and power positions in which they are located. Not all actors have recourse to the same gamut of possible actions because they do not all have equal access to the same material and symbolic resources. Higher levels of capital offer a wider choice of behaviours. Dispositions will also be diversified according to people's positions within the social hierarchy, depending on the types of information and systems of value to which they are exposed and the behaviours that they consequently perceive as imaginable and legitimate for themselves and for others. Thus, practices are conditioned by habitus: the vast range of unconscious attitudes and competencies into which people in specific groups are socialized. These, in turn, enable them to navigate everyday life and cope strategically with unexpected and constantly evolving situations (Bourdieu, 1977). These dispositions are the product of collective, historically sedimented behaviours and experiences inherited from and transmitted to other actors over time. Looking at informalities from a Bourdieusian perspective, therefore, anchors the analysis of informal practices within locally distinct historicized dynamics of power. It draws our attention to how specific economic interests and political equilibria influence the crafting and moulding of rules and laws over time and at different scales. It is also essential to understanding how social attitudes evolve in relation to them (Bourdieu, 1987). This enables us to identify which formal rules are widely accepted as legitimate, which may be bent (and by whom), how their symbolic weight and negotiability have shifted over time, and how some informal behaviours have become absorbed into the regulatory order while others have been delegitimized.

The "rules of the game" in any field are likely to be shaped to favour elite interests and perspectives (Bourdieu & Wacquant, 1992; Fligstein & McAdam, 2015), since, in rising to their position of dominance, these groups tend to construct its formal mechanisms – its official regulations, procedures, recognized roles – and the behaviours that are valued. The same symbolic power can be equally central to defining what informal strategies for advancement are also considered legitimate. Powerful actors may use informal practices to maintain their advantages, creating conditions whereby certain types of rule-breaking become the unquestioned, common-sensical way of operating, to which weaker actors must often adhere. By conforming to and perpetuating those informalities, the latter may unwittingly reinforce the doxa that naturalises inequalities, thereby collaborating in their own subordination (Danielsson, 2015). Nevertheless, and contrary to common claims that Bourdieu's perspective is overly deterministic, he recognises that in all aspects of social life, rules – whether informally patterned or formal – are always open to subversion and circumvention (Crossley, 2005). "Playing with the rule is part and parcel of the rule of the game" (quoted in Bourdieu & Wacquant, 1992, p. 12). It is the constant potential of actors to resist against patterned orders, to soften structural rigidities and at times entirely overhaul them, that gives any field its "historical dynamism and malleability" (p. 18). Subordinate groups may very well challenge the informal activities of powerful actors while justifying their own. They may thereby contest dominant definitions and push to reformulate them in ways that respond to their own interests. Informal practices are thus not merely a reflection of existing inequalities but a means, a process, through which power is continuously negotiated and recalibrated.

Indeed, in Bourdieu's view, every field is in a constant state of tension, as actors with different amounts of capital vie to define its relative value and accrue more of it. I argue that informal negotiations are embedded within this conflict. They are a vector through which actors cultivate and mobilize their economic, social, cultural, and symbolic capital to advance their specific interests. The notion that capital can be converted in multiple and multidirectional ways is important here (Bourdieu, 1986; Pret et al., 2016). It allows us to trace, for example, how actors with high economic capital may transform that into the social capital required to convince others to formulate and enforce (or ignore) rules to their benefit. Elites may use informal negotiations within their social networks to perpetuate their dominance when formal rules are intended to check that power. Similarly, social networks – especially in the form of outwardly-projected *bridges* rather than intragroup *bonds* (Granovetter, 1973) – provide routes for subordinate actors to advance their position when they lack the cultural and economic capital to do so in formal and institutionalized ways.[8] Some forms are, however, more easily converted than others. For example, the embodied cultural capital of "long-lasting dispositions of the mind and body" (Bourdieu, 1986, p. 17) requires costly economic and temporal investment. Social capital may instead be more easily garnered since it is not conditional on financial resources or educational background (Light, 2004). Weak groups may focus on building ties with more highly positioned actors in order to influence regulatory processes to their advantage. Investments in social capital may also seek to redefine what characteristics are acknowledged as symbolic capital, aiming to enhance the prestige or recognition of attributes possessed by weaker actors. People working in informal economic niches, for example, may use their relationships with NGOs campaigning for social justice or environmental issues to reframe their stigmatized activities as a contribution to the social good.

An alternative way in which people make claims to rights and status emerges through the empirical case studies in this book. This is *temporal* capital; an additional typology of capital not proposed by Bourdieu, but which is mobilized by numerous actors to promote the legitimacy of their informal practices, especially when alternative forms of prestige are blocked off. It is a form of symbolic capital which rests on the longevity of a person's activity in a given field, irrespective of their lack of formal authorization. It is on the basis of long-term physical presence and the accumulated expertise that comes with it, that actors claim the right to continue their activities and for these to be valued in negotiations with the authorities. Temporal capital is therefore often a crucial resource that individuals at the lowest levels of the social hierarchy can harness to advance their position and to transform rule-breaking from a source of vulnerability to one of symbolic worth.

A Bourdieusian field is a specific and autonomous social arena (such as education or high fashion) ordered around its own rules, institutions, elites, and shared assumptions about what is important and what possibilities for action exist within it (Bourdieu & Wacquant, 1992; Hilgers & Mangez, 2014). Mapping a field in its entirety requires studying every element of its genesis and evolution, its stakes and doxa, the habitus of all the social groups involved and their positions within it. To build a complete genealogy of the macro fields considered in this book – housing, waste management, economics of trade and credit – would exceed the scope of identifying the roles played by informal negotiations in the governance of these sectors in Rome. Nevertheless, some elements of Bourdieu's field sociology – and those of scholars who have adapted his work – are useful in analyzing how informal practices both reflect and contribute to the local political economy. In particular, I view the sectors explored in the case studies as sub-fields that both depend on the dynamics of the higher-level field but also present their own internal logics (Fligstein & McAdam, 2015). Street trade, for example, has its own rules and regularities of practice, institutions, units of governance, but its hierarchies and opportunities are strongly influenced by the state and by forces in the local, national, and international economy. Each sub-field is a space of strategic action tied through a "complex latticework of relations," vertically to its macro-level field and horizontally to other proximate sub-fields (Fligstein & McAdam, 2015, p. 7, see also Schmitz et al., 2017). In this framework, the state bureaucracy holds "a sort of meta-capital granting power over other species of capital and over their holders" (Bourdieu et al., 1994, p. 4). It penetrates other (sub)-fields via its public policies, regulations, systems of categorization and distribution of public goods (Wacquant, 2019a, p. 37). Yet, it too is made of bureaucratic sub-fields where actors wrestle over "the power to rule via legislation, regulations, administrative measures" in their effort to gain control over "the monopoly of legitimate symbolic violence" (Bourdieu & Wacquant, 1992, pp. 111–112). The state is therefore a space of intense battle as different actors endeavour to shape its definitions and policies to reflect their own perspectives and positions (Dubois, 2015). Consequently, it is here that many informal negotiations and practices are concentrated, through short-term manoeuvrings around rules to benefit specific actors and through longer-term struggles over the very definition and impacts of those rules.

While Bourdieu saw actors in each field engaged primarily in conflict, more recent scholars have highlighted the possibilities for cooperation and solidarity that also emerge as agents coalesce to advance their shared concerns (Fligstein & McAdam, 2015; Friedland, 2009). Such alliances may be woven not only within but also between different fields. Actors, in fact, often operate in multiple fields at once and transfer understandings, competencies, and resources from one to the other. Thus, informal patterns of behaviour that become consolidated in one field may be mimicked in proximate ones or, conversely, the symbolic condemnation of such practices in one domain may spread to others as actors compete to define what actions are legitimate. Thinking in terms of (sub-)fields helps us to understand how informal practices are embedded within specific spheres of governance while recognizing that none of these fields is fully autonomous. This enables us to avoid identifying certain social groups as particularly prone to informality or viewing such practices as homogeneously spread across the city's mechanisms of governance. Rather, it prompts an analysis of power relations within each domain to explain how informal practices emerge, what purposes they serve and for whom, and why in some sectors they remain remarkably resilient while in others they are repressed. Informal practice thus lies in the hinge that connects agency and structure: it is a means of moving within the restrictions of structure and its patterned inequalities, bending its rigidities and taking advantage of that "play". If done repeatedly enough and with effective mobilization of capital, it can produce long-term change in the field's rules and logics of practice.

Temporal dimensions of informality

Some studies of informal practices have highlighted the centrality of time in how weak social actors construct their identities and manage their interactions with institutional agents (Auyero, 2012; Lombard, 2013; Moatasim, 2019). More analysis is needed, though, of the way institutional timeframes produce and reinforce inequalities, sometimes directly forcing people into rule-bending. How they generate diverse experiences of informality depending on how temporally pervasive it is in individuals' lives also requires further consideration. The processes through which we continuously "do" or "make" time in our everyday practices – *temporalization* in Bourdieu's terminology (2000) – are so embedded as to have become naturalized (Fitzpatrick, 2004). Yet, the ability to control and manipulate temporal rhythms and meanings lies at the heart of power (Bourdieu, 2000; Grabham, 2016), of state discipline and governance. The temporalities intrinsic to formulating and enacting regulations largely condition how informal practices are generated and experienced. It is hard to think of any rule that does not involve a defined implementation date, deadlines for compliance, or a rhythm of required behaviours. Regulations demand synchronism between social and institutional actors. Yet one simply may not be able to comply with the temporal demands of those in power by producing the right documents on time, attending a crucial appointment, or fulfilling dominant expectations of what constitutes permanent housing or a stable job (Vrăbiescu, 2019). To be "out of synch" frequently means being outside the rules – irregular –, treated as deviant and exposed to punishment or intensified obligations to conform in order to access core necessities.

It is when people's needs or priorities are incompatible with institutionalized time-rules that situations of informality often emerge or become most visible. Given the punitive repercussions that can come with being out of regulatory synchrony, many of the manoeuvres that constitute informal practices are negotiations over time. Strategies of temporalization include patiently waiting for institutional situations to change (Lombard, 2013), seeking extensions to deadlines or decelerating their enforcement, pushing for speedier paperwork or service provision. Since political and economic institutions of the state control much time-making, its representatives are those most able to dilate and contract regulatory timeframes. Such negotiations between bureaucrats and citizens are of course hierarchically inflected; nevertheless, as Ghertner demonstrates, people are able to "reach into the space of the state" (2017, p. 733), not simply by weaving ties with bureaucrats but by knowing *when* the configurations of power offer the most opportune moments for mobilizing those ties. Formally weak political actors thereby exert agency through a "keen spatiotemporal sensibility" (Ghertner, 2017, p. 733) that responds to shifting political conjunctures, exploiting the moments when power moves into the hands of the bureaucrats most accessible to them. Where time is elastic, therefore, it is not only state functionaries that manipulate it to their advantage, but any actor needing to incrementally improve their prospects.

Indeed, the state and its rules are not continuously present in people's lives. They appear and disappear through the actions of, and citizens' encounters with, officials in specific periods or moments (Dalsgaard, 2013). For prolonged durations the state may be experienced as absent, and that absence may take on visible, material qualities. Waste may pile up and infrastructure fall into disrepair (or never arrive), and activities outside state regulation may spread. The informal practices that replace the state's role of providing welfare, social order, economic and housing stability are particularly likely to flourish in such phases. When its own temporal logics induce the state to then (re)surface, reappearing in the personified form of politicians or functionaries, it must work to restore its authority and relevance. In contexts where the target population has political weight, this legitimacy may be achieved through offering gifts or concessions, or quickly providing long-awaited services. When dealing with politically weak groups, instead, the state is likely to flex its punitive muscles, reaffirming its power through repression and discipline. It is in these junctures when regulations are changed or enforced, when formalization initiatives are activated, that the informal practices through which actors organize their lives are potentially exposed to violent disruption. Positions of informal power built up over time may be destabilized, long-term financial investments suddenly undone, homes and livelihood displaced, effective tactics of citizenship and self-organization quashed (Verloo, 2017). Incrementally built stability may suddenly be replaced by precarity and insecurity. The politics of informality therefore involve cycles between the everyday activities of life and episodic moments of violence and rupture (Kudva, 2009).

There are profound qualitative disparities between the inherent temporalities of different types of informal practices and conditions. While many activities and encroachments are ephemeral, easily withdrawn or hidden in the face of institutional (re)surfacing, others are far more durable and structured. Unauthorized homes or irregular documentary statuses, for example, cannot simply be made to disappear. The time-scapes of informalities are intertwined with the vulnerability to which their irregularity exposes people. Each informal act is suffused, therefore, with implicit calculations concerning the perpetual possibility of a repressive backlash. These draw on observation of past rhythms and behaviours of the state in its multiple and fragmented expressions. Such knowledge also shapes expectations and orientations about the future. The intrinsic precarity of those who live in situations of protracted informality gives the future an exacerbated sense of unpredictability and insecurity. Not knowing whether regulatory shifts may affect one's access to housing, to work, or other necessities, weakens the ability to plan and to aspire that are essential to life in the present. Informal actors therefore often lack "the temporal 'affordances'" that make it possible to organize for the future beyond the most pressing immediate needs (Atkinson, 2019, p. 13). It is because of this insecurity that vulnerable actors so often labour to build a sense of legitimacy, collective identity, tenure, and rights centred on the longevity of their informal practices. Continuity in the past is a means of projecting some stability into the future, of demanding guarantees that are not formally bestowed, to achieve some sense of control.

Liminal informalities

However much people may seek predictability – that meshing together of past and future – not all social change is gradual or path-dependent. Sudden, dramatic upheavals may entirely disrupt all the dynamics and certainties of a field. Moreover, not all situations of indeterminacy are equal in their intensity and temporality. Recent discussions in the field of liminality studies help to unpack the gradations that precarity and ambiguity may take on, particularly foregrounding what happens when actors find themselves suspended outside normal social structures and clearly defined statuses. Many informalities exist in exactly the kind of threshold situations that the notion of liminality encapsulates, positioned in-between the certainty of what is fully authorized or evidently outside the rules, what is licit and normatively spurned. It is in such situations of indeterminacy – at once incorporated and separate, and where the future often appears unfathomable – that vulnerability and anxiety may be experienced particularly acutely (Andrews & Roberts, 2012; Szakolczai, 2014; Thomassen, 2009). Understanding how people cope with and act in such circumstances, striving to impose a sense of order and control, is fundamental to analyzing the logics and grammars through which actors create form in the apparent formlessness of informality.

Originally developed by Van Gennep (1960/2004) to identify the middle period in rites of passage – the phase in which one is suspended between two distinct statuses, social situations, places or times – the term liminality has in recent years been employed to make sense of a wide variety of conditions of in-betweenness; voluntary and involuntary, individual and collective, fleeting and epochal (Andrews & Roberts, 2015; Horváth et al., 2015; Stenner, 2018; Szakolczai, 2000, 2014; Thomassen, 2018).[9] Similarly to discussions of informality, its spatial dimensions have been the focus of much attention, partly due to the contemporary proliferation of physical zones that are ambiguous or contested, positioned outside normal social life, such as holding centres for asylum seekers (Andrews & Roberts, 2012; Downey et al., 2018; Horváth et al., 2019). It is in many such liminal spaces that regulations are at their least clear or, conversely, so rigid that informal practices are likely to emerge within or around them. Thus, it is in urban borderlands that many such activities may be found: on the edges of formal markets, in the indistinct zones around waste dumps, in peri-urban landscapes, and in buildings whose uses defy formal planning processes. These spatial dimensions are important in mapping the physical terrains of informality, their symbolic and economic value, and the social relations that play out within them.

It is when these are combined with an analysis of time and scale, however, that liminality can help us better focus on degrees of informality. Thomassen (2009, p. 17) has identified the differing social, temporal, and spatial scales that experiences of liminality may reach. It can concern individuals, groups (such as minorities), or entire populations. Its spaces may be small-scale (e.g. a doorway), mid-level zones, or macro-areas, such as regions. Most importantly for our purposes, time scales of liminality can range between the momentary, across periods of varying duration, to the permanent. As we have seen, informal activities may be short-term and quickly resolved, with individuals moving in and out of them with relative ease, like when workers merge informal and formal employment in their daily lives. Their fleetingness makes them difficult for institutions to intercept as they occur. It is instead when informal practices happen at the group level, taking on visible material forms and building up over time, that they are most susceptible to measures aimed at repressing or formalizing them and are most exposed to social turmoil when they are disrupted. Finally, liminal situations may become protracted, with no possibility of resolution in sight: "where the temporary and transitory become enduring and lasting" (Szakolczai, 2019, p. 8). While others have argued convincingly that permanent liminality is a defining feature of the entire epoch of modernity (Szakolczai, 2000, 2019; Thomassen, 2018), the empirical scale of attention in this book is at the meso-level, where specific groups of actors find themselves protractedly or indefinitely suspended outside the normal, ongoing regulatory systems of society.

We are not dealing here with the voluntary informal practices involved in advancing one's interests or "getting things done" (Ledeneva, 2018), or social contexts in which working around the rules is widespread or normatively sanctioned. Those are conditions where informalities are embedded in and work with existing structures. Liminality is instead "an interstructural situation" (Turner, 1967, p. 93) where one is located outside the stable, culturally recognized states through which people are granted clearly defined rights and obligations. It is about being unclassified and unclassifiable, and is consequently accompanied by a "scarcity of jurally sanctioned relationships" (p. 101). Liminal informalities are those in which actors have little agentive choice, forced – because of their documentary status or lack of economic resources – into living in a pervasive condition of precarity, often lacking any form of legal protection: in housing that is under constant threat of eviction, working in perpetual danger of arrest or losing one's assets, risking deportation or imprisonment for lack of papers. It is in such situations that vulnerability becomes an existential part of normality and where, very often, multiple types of informality reinforce each other, such that housing, bureaucratic, and economic informalities become intertwined and their intensity accumulates. Here the lack of clearly recognized statuses may breed continuous tension and convulsion, as crackdowns and displacements become the stuff of everyday life. Actors in such contexts must often dedicate time and money to averting institutional attention, activating strategies of invisibility or securing bureaucrats' forbearance to survive.

Turner (1967) argues that liminal *personae* are structurally "invisible" because of their unclassifiable status; it is that social non-being that makes liminal subjects symbolically charged and that requires ritual to exert order and predictability on the condition and an avenue for exiting it. A master of ceremonies is therefore often essential in guiding subjects through the strict phases of the rite, to the other side. This view assumes, however, that liminality is eventually resolved and a new stable status is achieved. It is now recognized though that this is not always the case. When liminality has no clear end, it may become so crystallized as to be widely acknowledged and institutionalized: hyper-visible and built into the social order (Thomassen, 2015). In such situations people may become "stuck" in liminality and escape routes or alternatives become difficult to contemplate. In the case of long-term informal statuses, public policies appear unable to unravel the regulatory gaps and contradictions upon which the informalities are built and become progressively more entangled. This is not the kind of "holy", integrated state evoked by Turnbull (1968), where opposites come together and actors learn to move between the parallel universes of the liminal and the normal. Rather, protracted informalities carry with them the same sense of danger and pollution that so many equivocal positions produce (Douglas, 2002; Turner, 1967), their negative connotations solidifying over time in ways that make the subjects' outsider status appear natural, ineluctable. Thus, many actors in situations of prolonged informality are subjected to the symbolic violence of continuous distancing and denigration, constructed as a threat to be avoided or perpetually quarantined. Indeed, marginality and liminality, though conceptually distinct conditions, often go hand in hand (Andrews & Roberts, 2012). Szakolczai (2000) argues that this merging is core to modernity's emphasis on regularity and conformity – and its fundamental construction of binary divisions; good and bad, legal and illegal – which results in the fixing of permanent, negative identities onto people who transgress such dualisms. Protracted informality, in its blurring of the authorized and the unauthorized, its muddying of formal roles and powers, disturbs and lays bare the fiction of transparent institutional and legal orderings. Thus, it must be institutionalized, its deviance made visible and visibly managed, in order for its opposite to be continuously reaffirmed.

Despite the danger to which individuals stuck in informality are exposed, this is not a static, passive situation. As with all liminal conditions, it holds within it the potential for upending taken-for-granted social logics and producing novel ones. Its separation from ordinary structures means that hierarchies may be questioned, doxa unmasked, and new forms of practice developed. Liminality brings with it not only transition, therefore, but deep transformation (Szakolczai & Thomassen, 2019; Turnbull, 1968); a potential new structuring of individual identities and social relations, new institutions and interactions. It thus appears to confound Bourdieusian linear-progressive explanations of the dynamics between social order and change (Szakolczai, 2014), agency and structure (Thomassen, 2009). However, Dobry (2015) has argued against abandoning the usual social scientific tools of analysis when examining such periods of upheaval, as if these liminal phases were on an entirely different plane from "normal" social life. Instead he calls for an exploration of "the fate of 'structures' in critical periods [...] the transformations to which they can be subjected, and [...] the possible effects of these transformations" (p. 95). We must identify the lasting features of dynamics built up during liminal situations (Mälksoo, 2012). We must tease out how protracted informalities produce their own logics and patterns, their own "grammars", and how these constrain how actors think and operate within them. Just as people in periods of upheaval will implement coping and sense-making strategies learned in the pre-liminal period and adapt them to the new situations, actors in durable positions of informality will borrow ordering mechanisms from "formal" life where appropriate and tailor them to the requirements of their immediate reality. If the situation of informality ends, they are likely to then take many of the behaviours and meanings developed there into their new reality. In discerning the continuities and differences in how people behave and the calculations they make in their changed circumstances, we can also focus on what types of capital are accrued during periods of liminality; which social ties, forms of knowledge, financial strategies and investments in temporal capital are maintained or converted in post-liminal conditions.

Conclusion

Bridging political economy approaches to informality with a time-sensitive focus on practices and their cumulative effects is central to the multi-scalar analysis presented in the next chapters. The attention to timings allows us to home in on the unsteady balance between stability and upheaval that so often marks informalities. On the one hand the Bourdieusian lens helps to trace the long-term interconnections between power positions, shared assumptions, and knowledge, and the perpetuation of these through practices. The liminality lens, on the other, highlights the often massively disruptive impacts that apparently minor shifts in regulatory definitions and statuses can have on that equilibrium. It emphasizes the lived experiences and coping strategies of people who find themselves in ambiguous positions. Whether these are protracted, permanent even, or whether a route into clarity is offered through formalization initiatives, this lens foregrounds the power and danger of the "in-between".

Notes

1 See, for example, the many typologies outlined in Ledeneva (2018).
2 For example, special issues focusing on various dimensions of informality have been published in *International Sociology* (2017), *Current Sociology* (2017), *The Journal of Development Studies* (2018), *International Journal of Urban and Regional Research* (2019), *Urban Studies* (2019), *Cities* (2019), and *International Journal of Housing Policy* (2020).
3 For an overview of the evolution of informality studies since the 1970s, see AlSayyad, 2004.

4 Picker (2021) points out the danger of using this chromatic metaphor which involuntarily perpetuates the racialized and colonial equation of whiteness as synonymous with order and transparency, and blackness as its opaque and violent opposite.
5 See, for example, Solimene's (2013) study of how Roma groups in Italy use "circumspect agency," engaging with state officials through humanising tactics that serve to bridge the power gap while also maintaining their autonomy and political disengagement.
6 Tuckett (2018), for example, highlights that Italian authorities rarely investigate whether migrants' work or residency declarations are true. Similarly, Esposito and Chiodelli (2020) note that the "fraudulent takeover" system that privatizes public housing operates effectively because officials do not monitor whether the stated composition of the households reflects reality.
7 Note that Italian law distinguishes between a criminal association (*associazione per delinquere*), and a mafia-type association (*associazione di tipo mafioso*). The former is applicable "when three or more persons associate in order to commit several criminal offences" (Art. 416 of the Penal Code). The latter "is said to exist when the participants take advantage of the intimidating power of the association and of the resulting conditions of submission and silence to commit criminal offences, to manage or at all events control, either directly or indirectly, economic activities, concessions, authorizations, public contracts and services, or to obtain unlawful profits or advantages for themselves or for others, or with a view to prevent or limit the freedom to vote, or to get votes for themselves or for others on the occasion of an election" (Art. 416.bis. Translation: UNODC).
8 This utilitarian view does not exclude the possibility that social networks may also serve to develop solidarity, trust, resource sharing and community development (Putnam, 2000). Nevertheless, in the highly unequal terrains discussed in these chapters, where institutional legitimacy and trust are generally weak and many vulnerable actors unable to invest time in civic participation, the emphasis is necessarily on individual negotiations of value rather than community-wide benefits.
9 See Thomassen (2009) for a thorough overview of the evolution in the term's conceptual development and application.

References

Acuto, M., Dinardi, C., & Marx, C. (2019). Transcending (in)formal urbanism. *Urban Studies*, 56(3), 475–487. https://doi.org/10.1177/0042098018810602.

AlSayyad, N. (2004). Urban informality as a "new" way of life. In A. Roy & N. AlSayyad (eds), *Urban informality: Transnational perspectives from the Middle East, Latin America, and South Asia* (pp. 7–30). Lexington Books.

Alsayyad, N., & Roy, A. (2006). Medieval modernity: On citizenship and urbanism in a global era. *Space and Polity*, 10(1), 1–20. https://doi.org/10.1080/13562570600796747.

Altrock, U. (2016). Conceptualising informality: Some thoughts on the way towards generalization. In C. McFarlane & M. Waibel (eds), *Urban informalities: Reflections on the formal and informal* (pp. 171–193). Routledge. https://doi.org/10.4324/9781315548814.

Andrews, H., & Roberts, L. (2012). Introduction: Re-mapping liminality. In H. Andrews & L. Roberts (eds), *Liminal landscapes: Travel, experience and spaces in-between* (pp. 1–17). Routledge. https://doi.org/10.4324/9780203123164-7.

Andrews, H. & Roberts, L. (2015). Liminality. In N. J. Smelser & P. B. Baltes (eds), *International encyclopedia of the social and behavioral sciences* (pp. 131–137). Elsevier. https://doi.org/10.1016/c2010-1-67141-6.

Atkinson, W. (2019). Time for Bourdieu: Insights and oversights. *Time & Society*, 28 (3), 951–970. https://doi.org/10.1177/0961463X17752280.

Auyero, J. (2012). *Patients of the state: The politics of waiting in Argentina*. Duke University Press.

Banks, N., Mitlin, D., & Lombard, M. (2019). Urban informality as a site of critical analysis. *Journal of Development Studies*, 56(2), 223–238. https://doi.org/10.1080/00220388.2019.1577384.

Bayat, A. (2004). Globalization and the politics of the informals in the Global South. In A. Roy & N. AlSayyad (eds), *Urban informality: Transnational perspectives from the Middle East, Latin America, and South Asia*, pp. 64–80. Lexington Books.

Boels, D. (2016). *The informal economy: Seasonal work, street selling and sex work*. Springer. https://doi.org/10.1007/978-3-319-43123-9.

Boudreau, J.-A. (2017). *Global urban politics: Informalization of the state*. Urban Futures.

Boudreau, J.-A., & Davis, D. (2017). Introduction: A processual approach to informalization. *Current Sociology*, 65(2), 151–166. https://doi.org/10.1177%2F0011392116657286.

Bourdieu, P. (1977). *Outline of a theory of practice*. Cambridge University Press. https://doi.org/10.1017/cbo9780511812507.

Bourdieu, P. (1986). The forms of capital. In J. G. Richardson (ed.), *Handbook of theory and research for the sociology of education* (pp. 241–258). Greenwood Press.

Bourdieu, P. (1987). The force of law: Toward a sociology of the juridical field. *Hastings Law Journal*, 38(5), 814–853.

Bourdieu, P. (2000). *Pascalian meditations*. Polity.

Bourdieu, P., & Wacquant, L. (1992). *An invitation to reflexive sociology*. Polity.

Bourdieu, P., Wacquant, L. J. D., & Farage, S. (1994). Rethinking the state: Genesis and structure of the bureaucratic field. *Sociological Theory*, 12(1), 1. https://doi.org/10.2307/202032.

Brown, A. (ed.). (2017). *Rebel streets and the informal economy*. Routledge. https://doi.org/10.4324/9781315641461.

Calavita, K. (2005). *Immigrants at the margins: Law, race and exclusion in Southern Europe*. Cambridge University Press. https://doi.org/10.1017/cbo9780511493942.

Canclini, N. G. (2019). A culture of informality. *Urban Studies*, 56(3), 488–493. https://doi.org/10.1177/0042098018782635.

Chiodelli, F., & Moroni, S. (2014). The complex nexus between informality and the law: Reconsidering unauthorised settlements in light of the concept of nomotropism. *Geoforum*, 51, 161–169. https://doi.org/10.1016/j.geoforum.2013.11.004.

Chiodelli, F. (2019). The dark side of urban informality in the Global North: Housing illegality and organized crime in Northern Italy. *International Journal of Urban and Regional Research*, 43(3), 497–516. https://doi.org/10.1111/1468-2427.12745.

Chiodelli, F., & Tzfadia, E. (2016). The multifaceted relation between formal institutions and the production of informal urban spaces: An editorial introduction. *Geography Research Forum*, 36, 1–14.

Clough Marinaro, I., & Solimene, M. (2020). Navigating the (in)formal city: Roma, urban life and governance in Rome. *Cities*, 96. https://doi.org/10.1016/j.cities.2019.102402.

Crossley, N. (2005). *Key concepts in critical social theory*. Sage. https://doi.org/10.4135/9781446220702.

Dalsgaard, S. (2013). The time of the state and the temporality of the Gavman in Manus Province. *Social Analysis*, 57(1), 34–49. https://doi.org/10.3167/sa.2013.570103.

Danielsson, A. (2015). Fieldnotes on informality's culture of ubiquity: Recognition and symbolic power within informal economic practices in Kosovo. In J. Morris & A. Polese (eds), *Informal economies in post-socialist spaces: Practice, institutions and networks* (pp.117–138). Palgrave Macmillan. https://doi.org/10.1057/9781137483072.

Davoli, C. (2018). Le occupazioni abitative a Roma: Una "pratica di movimento" per il diritto all'abitare. In A. Coppola & G. Punziano (eds), *Roma in transizione. Governo, strategie, metabolismi e quadri di vita di una metropoli* (pp. 303–316). Planum. www.planum.net/planum-magazine/planum-publisher-publication/roma-in-transizione_coppola_punziano.

Demirtas-Milz, N. (2013). The regime of informality in neoliberal times in Turkey: The case of the kadifekale urban transformation project. *International Journal of Urban and Regional Research*, 37(2), 689–714. https://doi.org/10.1111/1468-2427.12005.

Dobry, M. (2015). Critical processes and political fluidity: A theoretical appraisal. In A. Horváth, B. Thomassen, & H. Wydra (eds), *Breaking boundaries: Varieties of liminality* (pp. 93–111). Berghahn. https://doi.org/10.2307/j.ctt9qcxbg.

Dorn, N., & Meerts, C. (2009). Corporate security and private settlement: An informal economy of justice. In J. Shapland & P. Ponsaers (eds), *The informal economy and connections with organised crime: The impact of national social and economic policies* (pp. 113–129). Boom Juridische Uitgevers.

Douglas, M. (2002). *Purity and danger: An analysis of concepts of pollution and taboo.* Routledge. https://doi.org/10.4324/9780203361832.

Downey, D., Kinane, I., & Parker, E. (2018). *Landscapes of liminality: Between space and place.* Rowman & Littlefield.

Dubois, V. (2014). The fields of public policy. In M. Hilgers & E. Mangez (eds), *Bourdieu's theory of social fields: Concepts and applications* (pp. 199–220). Routledge.

Durst, N. J., & Wegmann, J. (2017). Informal housing in the United States. *International Journal of Urban and Regional Research*, 41(2), 282–297. https://doi.org/10.1111/1468-2427.12444.

Esposito, E., & Chiodelli, F. (2020). Juggling the formal and the informal: The regulatory environment of the illegal access to public housing in Naples. *Geoforum*, 113, 50–59. https://doi.org/10.1016/j.geoforum.2020.05.002.

Friedland, R. (2009). The endless fields of Pierre Bourdieu. *Organization*, 16(6), 887–917. https://doi.org/10.1177/1350508409341115.

Fitzpatrick, T. (2004). Social policy and time. *Time and Society*, 13(2/3), 197–219. https://doi.org/10.1177/0961463X04043502.

Fligstein, N., & McAdam, D. (2015). *A theory of fields.* Oxford University Press. https://doi.org/10.1093/acprof:oso/9780199859948.001.0001.

Ghertner, A. (2017). When is the state? Topology, temporality, and the navigation of everyday state space in Delhi. *Annals of the American Association of Geographers*, 107(3), 731–750. https://doi.org/10.1080/24694452.2016.1261680.

Gillespie, T. (2017). From quiet to bold encroachment: Contesting dispossession in Accra's informal sector. *Urban Geography*, 38(7), 974–992. https://doi.org/10.1080/02723638.2016.1191792.

Giordano, C., & Hayoz, N. (2013). *Informality in Eastern Europe: Structures, political cultures and social practices.* Peter Lang AG. https://doi.org/10.3726/978-3-0351-0651-0.

Graaff, K., & Ha, N. (2015). *Street vending in the neoliberal city. A global perspective on the practices and policies of a marginalized economy.* Berghahn.
Grabham, E. (2016). *Brewing legal times: Things, form, and the enactment of law.* University of Toronto Press. https://doi.org/10.3138/9781442663909-002.
Granovetter, M. (1973). The strength of weak ties. *American Journal of Sociology*, 78(6), 1360–1380.
Grashoff, U. (2019). Cautious occupiers and restrained bureaucrats: Schwarzwohnen in the German Democratic Republic. Somewhat different from squatting. *Urban Studies*, 56(3), 548–560. https://doi.org/10.1177/0042098017734813.
Gurran, N., Maalsen, S., & Shrestha, P. (2020). Is 'informal' housing an affordability solution for expensive cities? Evidence from Sydney, Australia. *International Journal of Housing Policy.* Advance online publication. https://doi.org/10.1080/19491247.2020.1805147.
Haid, C. G. (2017). The Janus face of urban governance: State, informality and ambiguity in Berlin. *Current Sociology*, 65(2), 289–301. https://doi.org/10.1177/0011392116657299.
Haid, C. G., & Hilbrandt, H. (2019) Urban informality and the state: Geographical translations and conceptual alliances. *International Journal of Urban and Regional Research*, 43 (3), 551–562. https://doi.org/10.1111/1468-2427.12700.
Herrle, P., & Fokdal, J. (2011). Beyond the urban informality discourse: Negotiating power, legitimacy and resources. *Geographische Zeitschrift*, 99(1), 3–15. https://elibrary.steiner-verlag.de/article/99.105010/gz201101000301.
Hilgers, M., & Mangez, E. (eds). (2014) *Bourdieu's theory of social fields: Concepts and applications.* Routledge.
Hillenkamp, I., Lapeyre, F., & Lemaître, A. (eds). (2013). *Securing livelihoods: Informal economy practices and institutions.* Oxford University Press. https://doi.org/10.1093/acprof:oso/9780199687015.001.0001.
Holland, A. (2017). *Forbearance as redistribution: The politics of informal welfare in Latin America.* Cambridge University Press. https://doi.org/10.1017/9781316795613.
Horváth, A. Thomassen, B., & Wydra, H. (eds). (2015). *Breaking boundaries: Varieties of liminality.* Berghahn. https://doi.org/10.2307/j.ctt9qcxbg.
Horváth, A., Benta, M. I., & Davison, J. D. (eds). (2019). *Walling, boundaries and liminality: A political anthropology of transformations.* Routledge. https://doi.org/10.4324/9781315105338.
Ivasiuc, A. (2015). Watching over the neighbourhood: Vigilante discourses and practices in the suburbs of Rome. *Etnofoor*, 27(2), 53–72.
Jaffe, R., & Koster, M. (2019). The myth of formality in the Global North: Informality-as-innovation in Dutch governance. *International Journal of Urban and Regional Research*, 43(3), 563–568. https://doi.org/10.1111/1468-2427.12706.
Joassart-Marcelli, P. (2019). Neoliberalism, globalization, and magnification of the informal economy. City Rising. *KCET.* www.kcet.org/shows/city-rising/neoliberalism-globalization-and-the-magnification-of-the-informal-economy.
Kubal, A. (2013). Conceptualizing semi-legality in migration research. *Law & Society Review*, 47(3), 555–587. https://doi.org/10.1111/lasr.12031.
Kudva, N. (2009). The everyday and the episodic: The spatial and political impacts of urban informality. *Environment and Planning A*, 41(7): 1614–1628. https://doi.org/10.1068/a41101.
Langegger, S., & Koester, S. (2017). Moving on, finding shelter: The spatiotemporal camp. *International Sociology*, 32(4), 454–473. https://doi.org/10.1177/0268580917701584.

Ledeneva, A. (ed.). (2018). *The global encyclopaedia of informality: Understanding social and cultural complexity* (vols 1 & 2). UCL Press. https://doi.org/10.14324/111.9781911307907.

Lendaro, A. (2019). Nothing to lose: The power of subtle forms of resistance in an immigration detention centre. In A. Polese, A. Russo, & F. Strazzari (eds), *Governance beyond law: The immoral, the illegal, the criminal* (pp. 309–322). Palgrave Macmillan. https://doi.org/10.1007/978-3-030-05039-9_16.

Light, I. (2004). Social capital's unique accessibility. *Journal of the American planning Association*, 70(2), 145–151.

Lombard, M. (2013). Struggling, suffering, hoping, waiting: Perceptions of temporality in two informal neighbourhoods in Mexico. *Environment and Planning: Society and Space*, 31(5), 813–829. https://doi.org/10.1068/d21610.

Lombard, M. (2019). Informality as structure or agency? Exploring shed housing in the UK as informal practice. *International Journal of Urban and Regional Research*, 43(3), 569–575. https://doi.org/10.1111/1468-2427.12705.

Mälksoo, M. (2012). The challenge of liminality for international relations theory. *Review of International Studies*, 38(2), 481–494. https://doi.org/10.1017/S0260210511000829.

Marcelli, E., Williams, C., & Joassart, P. (2014). *Informal work in developed nations.* Routledge. https://doi.org/10.4324/9780203874455.

Marx, C., & Kelling, E. (2019). Knowing urban informalities. *Urban Studies*, 56(3), 494–509. https://doi.org/10.1177/0042098018770848.

McFarlane, C., & Waibel, M. (2016). *Urban informalities: Reflections on the formal and informal*. Routledge. https://doi.org/10.4324/9781315548814.

Menjívar, C. (2006). Liminal legality: Salvadoran and Guatemalan immigrants' lives in the United States. *American Journal of Sociology*, 111(4), 999–1037. https://doi.org/10.1086/499509.

Mica, A. (2016). Towards a typology of hybrid formalities and informalities. *Polish Sociological Review*, 194(2), 139–153.

Mica, A., Winczorek, J., & Wisniewski, R. (2015). *Sociologies of formality and informality.* Peter Lang. https://doi.org/10.3726/978-3-653-04521-5.

Moatasim, F. (2019). Informality materialised: Long-term temporariness as a mode of informal urbanism. *Antipode*, 51(1), 271–294. https://doi.org/10.1111/anti.12434.

Moini, G. (ed.). (2015). *Neoliberismi e azione pubblica. Il caso italiano.* Ediesse.

Moini, G., & d'Albergo, E. (2015). *Il regime dell'Urbe. Politica, economia e potere a Roma.* Carocci.

Morris, J., & Polese, A. (Eds.). (2015). *Informal economies in post-socialist spaces: Practice, institutions and networks.* Palgrave Macmillan. https://doi.org/10.1057/9781137483072.

Mukhija, V. & Loukaitou-Sideris, A. (eds). (2014). *The informal American city: Beyond taco trucks and day labor.* MIT Press.

Müller, F. I. (2017). Urban informality as a signifier: Performing urban reordering in suburban Rio de Janeiro. *International Sociology*, 32(4), 493–511. https://doi.org/10.1177/0268580917701585.

Naqvi, I. (2017). Governance as an emergent compromise: Modernization and flexibility in the Pakistani electrical power sector. *Current Sociology*, 65(2), 195–208. https://doi.org/10.1177/0011392116657290.

Nasreen, Z., & Ruming, K. J. (2020). Informality, the marginalised and regulatory inadequacies: A case study of tenants' experiences of shared room housing in

Sydney, Australia. *International Journal of Housing Policy*. Advance online publication. https://doi.org/10.1080/19491247.2020.1803531.
Peck, J. (2010). *Constructions of neoliberal reasoning*. Oxford University Press. https://doi.org/10.1093/acprof:oso/9780199580576.001.0001.
Picker, G. (2019). Sovereignty beyond the state: Exception and informality in a Western European city. *International Journal of Urban and Regional Research*, 43(3), 576–581. https://doi.org/10.1111/1468-2427.12704.
Picker, G. (2021). Discussion intervention. Houses of Cards: The Rules and Institutions of Housing Illegality/Informality in Western Countries, 19–21 April. University of Cambridge and University of Turin. Online Conference.
Pizzo, B., & Altavilla, E. (2018). Embedding illegality, or when the illegal becomes licit: Planning cases and urban transformations in Rome. In F. Chiodelli, T. Hall, & R. Hudson (eds), *The illicit and illegal in regional and urban governance and development: Corrupt places* (pp. 164–180). Routledge. https://doi.org/10.4324/9781315317663-10.
Polese, A., Kovacs, B., Morris, J., & Reviakhshvili, L. (eds). (2017a). *Post-socialist informalities: Power, agency and the construction of extra-legalities from Bosnia to China*. Routledge. https://doi.org/10.4324/9781315100135.
Polese, A., Williams, C., Horodnic, I., & Bejaković, P. (eds). (2017b). *The informal economy in global perspective: Varieties of governance*. Palgrave. https://doi.org/10.1007/978-3-319-40931-3.
Polese, A., Russo, A., & Strazzari, F. (2019). Introduction: "The good, the bad and the ugly": Transnational perspectives on the extralegal field. In A. Polese, A. Russo, & F. Strazzari (eds), *Governance beyond the law: The immoral, the illegal, the criminal* (pp. 1–26). Palgrave. https://doi.org/10.1007/978-3-030-05039-9_1.
Pratt, A. (2019). Formality as exception. *Urban Studies*, 56(3), 612–615. https://doi.org/10.1177/0042098018810600.
Pradel-Miquel, M. (2017). Crisis, (re-)informalization processes and protest: The case of Barcelona. *Current Sociology*, 65(2), 209–221. https://doi.org/10.1177/0011392116657291.
Pret, T., Shaw, E., & Drakopoulou, D. S. (2016). Painting the full picture: The conversion of economic, cultural, social and symbolic capital. *International Small Business Journal: Researching Entrepreneurship*, 34(8), 1004–1027. https://doi.org/10.1177/0266242615595450.
Putnam, R. D. (2000). *Bowling alone*. Simon & Schuster.
Roy, A. (2009). Why India cannot plan its cities: Informality, insurgence and the idiom of urbanization. *Planning Theory*, 8(1), 76–87. https://doi.org/10.1177/1473095208099299.
Roy, A. (2018). The potency of the state: Logics of informality and subalternity. *Journal of Development Studies*, 54(12), 2243–2246. https://doi.org/10.1080/00220388.2018.1460470.
Rubin, M. (2018). At the borderlands of informal practices of the state: Negotiability, porosity and exceptionality. *Journal of Development Studies*, 54(12), 2227–2242. https://doi.org/10.1080/00220388.2018.1460466.
Schmitz, A., Witte, D., & Gengnagel, V. (2017). Pluralizing field analysis: Toward a relational understanding of the field of power. *Social Science Information*, 56(1), 49–73. https://doi.org/10.1177/0539018416675071.
Schoon, S., & Altrock, U. (2014) Conceded informality: Scopes of informal urban restructuring in the Pearl River Delta. *Habitat International*, 43, 214–220. https://doi.org/10.1016/j.habitatint.2014.03.007.

Sciarrone, R. (2019). The economic dimension of mafias, social capital and the "grey area". In F. Allum, I. Clough Marinaro, & R. Sciarrone (eds), *Italian mafias today: Territory, business and politics* (pp. 76–90). Edward Elgar. https://doi.org/10.4337/9781789904147.00014.

Scott, J. C. (1976). *The moral economy of the peasant: Rebellion and subsistence in Southeast Asia*. Yale University Press.

Scott, J. C. (1985). *Weapons of the weak: Everyday forms of peasant resistance.* Yale University Press.

Scott, J. C. (2009). *Domination and the arts of resistance: Hidden transcripts.* Yale University Press.

Shapland, J., & Ponsaers, P. (2009). Potential effects of national policies on the informal economy. In J. Shapland & P. Ponsaers (eds). *The informal economy and connections with organised crime: The impact of national social and economic policies* (pp. 1–21). Boom Juridische Uitgevers.

Simone, A. M., & Pieterse, E. (2017). *New urban worlds.* Polity. https://www.wiley.com/en-us/New+Urban+Worlds%3A+Inhabiting+Dissonant+Times-p-9780745691565.

Smart, A., Smart, J., & Zerilli, F. (2017). Foreword. *ANUAC*, 6(2), 45–108.

Solimene, M. (2013). Undressing the gagé clad in state garb: Bosnian xoraxané romá face to face with the Italian authorities. *Romani Studies*, 23(2), 161–186. https://doi.org/10.3828/rs.2013.9.

Solimene, M. (2019). The (in)formal, the (il)legal and the (il)licit. Roma informal settlements and institutional pragmatics of compromise and compassion in a Roman periphery. *Cities*, 95. https://doi.org/10.1016/j.cities.2019.05.038.

Stenner, P. (2018). *Liminality and experience: A transdisciplinary approach to the psychosocial.* Palgrave Macmillan. https://doi.org/10.1057/978-1-137-27211-9.

Szakolczai, A. (2000). *Reflexive historical sociology.* Routledge. https://doi.org/10.4324/9780203193617.

Szakolczai, A. (2014). Living permanent liminality: The recent transition experience in Ireland. *Irish Journal of Sociology*, 22(1), 28–50. https://doi.org/10.7227/ijs.22.1.3.

Szakolczai, A. (2019). *Permanent liminality and modernity: Analysing the sacrificial carnival through novels.* Routledge.

Szakolczai, A., & Thomassen, B. (2019). *From anthropology to social theory: Rethinking the social sciences.* Cambridge University Press. https://doi.org/10.1017/9781108529426.

Thomassen, B. (2009). The uses and meanings of liminality. *International Political Anthropology*, 2(1), 5–27.

Thomassen, B. (2015). Thinking with liminality: To the boundaries of an anthropological concept. In A. Horváth, B. Thomassen, & H. Wydra (eds), *Breaking boundaries: Varieties of liminality* (pp. 39–60). Berghahn. https://doi.org/10.2307/j.ctt9qcxbg.6.

Thomassen, B. (2018). *Liminality and the modern: Living through the in-between.* Routledge. https://doi.org/10.4324/9781315592435.

Tuckett, A. (2018). *Rules, paper, status: Migrants and precarious bureaucracy in contemporary Italy.* Stanford University Press. https://doi.org/10.1515/9781503606500.

Turnbull, C. (1968). *The forest people.* Simon & Schuster.

Turner, V. (1967). *The forest of symbols: Aspects of Ndembu ritual.* Cornell University Press.

Van Gelder, J.-L. (2013). Paradoxes of urban housing informality in the developing world. *Law & Society Review*, 47(3), 493–522. https://doi.org/10.1111/lasr.12030.

Van Gennep, A. (1960/2004). *The rites of passage.* Routledge.

Varley, A. (2013). Postcolonialising informality? *Environment and Planning: D, Society and Space*, 31(1), 4–22. https://doi.org/10.1068/d14410.

Varriale, A. (2014). Informal practices, formal regulations: Understanding informality as spatial dialectics. *Advanced Engineering Forum*, 11, 136–141. https://doi.org/10.4028/www.scientific.net/aef.11.136.

Verloo, N. (2017). Learning from informality? Rethinking the mismatch between formal policy strategies and informal tactics of citizenship. *Current Sociology*, 65(2), 167–181. https://doi.org/10.1177/0011392116657287.

Vrăbiescu, I. (2019). Dwelling in limbo. Temporality in the governance of Romani migrants in Spain. In T. Magazzini & S. Piemontese (eds), *Constructing Roma migrants: European narratives and local governance* (pp. 109–128). Springer. https://doi.org/10.1007/978-3-030-11373-5_7.

Wacquant, L. (2008). Ordering insecurity: Social polarization and the punitive upsurge. *Radical Philosophy Review*, 11(1), 9–27. https://doi.org/10.5840/radphilrev20081112.

Wacquant, L. (2019a). Class, ethnicity and state in the making of urban marginality. In J. Flint & R. Powell (eds), *Class, ethnicity and state in the polarized metropolis: Putting Wacquant to work* (pp. 23–50). Springer. https://doi.org/10.1007/978-3-030-16222-1_2.

Wacquant, L. (2019b) Dispossession and dishonour in the polarized metropolis: Reactions and recommendations. In J. Flint & R. Powell (eds), *Class, ethnicity and state in the polarized metropolis: Putting Wacquant to work* (pp. 309–323). Springer. https://doi.org/10.1007/978-3-030-16222-1_13.

Yiftachel, O. (2009a). Critical theory and 'gray space': Mobilization of the colonized. *City*, 13(2/3), 246–263. https://doi.org/10.1080/13604810902982227.

Yiftachel, O. (2009b). Theoretical notes on 'gray cities': The coming of urban apartheid? *Planning Theory*, 8(1), 88–100. https://doi.org/10.1177/1473095208099300.

2 Residing in liminality

Housing informalities and the public sector

Introduction

As urbanization has expanded relentlessly across the globe in recent decades, unauthorized, legally ambiguous, or improvised housing has inevitably proliferated with it.[1] The United Nations estimates that over a billion people currently live in slums or low-quality informal settlements, primarily in the megalopolises of the Global South (UN-Habitat, n.d.). Because of the ties between precarious housing and residents' health and economic survival, scholarly attention has tended to focus on this dimension. Nevertheless, the role played by elite actors – especially real-estate developers and public authorities – in bending regulations to generate high-revenue property has also drawn scrutiny for its part in shaping today's cities (Moatasim, 2019; Pow, 2017; Roy, 2005, 2009). A similar diversity of informal housing situations exists in Italy. This ranges from shacks built by migrants among vegetation on the fringes of cities or agricultural land to unauthorized construction or expansion of private homes often visually indistinguishable from authorized buildings (Chiodelli et al., 2020).

Rome's urban development since it became capital in 1871 has in many ways been driven by informal housing production, of both the survival and financially speculative types. The mechanisms that have spurred its private forms have been widely studied (Berdini, 2010; Cellamare, 2014; Coppola, 2017, 2018). Far less consideration has been given to informalities within publicly built and managed housing, where residents are exposed long-term to the fluctuating attentions of multiple institutions. This chapter connects macro-level shifts in the field of housing policy to the lived experiences of residents, particularly those in state-built accommodation. It demonstrates that the city's informalities are primarily driven from "above." The contradictory behaviours of different institutions, gaps between regulations, and other governance ambiguities directly condition the daily lives and tactics of some of the city's most disadvantaged residents. The analysis reveals not only the multi-layered processes of "grey governance" (Chiodelli & Tzfadia, 2016) but also traces how residents order their lives and adapt in response, negotiating power and seeking to mould institutional actions from "below."

DOI: 10.4324/9780429353321-3

The chapter first maps out how the field has evolved in Rome since the post-war period, highlighting the political emphasis that has been placed on supporting and expanding the private housing sector. The consequent lack of sustained public provision of low-cost accommodation has created an environment in which informal solutions have become normalized: the taken-for-granted practices adopted by myriad urbanites to fill this vast gap. The varied levels of capital available to these actors have generated many types of informal housing production, the most prevalent and problematic of which are outlined in the first part of the discussion. A hierarchical ordering of these typologies can be identified, based on how public institutions have responded to them. Some manifestations have been stigmatized and repressed, some have been absorbed into the formal order, while others have been tacitly accepted by the authorities for decades. In fact, many inhabitants have been placed in situations of protracted liminality, their status often remaining chronically unaddressed and unresolved. This historical and sectoral overview provides the context, then, for the chapter's main case study, which focuses on Corviale, a public housing complex built in the late 1970s to accommodate thousands of low-income residents. The multiple informalities that have evolved there over forty years result from – and are emblematic of – broader institutional management of Rome's low-income population. Oscillations in regulations and bureaucratic timeframes have had notable repercussions on Corviale residents' access to services and on their everyday security and stability. They have also further fuelled the latter's informal self-help strategies.

A localized formalization initiative has now been launched with the aim of undoing of some – but not all – entrenched informalities in the complex. Exploring the pre-formalization situation and the current regularization policy offers rich material for analyzing how institutional allocations of time underpin the production, perpetuation, and attempted resolution of informal housing. The case study also demonstrates how residents respond to long-term informalities by developing coping mechanisms and social structures to impose control and predictability on their unsettledness. It argues that the success of the formalization initiative will ultimately depend on whether the agencies involved meet inhabitants' demands for security, welfare, and the preservation of their social networks, offering a route out of liminality without producing new forms of uncertainty. The conclusion underlines how the management of Corviale is part of a broader mechanism whereby local institutions negotiate with some residents, without resolving the overarching problems or destabilizing the hierarchical structure of the field.

The case study is based on six months of fieldwork in Corviale during 2019, involving participant observation, attendance at numerous public meetings, and loosely structured interviews with 26 local actors: squatters, formal tenants, neighbourhood activists, artisans and artists, and two institutional representatives. Given the sensitive topics under discussion and the legal vulnerability of many actors, all interviews were intimate, informal conversations organized around open, thematic questions to avoid the potential discomfort of direct questioning. It is consequently difficult to reach generalizations about social relations within the large and diverse population that lives in the complex. Nevertheless, a composite picture does emerge of the extended liminal situations that many residents find themselves in and the upheavals that formalization policies can unleash on the tenuous stabilities they have built over time. As the next section highlights, these liminalities are not anomalous. They are the outcome of a city-wide dynamic that perpetuates long-term informalities as a calculated means of governing the urban poor.

Rome's housing informalities in context

Informal housing is pervasive throughout Italy. Far from being a marginal feature, it has long been a structural, systemic element in the production and availability of affordable accommodation. Numerous factors have contributed to its scale and range, but three national-level patterns are particularly important. First, social policies since World War II have prioritized family-based private homeownership as the main housing model, deeply intertwined with its broader familistic approach to welfare (Allen et al., 2004). Consequently, public housing provision has often been inadequate, especially in cities like Rome that have proven unable to respond effectively to major population growth. This problem has been further exacerbated by an active withdrawal from public housing by local authorities since the 1990s, with many selling off large parts of their stock and effectively ceasing any new construction, at the same time incentivizing private real estate development (Puccini, 2016; Storto, 2018).[2] In the case of Rome, the interests of the private construction sector have long been promoted in planning policy by an urban regime: a historically stable alliance between major landowners, real estate developers, and the city's political class of both the right and left (D'Albergo & Moini, 2015). Second, local authorities in many areas of the country lack the capacity to counteract the diverse ways in which unauthorized housing manifests itself, due to a shortage of personnel and "cognitive resources" (Chiodelli et al., 2020, p. 35), as well as chronic slowness of bureaucratic and judicial procedures. Moreover, there are often strong political incentives to ignore the situation. A third major counterforce, in fact, lies in the broad range of actors (brokers, construction companies, residents' consortia, etc.) involved in informal housing production who have an interest in perpetuating the status quo. Their electoral weight and informal negotiating power are such that politicians will often accommodate their demands rather than campaign for planning and building regulations to be enforced (Chiodelli et al., 2020; Coppola, 2018; Pizzo & Altavilla, 2018). Italy's vast informal housing market is, therefore, a direct product of formal housing policies, an incapacity to promote legal alternatives, and entrenched mechanisms of political clientelism. As Chiodelli et al. (2020) underline, though, the tolerance that perpetuates such housing is selective: strategic neglect of some informalities occurs in parallel with clampdowns, evictions, or formalizations when the electoral calendar or other political pressures require the performance of a "tough on illegalities" agenda.

Abusivismo: unauthorized housing construction and expansion

Known as *abusivismo*, unauthorized construction is the most common category of housing informalities and involves two main typologies. First, the building of entire houses in violation of land use laws or housing codes. The size and quality of these houses varies massively, from small units with minimal amenities to luxury villas (Berdini, 2010; Cellamare, 2014; Chiodelli et al., 2020). The second – even more widespread – form involves changing or extending the structure of a building without permission. Again, this can vary from opening up a window to adding entire storeys. An exact quantification of the phenomenon is impossible since much of it is not reported. Nevertheless, in 2018 the proportion of reported violations was 18.9 for every hundred authorized constructions (ISTAT, 2019a). Strikingly, this figure was lower than in previous years: infractions peaked at 19.9% in 2015 (Chiodelli et al., 2020). These statistics do not convey the actual long-term accumulation of illegally built housing, though. Most such constructions are never pulled down, either because orders are rarely implemented – only 19.6% of buildings ordered for demolition between 2004 and 2018 were actually razed (Legambiente, 2019) – or because repeated national amnesties and other local planning mechanisms have shifted their status to legal. Scholars of urban planning, as well as environmental and sustainability campaigners, widely agree that such regularization tools have had the effect of incentivizing further violations in anticipation of future amnesties, aggravating rather than solving the problem. Indeed, such post hoc periodic formalization has come to replace the development of a sustained official housing policy in many parts of the country.

In 2018, the region of Lazio ranked fourth nationally – behind the main southern regions – in terms of new illegal construction (Legambiente, 2019). *Abusivismo* has spread along its coasts and in the provinces, but it is Rome that stands out as particularly critical. One study claims that, if we consider all forms of *abusivismo*, including minor infractions, "more than 50 per cent of the existing buildings in Rome are somehow illegal" (Pizzo & Altavilla, 2018, p. 167). Even more notably, it is estimated that nearly 30% of the current city was originally constructed illegally (Cellamare, 2014). Much of its contemporary layout and sprawl are the result of this unplanned and spontaneous creation of homes and, indeed, of entire neighbourhoods built to compensate for a lack of municipal programming. Illegal building is therefore "one of the basic structural modalities of the city's development"; it "forms a part of the very nature of the city and its mode of governance" (Cellamare, 2014, p. 205 & 215).

Since it became capital, Rome has attracted numerous waves of migration from rural areas. Its population first exploded from around 210,000 in 1871 to over a million by the outbreak of World War II. The creation of some low-income neighbourhoods close to the city's emerging industrial zones was not sufficient for all its newly arriving workers, especially those at the lowest income levels. Poor-quality self-built dwellings thus proliferated at the city's edges and in interstitial spaces at its centre. Although the fascist regime did expand public housing in the interwar period,[3] and there was an effort to significantly increase provision in subsequent decades – especially the 1970s –, the supply never fulfilled demand as the population continued to multiply, reaching almost three million by 1981.[4] In the early post-war decades, self-construction was therefore marked primarily by need. Living conditions within these homes were often minimal, lacking sewage infrastructure, running water, paved roads, or access to public transport. Although need-based building continued into the 1980s – and, as we will see below, has not entirely disappeared – in the boom years of the 1960s the phenomenon entered a second phase, becoming much more systematic and speculative. In particular, there was an intensification in landowners selling swathes of property officially zoned for agricultural use on which unauthorized housing then mushroomed. These rent-seeking strategies combined with the desire of many working- and middle-class families to acquire good-quality housing, often with gardens, at an affordable price to pass on to future generations (Cellamare, 2014), or from which to extract rents themselves (Pizzo & Altavilla, 2018). The phenomenon was so vast – "hegemonic," in fact (Mudu, 2014, p.66) – that "at the end of the 1960s the illegal construction sector [...] was larger than its legal counterpart" (Marchini & Sotgia, 2017, p. 71). In the third and current phase, the sector has evolved to become even more professionalized and "industrialized," with technicians and lawyers colluding to develop entire complexes that in multiple ways violate planning laws (Cellamare, 2014, p. 210).

The city administrations' responses have taken two main directions: on the one hand, much of the historic subsistence housing was demolished in the 1970s and its residents moved to public complexes. On the other hand, many of the higher-quality self-built settlements have been regularized over time and integrated into formal urban plans, with utility grids gradually extended to reach them. Since some of these buildings are spatially spread out in Rome's hinterland, this has proven extremely costly for the public purse. Consequently, in recent years the city has required owners in peripheral zones to form consortia through which to identify their infrastructural needs and use publicly provided budgets to implement them in cooperation with the city authorities. The result of what should have been a process of participatory planning has, however, achieved little in terms of sustainable infrastructural development (Cellamare, 2014; Coppola, 2017; Pizzo & Altavilla 2018). At the same time, it has given these groups – and especially individual power brokers within them – disproportionate weight in negotiations with the authorities and the ability to mobilize votes at election time. It has thus contributed to consolidating clientelistic relations between politicians and specific power groups in the city, which include not only landowners and the construction sector but also residents of some of these self-built areas.

While the status of many buildings has been clarified over the years, thousands of other residents remain suspended in situations of prolonged liminality. Three national-level amnesties have been introduced since 1985. These have spawned so many regularization requests that the authorities are still processing those made in the 1980s.[5] In the interim, their status is frozen: neither legal nor illegal. The applications that are eventually rejected are unlikely to result in demolitions, allowing residents to continue living in them in indefinite illegality. Where regularization is forthcoming, people are still likely to wait years for basic services to arrive. In material terms, this means that large sections of the population continue to inhabit areas that are both part of the city and separated from it, deprived of pavements to walk along, places for sociality, shops, and public transport (Cellamare, 2014).

Many of Rome's residents have taken advantage of the opportunities for evading regulatory restrictions and the high costs that official housing construction entails. This has enabled some previously low-income groups to acquire secure housing and economic mobility over time. However, it has also fostered mechanisms of accumulation by dispossession, particularly in neighbourhoods where the most precarious needs-based shelters have been razed and replaced by speculative real-estate developments. Those original residents have been stripped of their investments, their communities and systems of solidarity erased, and left with no say in the location and forms of their future homes. In fact, the outcomes of this vast informal market have not been widely redistributive and have only partially mitigated the city's shortage of affordable accommodation. They have not lowered prices in the legal sector, and those who lack the financial capital to buy or build informally remain excluded (Pizzo & Altavilla, 2018). Indeed, the sector has become highly stratified. Its historic evolution shows that the groups with the highest economic capital to expend in illegal construction have benefitted the most; their informality laundered through regularization initiatives which have further increased the value of their assets by allowing them to be traded in the legal market.

The root causes of these diverse expressions of *abusivismo* and the liminality that often accompanies it are institutional, founded on local authorities' enduring failure to meet demand for low-cost housing through formal policy. The magnitude and durability of the phenomenon show that its mechanisms are not accidental. They constitute a calculated mode of informal governance that is actively maintained through amnesties, bureaucratic slowness, and selective enforcement that primarily targets the politically and socially weak. Rome's public institutions have thus avoided the expense of developing an adequate and sustainable housing policy, while at the same time reducing conflict with large sections of the electorate. Meanwhile, the dominance of the city's urban regime of private landowners, developers, and their political allies remains intact.

Makeshift housing solutions

Rome's long-term shortage of public housing for those unable to enter the private market has meant that makeshift shelters remain a significant phenomenon, albeit now more hidden than in the post-war period. These homes conform to UN definitions of slums or inadequate housing and as such violate inhabitants' human right to adequate accommodation.[6] Especially since the post-2008 financial crisis, rising numbers of people have been exposed to homelessness or substandard housing conditions, including Italy's growing and increasingly vulnerable elderly population. Its middle class has shrunk with rising poverty levels, income precariousness, and the country's persistently high youth unemployment. In 2019, 4.6 million individuals were living in absolute poverty (ISTAT, 2019b); a situation whose gravity has been exacerbated by the COVID-19 pandemic, exposing as many as ten million to the risk of indigence (La Stampa, 2021). Difficulty in paying for housing costs is a major concern throughout the country, especially for poor households who spend on average 34.6% of their income on accommodation, with figures much higher among those in rented housing (FEANTSA, 2020). Rome's very steep rental prices are often unmanageable for the approximately 40% of residents living on less than 15,000 euro per year (Manna & Esposito, 2019) and the pandemic has worsened the strain; over 200,000 people now face housing deprivation in the capital (de Ghantuz Cubbe, 2020).

The problem is particularly acute for migrants and asylum seekers, who are massively over-represented in all indicators of poverty, inadequate housing, and excessive accommodation costs (FEANTSA, 2020).[7] More than 10,000 recent arrivals were living in makeshift housing nationally in 2016 (Montagna & Grazioli, 2019), subject to repeated and often violent forced evictions not followed by any alternative accommodation provisions (Belloni et al., 2020). Rejected asylum seekers are especially vulnerable, pushed into overcrowded conditions in the informal sub-letting market or onto the streets (FEANTSA, 2020). Those whose asylum requests are approved often fare little better, since there is no public system for helping them transition into integrated housing when they leave reception centres.

As Mudu (2014) has argued, we are dealing here not with an inability of the public authorities to provide adequate shelter but rather the ability *not to*. The Italian state disburses only 0.12% of GDP for housing needs (compared to the EU average of 1.5%: CNEL, 2018), with an expenditure of 6.97 euro per inhabitant per year (FEANTSA, 2020). What is widely defined as a housing crisis in Rome is the outcome of long-term, systematic failure by state institutions to intervene in the gaping disparity between the need for low-cost housing and its supply. Decades-long waiting lists for public housing (discussed below) mean that safety nets are lacking for those at risk of eviction or excluded from the private market.[8] Homelessness often follows. An estimated 8,000 people in the capital are sleeping rough, in shelters or in insecure housing (AGI, 2019; ISTAT, 2015).[9] In addition to those living in cars, caravans, cellars, caves, and abandoned buildings, hundreds have built shacks along its rivers and in wooded areas (Giudice, 2018). The problem is not exclusive to the capital; nationally, approximately 50,724 people were homeless in 2014, more than 58% of them foreigners (ISTAT, 2015).[10]

These conditions must also be contextualized within the broader reality that over 20% of Italy's housing stock has been consistently vacant since the 1980s (Gentili & Hoekstra, 2019). The reasons why potential homes remain officially empty are numerous and the numbers are complicated by a large proportion of dwellings being rented on the informal market.[11] High vacancy rates are, however, mostly a by-product of the fact that, in a country with limited welfare provisions, "homeownership [...] represents a form of social security" (Gentili & Hoekstra, 2019, p. 438). Investment in real estate is a means of assuring a future home or income for offspring or elderly relatives facing economic precarity. Consequently, accommodation costs have not been pulled down by high vacancy rates. This paradox is evident in Rome, where house prices are among the highest in the country despite an estimated 200,000 dwellings standing empty (Bisbiglia, 2017). The phenomenon thus contributes to the intense stratification of the housing field and the shortage of accessible private rentals for low-income groups.

Although it is not only foreigners who live in inadequate and insecure housing in Rome, migrants are those most vulnerable to exclusion from this family-based housing system. Those who turn to unauthorized self-built housing solutions, however, are not treated with the forbearance of earlier decades. In fact, subsistence housing is now largely criminalized and subject to demolition by a city that is determined to hide its gravest expressions of housing inequality. Since stable alternatives are lacking, unprotected residents of many backgrounds are forced into a continuous cycle of eviction, reconstruction, and eviction.[12]

Between informal shacks and publicly built slums: housing Roma people

One of the population groups most exposed to such precarious and substandard accommodation are Roma people.[13] Many of them are Italian or have lived in the country for decades, but the extreme racialized discrimination they face has produced a distinct system of housing marginalization. Nationally, an estimated 25,000 are confined in segregated and ethnically concentrated camps of different types. Of these, 15,000 live in officially designated camps where, despite being publicly managed, conditions are slum-like or provide inadequate services and infrastructure. Between 8,600 and 10,600 instead inhabit self-built shacks generally lacking the most basic amenities and largely indistinguishable from the makeshift housing discussed above (Associazione 21 luglio, 2020).[14] While some local authorities have facilitated Roma's access to public housing, others have offered few concrete alternatives to residence in camps. Lazio is in the latter category; approximately 41% of camp-dwelling Roma are in this region, mostly concentrated in

Rome (Associazione 21 luglio, 2015). The camps within which between 7,000 and 12,000 people are relegated have a spectrum of legal statuses. There are currently over three hundred unauthorized precarious encampments, ten "tolerated" informal settlements, and six publicly built but legally ambiguous camps. This panorama is the outcome of urban planning trajectories that have evolved, often in contradictory ways, over the last seventy years and that have repeatedly shifted the statuses of the settlements (Clough Marinaro, 2014). Rome is thus emblematic of a national problem of segregation and institutional neglect and its most extreme manifestation. Indeed, around 2,000 Roma live in gravely inadequate conditions in the city, usually in shacks hidden among vegetation, exposed to extreme weather conditions, and without access to hygiene facilities or public services (Associazione 21 luglio, 2020).

Roma families were among the many internal migrants who congregated in the shantytowns at the city's margins in the immediate post-World War II period. The slum clearance initiatives of the 1970s and 1980s forced many to build more hidden, fragmented and ethnically concentrated encampments, since they were mostly excluded from the public housing being developed at the time. Rather than facilitate this access, in 1985 regional legislation was passed requiring municipalities to build "nomad camps," under the misplaced assumption that Roma were inherently peripatetic.[15] Although the law required these camps to be integrated into the city's social and infrastructural fabric, in practice most settlements were simply formalized, without providing any of the legally mandated services. Their status thus shifted, but their exclusionary features remained unchanged. In 1993, a new administration introduced the first of Rome's many policies, known as "nomad plans," that targeted this population group in explicitly ethnicized terms. This and all subsequent "plans" set out to replace the informal settlements with much larger, official camps, labelled "villages." However, the absence of clear regulatory procedures, a shortage of available land, and the high cost of building these mega-camps, repeatedly resulted in too few structures being created to accommodate all the individuals intended. Instead, some illegal encampments were given temporary authorization while others were not, some "tolerated" ones were upgraded, some authorized ones were moved, while a small number became "villages." The status of camps was thereby repeatedly changed, creating such confusion about their relative in/formality that residents were often unclear about the legal status of their homes and whether they were vulnerable to eviction. Demolitions of unauthorized settlements meanwhile became a systematic practice, often violating legislation requiring the authorities to provide substitute accommodation to evictees.

Tightly intertwined with escalating political and media discourses criminalizing Roma, in 2008 the Italian government proclaimed the existence of a national "nomad emergency" and called for even more extreme policies of segregation and surveillance. In 2013, however, Italy's Supreme Court declared this policy ethnically discriminatory and therefore unlawful. The mega-camps built in Rome during the intervening years thus definitively shifted into the realm of illegality. Meanwhile, shortly beforehand – in 2012 – the government had bowed to EU pressure and instituted a National Strategy for Inclusion of Roma, Sinti and Caminanti (UNAR, 2012). The document acknowledged that segregation in camps hampers inclusion and fuels anti-Roma prejudice. Among its objectives for 2020 was to develop a range of appropriate accommodation solutions "to definitively overcome emergency approaches and large-sized mono-ethnic settlements" (UNAR, 2012, p. 48). Although the Strategy was not legally binding, local authorities were expected to develop long-term planning mechanisms to achieve this goal. In 2017, Rome's mayor, Virginia Raggi, unveiled a new policy that, on paper, conformed to the Strategy's guidelines, committing the municipality to tackling Roma's interlinked marginalization from adequate housing, healthcare, education, and work opportunities.[16]

However, today's continued presence of illegal, tolerated, and official camps demonstrates that the city has not supplanted its ethnicized and exclusionary management of Roma housing. Since the Strategy went into effect, few families have been helped to transition into mainstream housing. Meanwhile, the municipality has neglected the upkeep of formal "villages" and has begun to wind three of them down, while persevering with forced evictions of unauthorized ones.[17] As a result, Roma communities are now fragmenting into even more numerous but smaller groupings, living in car-parks or hidden from view, further reducing their access to services, with significant consequences for health, education, and employment (Associazione 21 luglio, 2020). An illustrative case is that of the Camping River "village," built by the municipality on a privately owned, isolated campsite. On 30 September 2017, the city's contract with the NGO managing the camp expired. Its 420 residents were told to leave, and the water supply was cut off six weeks later. The municipality presented this as part of its implementation of the National Strategy, promising to support residents' rent in mainstream housing if they were able to obtain legal rental contracts. Most families, however, were unable to find private accommodation due to anti-Roma hostility among landlords (Bisbiglia, 2018), or were refused contracts because they could not provide evidence of their ability to pay rent long-term. They could, circularly, only receive such documentation from the municipality if they already held a rental contract (Associazione 21 luglio, 2018). Thus, residents remained in the space that had been their home for 12 years, but other elements of their daily lives were gravely disrupted, such as school attendance, which fell by 55% compared to the previous year (Associazione 21 luglio, 2018). In legal terms, they were now squatting their previously formal, publicly provided homes. On 21 June 2018, the municipality destroyed 17 of the prefabricated dwellings which it had installed at taxpayers' expense, with an estimated market value of 20,000 euro each (Favale, 2018). Although the European Court of Human Rights (ECHR) imposed a suspension of the camp's full eviction until 27 July, the municipality violated the order and demolished the rest on the 26th.

In less than a year, therefore, the city administration transformed the status of a legal and publicly funded camp into one of regulatory void and informality, and finally into illegality. In the process, it violated all the provisions for schooling, stability, and anti-discrimination enshrined in the National Strategy. Following the eviction, only 12% of the residents accessed mainstream housing; 52% were left entirely homeless.[18] These infringements of the Strategy and the ECHR order were, nevertheless, presented by the mayor and the interior minister as imposing law and order (Magliaro, 2018). The case is illustrative of how Rome's authorities have shaped informality and marginality through their selective allocation of resources, through legitimizing their own informal or illegal practices, while punishing those of vulnerable subjects, thereby materializing and perpetuating hierarchies of power.

The concentration of migrants in inadequate housing, violation of obligations to safely accommodate asylum seekers and refugees, and methodical segregation of Roma in ethnic ghettos are all components of an overarching racialized system of "grey governance." The tens of thousands of marginalized minority group members living in substandard informal housing are not a mere side-effect of policy but a governance tool that ensures they are unable to collectively organize to demand recognition of their legally enshrined housing rights. Their residence in such dwellings not only exposes them to the constant fear of eviction and potential deportation. It also directly affects their possibilities to access citizenship rights and legal work, producing intersecting informalities – and vulnerabilities – in related spheres such as income generation.

Organized squatting of abandoned buildings

Since the 1970s, organized squatting movements have evolved as a major grassroots response to Italy's affordable housing problem. While in the early decades they focused primarily on occupying public housing whose formal allocation was slow and opaque, more recently their operations have shifted to taking over entire abandoned buildings, often unoccupied office blocks or disused factories (Belotti & Annunziata, 2018). These activities have intensified further since 2010, due to the escalating housing crisis (Di Feliciantonio, 2017). It is estimated that Rome is now home to around a hundred such squats (Médecins sans Frontières, 2018), although the phenomenon is in constant flux. These collective movements employ a range of political actions that not only provide accommodation but also contest the neoliberalization of housing, erosion of welfare, and non-recognition of migrants' rights more generally (Davoli, 2018). Most such squats bring together foreigners excluded from the rest of the housing market with Italian families in similar situations, although some mono-ethnic self-organized ones – housing Eritreans and Roma in particular – have also emerged (Associazione 21 luglio, 2018; Belloni et al. 2020).These collectivities produce an infrastructure of care and solidarity, with members working together to promote the visibility and active political subjecthood of people otherwise silenced in contemporary urban life (Vasudevan, 2021). They are thus embedded within a broader multi-issue social justice movement that works to undermine the city's deep and often racialized inequalities (Di Feliciantonio 2017; Grazioli, 2017, 2021; Mudu, 2014; Mudu & Chattopadhyay, 2016).

The response of Rome's authorities to organized squatting has reflected their traditional ambivalence towards informal housing. On the one hand, they have long treated the phenomenon with benign neglect. Many large-scale squats, accommodating as many as 800 people, have existed for over ten years with little institutional action apart from providing residence permits to some inhabitants (Belloni et al., 2020). On the other hand, a series of high visibility demonstrations and mass squatting initiatives in the last decade have forced the region and the municipality to publicly acknowledge that a housing crisis exists (Davoli, 2018). The Lazio region introduced a plan in 2014 to address the emergency.[19] Among its provisions were the refurbishment of unused public buildings, construction of new ones, and the acquisition, at controlled prices, of private housing. This increased public stock was intended to accommodate families stuck in waiting lists for public housing, but also to provide legal alternatives to some groups living in squatted accommodation. Despite the urgency of the situation, however, the plan remains largely unimplemented (Davoli, 2018; Grazioli, 2017), notwithstanding a few exceptions such as the formalization of parts of the Corviale housing project explored below. Paradoxically, though, the same year that the Lazio region acknowledged the structural causes of squatting, national legislation was passed that effectively stripped squatters of fundamental civil rights and criminalized their poverty (Belotti & Annunziata, 2018: Davoli, 2018).[20] The law bans squatters from obtaining residency papers – upon which the rights to healthcare, social services, schooling, and voting hinge – or sign contracts for essential utilities such as water and electricity. It thus adds a further layer of marginalization to housing deprivation. The law dovetailed with a more general criminalization of squatting and an escalation in violent and highly mediatized evictions of large squats.[21] This trend was compounded in 2018 by Matteo Salvini's introduction of an "eviction plan" for Rome during his tenure as interior minister. Nevertheless, the Lazio region, run by the left-wing Democrat Party, has since taken a more moderate line, acknowledging that evicting squats without providing alternative housing is not only fruitless but violates basic housing rights (Arzilli, 2019a). The municipality has similarly recognized the structural nature of the problem and has made gradual moves towards acquiring empty buildings to mitigate the crisis (AdnKronos, 2017), although these have not yet produced a significant improvement in the availability of low-cost accommodation. These small-scale measures serve to temporarily appease protesters but do nothing to overcome the systemic problems of the city's affordable housing market.

Individualized squatting of public housing

Since the 1990s, the Italian public sector has sold off 22% of its housing stock (Belotti & Annunziata, 2018; Puccini, 2016). State-built and rent-subsidized accommodation has now dwindled to less than 5% of the nation's supply, home to approximately two million individuals (Chiodelli et al., 2020). At the same time, rent-capped apartments owned by state or para-state institutions have also been dramatically reduced, exposing middle-income families to housing precariousness (Rigucci, 2019). There are now 650,000 eligible households waiting to receive public housing nationally (Chiodelli et al., 2020), nearly 13,000 of them in Rome (Federcasa-Nomisma, 2016). Many of these are in conditions of economic distress which risks becoming protracted: since only about five hundred apartments are assigned each year, the wait can last up to 25 years (Arzilli, 2019b). Yet, many flats remain unassigned because they were originally designed for large families and have not been adapted to contemporary demographics (Bisbiglia, 2019). Meanwhile, an estimated 254 million euro of funding for public housing has gone unspent in Lazio since 1996.[22]

Although squatting of public housing is not a new phenomenon, it has intensified in the last two decades. Approximately 48,000 of Italy's 750,000 public housing units are squatted (AGI, 2019), while in Rome the proportion is much higher: around 9,000 of the city's 71,000 public apartments (Roma Capitale, 2017). Unlike the coordinated squatting movements previously discussed, most unauthorized public housing occupations are fragmented and individualized, and take on a multiplicity of forms. In some cases, assignees stay on despite eviction orders when they fall into rent arrears (in Rome around 40% of public housing tenants do not pay regularly: Puccini, 2019). In others, apartments are taken over by relatives or friends claiming to be part of the same household (see Esposito & Chiodelli, 2020). Alternatively, non-assignees sublet the flats or "buy" the keys from formal tenants who have moved out without informing the authorities. A fourth practice is simply to forcibly occupy a vacant unit before the official assignee can do so. Such actions rarely connect to a broader political agenda and tend not to advance practices of commoning and solidarity. On the contrary, in by-passing the points-based waiting lists for housing, such squatting contributes to the lack of units that can be allocated to eligible and often very vulnerable households. Nevertheless, such actions have been legitimized by public authorities through the implementation of seven amnesties since 1987 which have assigned many apartments to squatters, thereby further prolonging the wait for non-squatters (Rigucci, 2019).

A major problem faced in much public accommodation is a structural disconnection between housing authorities, employment policies, and other welfare services (Maranghi, 2016; Puccini, 2019). Indeed, Rome's public sector has so far made no attempt to map the conditions and needs of residents in low-income housing (Cubeddu & Puccini, 2020). Many tenants consequently receive no income support or reliable assistance in facing chronic healthcare or disability needs, making it difficult to cover essential expenses despite low rents, and triggering widespread non-payment of bills.[23] Much of Rome's social deprivation is concentrated in these public housing complexes, particularly in the very large ones such as Corviale and

Tor Bella Monaca (Puccini, 2019). Yet, these are often among the least multi-ethnic neighbourhoods, since migrants have historically been hindered from accessing such housing. Individual squatting within these estates has thus become a privatized strategy for Rome's most disadvantaged residents – foreigners and Italians who lack ties to organized housing movements – to reduce expenses in the face of inadequate welfare support. The half-century-long acceptance of this phenomenon by local authorities indicates that they treat squatting as a social buffer (Belotti & Annunziata, 2018): a de facto safety net that responds to the housing crisis without intervening in its causes. This institutional inaction deprives those authorities of rental income that could be invested in expanding the housing stock. As the director of Rome's Urban Planning Office admitted in 2005: "some time ago we gave up [...] managing [public housing estates] considered too difficult or too costly. This incomprehensible policy renunciation and waste of public resources has been going on for years" (quoted in Vidotto, 2017, p. 110). Little appears to have changed since.

The fragmented nature of this squatting and its lack of a politically active leadership contributes to the vulnerability that many unauthorized residents feel. They are often aware that housing and law enforcement authorities are more prone to act against single households than large squatting collectives. Their consequent fear of attracting institutional attention, coupled with the fact that these households tend to be spatially dispersed, has hindered much in-depth research into their practices and engagements with different layers of the state. The following section seeks to compensate for this gap, providing an ethnographic account of how life is organized and narrated in the unregulated spaces that have emerged within Corviale.[24] It then analyzes the Lazio region's recent initiative to regularize some of those informalities. It questions whether its implementation so far has addressed the needs and expectations of occupiers in ways that may realistically replace the informal practices developed over thirty years. Although the analysis is specific to this housing complex, the mechanisms of engagement between residents and representatives of public institutions are tightly intertwined with the wider national and Roman patterns discussed above.

Corviale: producing and perpetuating informalities

A massive linear building, almost one kilometre long and intended to house 8,500 people, Corviale has been described as "possibly the most important and symbolic public housing district in Italy" (ATER, 2015, p. 6). Built between 1975 and 1984 beyond the south-western edge of the city, the complex was part of short-lived drive by left-wing administrations to provide dignified housing to Rome's proletariat, rehouse communities uprooted by slum demolitions, and establish an alternative to the capital's rampant private real-estate speculation (Rhodes, 2008; Vidotto, 2017).[25] The housing project was designed with a utopian vision: intended to become a virtually self-sufficient environment, tenants were to be provided with integrated services, shops, sports facilities, bars, schools, elderly care, employment opportunities, and spaces for community building. Much has been written on the design mistakes that were instead made, the authorities' failure to furnish many of the services, and the institutional neglect that have contributed to its physical dilapidation and negative image from the start (Del Monaco, 2006; Gennari Santori & Pietromarchi, 2006; Rhodes, 2008; Vidotto, 2017). The monolith's sheer size and austere aspect (Figure 2.1), its spatial isolation, and its concentration of low-income residents have further fuelled its territorial stigmatization.

A central element in this stigmatization concerns pervasive squatting, which is scattered throughout the complex but is most visible along the entire kilometre of the fourth floor originally designed for the shops and services that never materialized. Unauthorized occupations began, in fact, before construction was even completed, as a major housing crisis swept the city from 1978, triggering vast numbers of evictions.[26] Almost half of Corviale's 1,200 housing units were therefore allocated in 1982, before much of its infrastructure was installed; only four of the 74 elevators were functioning and many flats lacked electricity, intercom, and telephone lines (Campanella, 1995). Around seven hundred people quickly followed, squatting unassigned apartments until they were evicted en masse in December 1983. With nowhere else to go, they set up tents outside the

Figure 2.1 Section of Corviale
Source: Clough Marinaro, I. (2020). Living the liminal life: Informalities in a utopian housing project. *International Journal of Housing Policy*. Reprinted and electronically reproduced by permission of Taylor & Francis.

building, remaining there for over a year (Campanella, 1995). While many subsequently found alternative housing, others moved into whatever squats they could find within the complex.

Hostile relations between the building's management agency, the IACP (now ATER),[27] and its inhabitants developed from the outset. Formal tenants resented paying heating and maintenance bills for the entire building, including squatted units, especially since many other services were still lacking. Non-payment thus became widespread, giving IACP/ATER an excuse to further reduce spending on amenities (Vidotto, 2017). The complex's chief architect, Mario Fiorentino (1985) had spelled out that Corviale's social project would only succeed with continuous institutional investment and participation in its daily running. Nevertheless, the few services initially provided gradually dwindled and institutional absence became the norm. By the early 1990s, squatters had regenerated the abandoned spaces of the fourth floor (Figure 2.2), employing actions supplementary to the state (Altrock, 2016) by compensating for its inadequate housing provision but also for its failure to guarantee security. As one interviewee recalls,

> we had to get organized because there was no sheriff. Kids from other neighbourhoods came here to take drugs because it was all open. So, the

Figure 2.2 Squatted spaces designed for shops on fourth floor
Source: Clough Marinaro, I. (2020). Living the liminal life: Informalities in a utopian housing project. *International Journal of Housing Policy*. Reprinted and electronically reproduced by permission of Taylor & Francis.

people here had to take possession, close it off. It was a normal reaction of residents who said, "If we don't manage this place, no-one will."

Indeed, the 1980s are described by many residents as having been a period of great turmoil: of high violence and crime rates, of mutual fear and distrust among residents, and a lack of policing or other sign of the state's presence. Since the 1990s, the complex has gradually become more integrated into Rome's urban fabric with the arrival of some municipal offices and services, bus routes, and social inclusion projects. Many of these developments have required decades of campaigning by locals or were achieved through self-help. The first medical facilities, for example, were set up by tenants themselves in abandoned spaces. Several services remain informal to this day: a community of priests providing spiritual support have been denied regularization for over two decades, despite paying rent and utilities. A self-service restaurant which feeds many public employees was opened in the mid-1990s, encouraged by city administrators, but was not formalized – constantly risking eviction – until 2020.[28] The local school has been shut since 2009 despite renovation in 2016 with state-of-the-art facilities, its new structures since left to degrade.[29] The farmers' market was temporarily closed in 2015 for lack of maintenance. It has not reopened. Temporally drawn-out institutional inaction has thus generated protracted liminality even in basic service provision such as education and food supply: not functional but never fully scrapped, suspended until some indeterminate future.

Faced with this institutional inertia, an established sense of do-it-yourself persists. Residents complain that police or social workers rarely visit, that ATER is unresponsive to reports of broken or malfunctioning services, and maintenance personnel appear infrequently, resolving emergencies but neglecting ordinary upkeep (Figure 2.3). It is widely recognized that evictions and sanctions are uncommon, and informal housing encroachments have consequently flourished. In addition to squatting along the fourth floor, six other typologies of rule-breaking are widespread. Some tenants have expanded legal apartments into public spaces to create patios and extensions (Figure 2.4), thereby blocking communal walkways. Many garages and cellars are illegally occupied.[30] Over a kilometre of unauthorized allotments have developed on public land. Artisans' workshops have moved in and are thriving. An estimated 80% of official occupiers do not pay their rent or utilities bills.[31] Public housing units are squatted as soon as they become free, through forced entry, assignees subletting them, or "selling" the keys.[32] It is consequently impossible to know Corviale's exact population: 1,204 formal flats are inhabited but by how many people remains unclear. Informally built apartments number around 140: 120 on the fourth floor and others in spaces originally designed for collective activities.

Most of these informalities are accepted by Corviale residents as the normalized status quo. Criticism is instead most vocally directed against ATER and municipal offices, accused of providing no alternatives or deterrents.[33] By

Figure 2.3 Example of maintenance
Source: Clough Marinaro, I. (2020). Living the liminal life: Informalities in a utopian housing project. *International Journal of Housing Policy*. Reprinted and electronically reproduced by permission of Taylor & Francis.

not maintaining infrastructure, they violate national safety standards and disabled tenants' rights to mobility. Their failure to intervene in the privatization of public housing negates the redistributive goals of the welfare state. Institutional legitimacy has thus corroded, prompting residents to justify their informal practices normatively in relation to these inadequacies.

Corviale's inhabitants are therefore sceptical about promises of change and were unconvinced when the Lazio region began to discuss a large-scale regularization initiative. These doubts were substantiated by an ATER manager: "when I was first given the formalization project in 2011, my bosses told me

Figure 2.4 Illegal extensions over lift shaft
Source: Clough Marinaro, I. (2020). Living the liminal life: Informalities in a utopian housing project. *International Journal of Housing Policy.* Reprinted and electronically reproduced by permission of Taylor & Francis.

not to worry, it would never be implemented."[34] Instead, increased attention to housing under the region's left-wing administration resulted in its inauguration of a Corviale "requalification" plan in January 2019[35]; 10.5 million of this was earmarked for demolishing the approximately 120 self-built homes on the fourth floor and replacing them with 103 legal apartments. The first families were moved out in December 2018 and construction began shortly thereafter, with the first four flats completed and assigned in summer 2019. The sections that follow analyze residents' accounts of how they experienced and organized long-term squatting on the floor and their reactions to this formalization initiative.

Building temporal capital in conditions of liminality

Corviale's fourth floor is spatially and temporally liminal. Sandwiched between "formal" housing above and below, it is defined in the negative, by the regulatory and design logics it defies: the homes that do not technically exist, the living configurations that remain unclear to the authorities, the walkways gated off, making its geographies difficult to navigate. Its time-frames have always been marked by temporariness and the constant possibility of eviction. And yet, this liminality is protracted. All the fourth-floor residents I interviewed had been living there for at least a decade. Most grew up in Corviale, their parents having been assigned legal flats in the 1980s and 1990s. Once they reached adulthood, many chose to start their own families there. Often ineligible for public housing themselves, they remained close for mutual support; aiding ageing parents in exchange for childcare, reflecting Italy's largely privatized and familistic welfare model. The social capital inherent in having long-established family and friendship networks in the complex enabled them to know when informal spaces became available and to move in quickly.

Family-based social capital emerges, moreover, as a key determinant of status and a sense of protection. To quote one long-term resident: "Everyone knows each other here. We may not like each other but we know who's who." This is starkly contrasted by another interviewee: "I've lived here for ten years but I've never felt integrated, because we're foreigners and outsiders aren't really welcomed. They only accept the old families." While all residents are security-conscious, investing in armoured doors and metal gates, the contrast between perspectives on risk is again striking. Many established inhabitants declare that they feel safe in most parts of the building despite the absence of reliable law enforcement. As one declared: "We've been here for so long that everyone recognizes us, including the criminals who don't play nasty tricks on us." However, this is not shared by some more recent squatters, who confirmed the sense of vulnerability articulated by one informant: "You come home and lock yourself in. You never know who you might find right next to you. You have to build gates around yourself or you can never leave. Someone may break down your door and move in or rent your flat to others while you're away."

Trust is highly individualized in Corviale, therefore. While forms of mutual support have blossomed on several landings between apartments, and some families share areas for childcare and socializing, most spaces originally designed for social interaction remain unused. Territorial stigmatization has been internalized and perpetuated by many who describe other sections of the fourth floor as "dirty, where nobody cleans the stairs and people leave their junk everywhere," "where bad people live," and where "the lifts are always broken because the criminals don't want the police to find them." Interviewees claim that a sense of community stretching beyond immediate neighbours or extended family is only shared by the oldest generation in Corviale – those who worked collectively to make the place liveable in the 1980s – and has been lost among the more socially mobile, younger generations. In a building where legality and illegality, ownership and appropriation, presence and absence are so blurred, temporal capital has become central to status hierarchies and legitimacy. Social prestige and belonging are measured by how long a family has lived in the complex and its accumulated expertise in managing the unpredictabilities of institutional action. It is on the basis of symbolically embodying the building's history that these actors claim rights and acquire recognition.

Temporalized economics of squatting

Although housing on the fourth floor is rent-free for those who squat autonomously, the initial move involves significant financial outlay. Apartments are bought from previous squatters at prices ranging from 10,000 to 50,000 euro, depending on size and condition. One occupant paid 10,000 euro for a section of terrace which she closed in and made habitable at further expense, creating a final living space of $25m^2$. Flats are frequently passed on in critical hygienic conditions and with makeshift amenities which incoming residents replace, often spending thousands of euro more. Some also paid to connect legally to the city's electricity grid – when this was still legally possible – rather than informally hooking up to the internal wiring which produces short-circuits, fires, and attracts law enforcement attention. Although flats can be cramped, a major attraction is the flexibility for further expansion if funds become available. One interviewee, for example, extolled having been able to create a new room on the balcony once her children required separate bedrooms. These financial investments highlight the protracted nature of the area's liminality. Such expenditures are a gamble in homes that could, in theory, be evicted at any moment. Yet they are the materialization of a calculation which prioritizes continuity and the determination to create a sense of security, where the odds that the authorities will "leave us in peace" are considered high enough.

Nevertheless, this relative stability and autonomy is not shared by all squatters. Some fourth-floor residents, primarily recent migrants, access apartments via a more organized informal market. Their legal vulnerability is much more pronounced since they often lack residency or employment papers, forcing them to adopt a strategy of invisibility to avoid institutional attention that may result in arrest or deportation. According to local activists, some have been duped, with fraudulent documentation, into believing they are legally purchasing a property. Others routinely pay rent to illegal entrepreneurs who have subdivided large tracts of the floor into small living units.[36] Fear of angering these informal landlords, who have a reputation for physical and psychological violence, no doubt contributes to their inconspicuousness. Indeed, they are excluded from the few support services that have developed in Corviale. Most have not applied for the regularization now underway and the organizations involved in facilitating those processes struggle to reach them. While migrants are greatly under-represented in the complex (only 3.6% of Corviale's official tenants are foreign: Puccini, 2019), observation of the comings and goings on the fourth floor indicates that their presence is proportionally much higher there than elsewhere in the building. The scarcity of affordable accommodation for migrants and their historic exclusion from public housing materializes in Corviale in their exposure to exploitative, illegal landlords. In the complex's hierarchy of vulnerability, they are positioned at the bottom, beneath Italian squatters and the foreigners who have occupied apartments independently. Their ambiguous documentary statuses intersect with a lack of financial, temporal, and social capital to deprive them of the autonomy that other occupants have built up.

Everyday politics of informality

In contexts where law enforcement and welfare institutions in Italy are inadequate, the possibility of organized criminal groups filling such voids is very real. Corviale hosts a variety of illegal activities, including drug dealing and the private letting of public property. A code of silence accompanies these businesses and residents are reluctant to name names. Indeed, those who have exposed Corviale's illegal housing market have experienced repeated intimidatory attacks. It is debatable, however, whether these constitute mafia-type power relations.[37] The territorial control of illegal housing entrepreneurs is limited to certain sections of the building. They do not have a monopoly of the market nor the ability to control competition. While these actors have known political affiliations, they cannot mobilize significant parcels of votes or influence institutional decision-making. On the contrary, the formalization of the fourth floor is set to uproot much of their influence. Residents widely claim that they spread misinformation about the regularization process, attempting to undermine a project which, if successful, will reduce demand and space for the unauthorized housing they supply.[38] Nevertheless, the need for informal housing has directly fed criminal power in this complex. These illegal entrepreneurs have taken on the role of "tricksters": figures that are "not really interested in solving the liminal crisis: they simply pretend. In fact, [...] their real interest often lies in perpetuating, rather than resolving, conditions of confusion and ambivalence" (Thomassen, 2015, p. 53). In Corviale, these actors provide a desperately needed resource, but with problematic outcomes. They enrich themselves while further dispossessing the poor and contribute to hiding housing deprivation from public view. They thus relieve pressure on the authorities to resolve the underlying housing shortage that circularly fuels their illegal wealth.

Familial and temporal capital also appear to trump other, more officialized, forms of political capital. Parties of the right and left historically garnered substantial electoral support throughout the complex. For decades, the left-wing forerunners of today's Democratic Party held political primacy until the success, in 2008, of the right-wing National Alliance which channelled frustrations in Rome's peripheries. Since the latter's electoral defeat in 2013, more radicalized groups such as Casa Pound have sought to mobilize discontent, while the Democratic Party is attempting to resurrect its legitimacy among working-class Romans.[39] Despite the mediatization of such campaigns, my interviewees were all sceptical about party activists' real interest in improving conditions in Corviale. Consequently, several pressure groups claiming to directly represent residents have emerged to bypass party-political rhetoric. However, they too are widely considered unable to resolve entrenched problems and, in some cases, are criticized for exploiting the building's visibility and internal divisions to advance their own political ambitions. Thus, political figures also act as "tricksters," partially alleviating locals' needs and discomforts in the short-term while failing to address the structural causes of precarity upon which their influence rests. Their legitimacy is, however, too limited to generate collectively shared norms or communication to contrast entrenched individualism and familism.

Like residents of unauthorized settlements in parts of the Global South (Chiodelli & Moroni, 2014), Corviale's squatters seek to achieve some security of tenure by incrementally conforming to whatever elements of regulatory formality they can, aware that housing recognition is often key to obtaining welfare services, voting rights, and formal employment. My fourth-floor interviewees recounted multiple attempts, over time, to formalize aspects of their living situations. Many were able to register official residency there before 2014, despite the illegality of their homes, and some repeatedly offered – unsuccessfully – to pay rent and utilities in exchange for formal rights. These techniques of encroachment into formality can be understood as individualized tactics to push out of liminality towards clarity of status and the relative security that this may bring. Thus, when the region initiated a housing amnesty in 2006, many enthusiastically applied and were approved. However, the authorities failed to act on the initiative until 2017, when some, but not all, of those regularizations were recognized. Eleven years of bureaucratic stalling had positioned those households in another variant of liminality: eligible for legality but suspended outside it.

A route out of liminality?

In 2016, three years before reconstruction work began, fourth-floor dwellers were invited to apply for another amnesty: those who could demonstrate residence in Corviale since 2004 would be allocated new homes in the building; others would be rehoused in alternative public accommodation. A week before Christmas 2018, inhabitants of the first section were abruptly informed that they had two weeks to move into temporary apartments before demolition began. This sudden temporal acceleration was dictated by ATER's concern about leaving renovated units uninhabited and exposing them to renewed squatting. Therefore, even in their drive to create formality, institutions operated in light of entrenched systems of informality. Many interviewees described the suddenness of this eviction as traumatic. After protracted institutional inaction, the need to rapidly pack up homes built over decades was deeply resented. The move into temporary flats was equally destabilizing; infrastructural conditions were often problematic (leaking pipes, unsafe wiring, faulty insulation) and replacement appliances and furniture had to be bought to fit new spaces. Residents now faced another set of unpredictable timings: while they knew their accommodation was temporary, its duration was not contractually specified. Their experience of institutional immobility made them unsure whether to settle in for the medium to long term. Some began to request that these temporary homes be made permanent, averting the upheaval of another move and further expenditures. Many remain in that liminal position today.

Given the crystallized mechanisms of self-help and mistrust, an external entity was brought in to improve relations between squatters and the authorities. Proposed by Roma Tre University and financed by the region since 2018, this "City Lab" has an office in Corviale, open to the public and run by two scholar-practitioners with expertise in the complex's social history and wider informal housing dynamics.[40] Its role is arguably that of "master of ceremonies" (Szakolczai, 2009: Turner, 1967), designated to guide fourth-floor occupants out of their liminal situation and into housing security, unravelling their often entangled regulatory statuses in the hope of making them conform to ATER's equally complicated bureaucratic requirements. The objective is to overcome reciprocal suspicions and to introduce a less conflictual, less punitive, and more citizen-focused approach to housing formalization than previously existed. These ambitions have been well received by many interviewees, who appreciate receiving clear information about their situations, as well as the Lab's ability to lobby ATER to provide timely responses to their concerns; a significant reversal of the agency's long history of non-communication. The Lab has also activated a "Memory Project,"[41] collecting photographs and artefacts from squats to help alleviate the trauma of uprooting, providing an emotional accompaniment in the transition out of liminality.

Nevertheless, it is also widely understood that the Lab's staff are powerless to resolve many of Corviale's enduring ambiguities. For example, some housing amnesty applicants remain stuck in regulatory limbo as different offices reach contrasting decisions about their status. Others have been refused regularization in situations almost identical to families who have been approved. One couple discovered that their residency papers were never recorded by the municipal officer that processed them. Others have been allocated apartments but not their associated garages, which remain illegally occupied. Meanwhile, some households have noted that the bills for their new formal homes are significantly higher than promised, and do not always correspond to the services provided. Thus, while individual situations vary, a composite pattern of institutionally generated uncertainty remains central to the building's management. Many residents are doubtful that the formalization project will be completed within five years as planned, predicting that funding and political attention will soon peter out. Meanwhile, squatting throughout the rest of the building remains unaddressed, with many other informal residents frustrated that they cannot be regularized too. Moreover, many official tenants still cannot afford the steep utility and maintenance bills.[42] They see no improvement in infrastructural conditions on their floors, perpetuating disincentives to pay and thereby fuelling further institutional neglect.

A clear irony of the initiative is that it regularizes only those who have squatted since 2005, giving greater rights to those who can demonstrate the longevity of their informality than to those whose rule-breaking is more recent. The process thus formally confirms the weight of temporal capital in the rights and opportunities of "informals." Moreover, in ignoring squatting on other floors, it continues to block eligible households from accessing public housing, thereby prolonging the structural causes of housing informalities and implicitly acknowledging their inevitability.

For Corviale residents who have benefitted from formalization so far, the outcomes have been mixed. Some are relieved about their newfound security; others are destabilized by the altered social geographies, finding themselves separated from support networks. Crucially, the financial costs accompanying formalization – including back-rent for the years of squatting and additional bureaucratic fees – are unmanageable for some. One interviewee argued: "only people who have money can get regularized. It's a privilege, not a right." Nevertheless, a significant novelty has emerged which may presage long-term change city-wide. Regional officials claim that in avoiding using police violence to carry out the Corviale evictions, and in ensuring that no low-income residents are left homeless, a new approach is emerging which recognizes squatters' needs rather than criminalizing them. Local housing activists are hopeful that this will become a policy blueprint for addressing squatting elsewhere in the city. Indeed, in working "with informality," it offers a much-needed step towards bridging the "competing rationalities" between modernist, techno-managerial "logics of governing" and impoverished urban inhabitants' "logics of survival" (Watson, 2009, p. 2268).

Informality is fundamentally a negotiation over value (Roy & AlSayyad, 2004); it is about potential loss and potential gain and the power of individuals to create and bend rules to reach their objectives. Residents' ability to manoeuvre around institutionally imposed constraints and discretionalities depends on the resources they can activate: their social, cultural, temporal, and symbolic capital. Some long-term squatters have successfully pressured the authorities to alter parts of the requalification process to meet their concerns. For example, they insisted that families who could most easily adapt to new housing be transferred first, giving more vulnerable residents longer to prepare. Some large families have also been allowed to stay despite being ineligible. Political pragmatism underlies the region's acquiescence to selected demands, as some inhabitants vocally denounce the institutional irregularities that have marked Corviale's history and the recent formalization process. Such experiences have become the basis for claims-making and a means to hold the authorities to account. Given weak institutional legitimacy in Corviale, residents now measure their approval according to the material benefits they are accorded. The region's couching of the formalization policy as evidence of a new, compassionate approach to squatters' needs arguably aims to build political consensus in a context where cynicism has long prevailed. Thus, social dynamics established under protracted liminality have produced some, albeit limited, "bottom-up" power to influence decisions.

By seeking to redistribute resources to at least some dwellers historically excluded from public services, this strategy attempts to mitigate conflictual relations. Whether this will be successful long term is hard to predict. The limited number of people benefitting from the policy may generate additional resentments, and the layers of regulations to which newly formalized residents are subjected may breed fresh informalities. On the other hand, by involving the "City Lab" in its efforts, the region has embarked on "collaborative governance" (Chiodelli et al., 2017, p. 12), building trust by incrementally addressing the complexities of lived informalities rather than implementing overly rigid or punitive policies. If this is sustained and applied equitably, localized institutional illegitimacy may wane; however, until a new city-wide public housing policy is enacted which meets the needs for low-cost accommodation with adequate supply, these efforts are unlikely to significantly uproot informal housing practices and their associated inequalities.

Conclusions

At least since World War II, informal housing has been used as a tool of grey governance in Rome to compensate for a lack of coherent planning and provision of low-income housing. Public institutional failure to fulfil this core responsibility of urban management, and to implement the regulations that do exist, lies at the root of the city's expansive and variegated informal housing sector. As the manifestations discussed in this chapter have shown, the same institutions have addressed self-developed housing by juggling tolerance with repression, their responses calculated to satisfy a range of political pressures. On the one hand inadequate public provision has ensured that Rome's ever-expanding private real-estate sector – with its close ties to political actors across the spectrum (Berdini & Nalbone 2011; D'Albergo & Moini, 2015; Erbani, 2013) – has never faced significant competition. On the other, political parties have long attracted grassroots support by voicing residents' frustrations, promising incremental improvements while failing to address system-wide inadequacies. Since a wholesale crackdown on the multiple informal housing typologies developed over seven decades is both logistically and politically unfeasible, regulations are enforced selectively. The more visible expressions – and especially those inhabited by racialized and politically weak minorities, such as migrants, refugees, and Roma – have been targeted more vigorously than the privatized encroachments of middle-class households. This management is a mode of rule that shores up entrenched social hierarchies. Nevertheless, shifts in the macro-level political context have modulated the trajectory of such practices. When it has served the municipality to demonstrate an adherence to inclusive policies for Roma, evictions have been counterbalanced by (generally unmet) promises to help obtain mainstream accommodation. When a left-wing regional government has needed to distinguish itself from a securitarian right-wing opposition, formalization of some squatting has replaced previous patterns of punishment or neglect. Such repositionings are ultimately a negotiation over symbolic capital: a strategy whereby elite actors manoeuvre to maintain their electoral and decision-making power by creating alliances with subordinate actors. Although some individuals in the latter group have benefitted from these shifts, the field's overarching power dynamics have remained untouched. External political pressures have thus had short-term impacts, modifying the "rules of the game" that dictate which informalities are condemned or condoned, while leaving open the possibilities for further calculated use of repression or toleration in the many situations left unresolved.

The Corviale case represents a microcosm of these city-wide dynamics. Although some residents are being guided out of the liminality of their squatter status, many others remain unaffected; their governability through protracted precarity is preserved. At the same time the ethnography shows that the "potency of the state" (Roy, 2018) is not absolute. Its need to periodically seek consensus creates spaces for negotiation over resource allocation in ways that can advantage some occupants, but which also aggravate inequalities *between* "informals," proving especially detrimental to those who lack social and political capital to leverage with the institutions. The case study demonstrates, moreover, how time is central to these power relations. The time spent in regulatory limbo, waiting for institutional actions (be they evictions, provision of services, or formalization), influences how "informals" build alliances and coping strategies – but also bolster social hierarchies – among themselves. Time emerges as a key factor in differential levels of vulnerability: people do not experience benefits and risks of informal housing equally. Some residents can use longevity of informality to successfully demand institutional recognition of their tenure and to bolster their social networks. It is mostly Italians who have recourse to this temporal capital, while migrants – who tend to be more recent residents – generally lack this asset and the protections and resources it entails. Time thus contributes to an ethnicized hierarchy that continues to relegate migrants to the most insecure positions, where their informality may be exploited by illegal power groups or other tricksters. Focusing on the gradational nature of liminality helps to underline that "in-between" situations are highly heterogeneous, as diverse categories of actors in similar contexts experience very different levels of contingency, threat, or possibility of resolution.

Any formalization policy must take these dynamics into consideration to be effective. Simply implementing rules and evicting rule-breakers is unlikely to reconfigure historically rooted relations and behaviours. At the same time, repeating the pattern of partial amnesties merely reinforces the expectations and competencies through which Rome's informal housing dwellers organize their lives and adapt to the opportunities offered. If the authorities begin to strictly enforce rules in ways that produce new contradictions, inequalities, and discretionalities, they will fail to undermine the social structures produced during informality or wrench legitimacy from the powerbrokers who thrive in regulatory ambiguity. Trickster figures will mobilize to undermine the effectiveness of regularization processes to defend their power built during the years of institutional absence. Employing "masters of ceremonies" like Corviale's "City Lab" to counter localized misinformation and mistrust may facilitate transitions into formality in the short-term. However, informal residents will ultimately evaluate the relative costs and benefits of adhering to formalization initiatives or reverting to informal solutions. Where informality serves as a source of welfare to compensate for lacking formal services, to provide some security, and to partially neutralize social conflict, formalization will be ineffective unless it can guarantee the same concrete benefits in the long term.

Notes

1 Some paragraphs of this chapter were previously published in the following two articles: Clough Marinaro, I. (2020). Living the liminal life: informalities in a utopian housing project. *International Journal of Housing Policy;* Chiodelli, F., Coppola, A., Curci, F., Zanfi, F., Belotti, E., Berruti, G., & Clough Marinaro, I. (2020). The production of informal space: A critical atlas of housing informalities in Italy between public institutions and political strategies. *Progress in Planning*.

2 Although the authorities often require private developers to include some low-income housing units in their projects, in practice this obligation is often bypassed (Grazioli, 2017).

3 Much of this took the form of isolated "*borgate*": public housing complexes located beyond the city's perimeter, where services and employment were often gravely lacking. See also Chianese (2017) on the slums of the fascist period.

4 Rome's official population was 1,651,754 in 1951. It rose to 2,781,993 in 1971 and peaked at 2,840, 259 in 1981 (Comune di Roma, 2004).

5 In 2019, Rome's municipality had yet to process 171,115 formalization requests made in 1985 (AdnKronos, 2019)

6 The UN defines slums households as any in which residents suffer at least one of these deprivations: "1. Lack of access to improved water source, 2. Lack of access to improved sanitation facilities, 3. Lack of sufficient living area, 4. Lack of housing durability and, 5. Lack of security of tenure" (UN-Habitat, n.d., p. 3). "For housing to be adequate, it must provide more than four walls and a roof and at a minimum, meet the following criteria": legal security of tenure; availability of services, materials, facilities and infrastructure; affordability; habitability, including protection against the elements; accessibility; safe location with access to employment opportunities and services; cultural adequacy (UN-Habitat, n.d., pp. 5–6). The international legal framework by which adequate housing is considered a human right is spelled out in OHCHR (n.d.).

7 30% of Rome's population in absolute poverty are migrants, although they make up only 13.4% of the city's residents (Manna & Esposito, 2019).

8 In 2018, 6,113 evictions were ordered in the Province of Rome of which the vast majority (4,457) in the capital were for rent arrears (Unione Inquilini, 2019).

9 FEANTSA's ETHOS framework of homelessness defines insecure housing as a situation of exposure to violence or eviction. Inadequate housing includes overcrowded, unfit for habitation or otherwise "unconventional" structures (FEANTSA, n.d.).

10 Unfortunately, more recent comprehensive data has not yet been collected.

11 An estimated 1.5 million rental contracts are illegal or informal (Gentili & Hoekstra, 2019). These dwellings officially figure as vacant despite being inhabited.

12 One emblematic case was the demolition of an encampment on the banks of the Aniene river in 2015 prior to the Catholic Jubilee. Two hundred people from North and Sub-Saharan Africa, Bangladesh, and Eastern Europe were evicted (La Repubblica, 2015). Within days, many had returned (Dellapasqua, 2015). Such evictions continue and affect migrants of all backgrounds, for example the demolition of the homes of thirty Filipino families in 2020 (De Santis, 2020).

13 The umbrella term "Roma" is used throughout the European Union to refer to a highly diverse set of ethnic groups with different histories, cultures, and socio-economic situations and who use various forms of self-ascription. In Italy they mostly define themselves as Roma, Sinti or Caminanti. Since Italy does not

collect ethnic-specific data, statistics are very approximate, with population estimates fluctuating between 120,000 and 180,000 (UNAR, 2012). Attempts in recent years to overcome the dearth of data have largely failed (Associazione 21 luglio, 2018). Methodological challenges in tracking people who often hide their identities because of stigmatization combine with difficulties in contacting those who live in precarious shanties repeatedly demolished by the police.

14 The most reliable statistics are produced by Associazione 21 luglio, a leading Roma rights NGO. While the organization has a political agenda and cannot be considered a neutral source, its data are nevertheless more complete than other sources, including governmental ones.

15 Legge regionale 24 maggio 1985, n.82.

16 See Associazione 21 luglio (2020) for a detailed report of the policy's concrete implementation.

17 In the 18 months following the unveiling of the new municipality's integration plan, it carried out 104 forced evictions with an estimated expenditure of 3,300,000 euro of public money (Associazione 21 luglio, 2020, p. 23.) Approximately 1,300 people were affected by these actions during 2018 (Associazione 21 luglio, 2018).

18 A further 14 families were placed in temporary shelters for two months and 12 others were assisted in returning to their countries of origin (Associazione 21 luglio, 2018, 2020), but many appear to have since returned to join relatives in informal encampments.

19 Regione Lazio Deliberazione 15 gennaio 2014, n. 18 Piano straordinario per l'emergenza abitativa nel Lazio e attuazione del Programma per l'emergenza abitativa per Roma Capitale.

20 Decreto legge 28 marzo 2014, n. 47, converted into Legge 23 maggio 2014, n. 80, known as the "Piano Casa Lupi."

21 Among these was the violent eviction of squatters from a building in Piazza Indipendenza, near Termini station in August 2017 (see Hung, 2019), which attracted international media attention (Busby, 2017).

22 See Floris (2019). Moreover, state authorities have identified at least 160 unused buildings in Rome (D'Albergo, 2019).

23 See, for example, Cubeddu & Puccini (2020) on poverty levels in Rome's Tor Bella Monaca housing estate.

24 A sociological study by Campanella (1995) remains the most recent and detailed exploration of relational dynamics in Corviale.

25 The city was governed by left-wing coalitions between 1976 and 1985, but then returned to the conservative Christian Democrat-led coalitions that dominated most of Rome's post-war political management until the early 1990s. Although various administrations developed public housing complexes, the most concerted drive occurred in those nine years of left-wing leadership.

26 The crisis followed rent-capping regulations introduced in 1978 (Legge 27 luglio 1978, n. 392, known as the Equo Canone Law) which had the paradoxical effect of reducing the availability of low-rent housing, especially in urban centres, thereby failing in its goal of fostering a more equitable private rental market.

27 The IACP (Istituto Autonomo Case Popolari) was converted into regional bodies in 1990. Lazio owns almost 2/3 of public housing units (46,000) in Rome, managed by ATER (Azienda territoriale per l'edilizia residenziale), while the municipality (Roma Capitale) owns 28,500 units and is responsible for allocating all apartments.

28 See http://arvalia.romatoday.it/corviale/punto-ristoro-corviale-m5s-bando-gestione.html.

29 See www.ediliziaeterritorio.ilsole24ore.com/art/progettazione-e-architettura/2016-06-09/a-roma-nuova-scuola-firmata-t-studio-e-quasi-pronta-il-rammendo-corviale-144655.php?uuid=ADO6B1Y and https://arvalia.romatoday.it/corviale/scuola-elementare-corviale-bando-periferie.html.

30 One resident stated: "Garages no longer correspond to the apartments. My neighbour leaves, I take his garage. And if you're a bit of a bully, not necessarily a criminal or a mafioso, but just a bit more arrogant and enterprising and you have two cars, well, you take over another space. You put up a wall, put in a gate and who's going to say anything? Nobody."

31 As stated by a representative of the Lazio Region at a public meeting in Corviale on 1 July 2019.

32 Several interviewees discussed individuals who had bought private housing outside Corviale with the income earned subletting their publicly allocated apartments. Selling of keys is widespread in Rome. See Angeli (2016).

33 Note that ATER's poor record of maintaining and managing its properties is not limited to Corviale. The institution has been described by one scholar as "increasingly on the verge of managerial disaster, perhaps now irreversibly so" (Rigucci, 2019, p. 173).

34 Declaration at a public meeting in Corviale, 1 July 2019.

35 This was part of larger project for which 21 million euro were allocated in total, the remaining finances reserved for redesigning its outdoor areas: www.lauraperettiarchitects.com/project/rigenerare-corviale/.

36 See also Angeli (2017).

37 Article 416 bis of the Italian Penal Code considers mafia-type association to involve intimidatory power that generates submission and silence, and the ability to control or influence economic activities, public contracts and services for profit or to manipulate electoral outcomes.

38 Almost half the fourth-floor population failed to regularize. It is unclear what proportion did so because of this misinformation.

39 Casa Pound mobilizes against evictions of Italians and the allocation of public housing to minorities. See, for example: https://it-it.facebook.com/casapoundroma/posts/vittoria-questa-mattina-a-corviale-scongiurato-sgombero-di-una-famiglia-italiana/990053511160367/ and Palma (2019).

The PD has been accused of neglecting low-income neighbourhoods in recent years. Lazio governor Zingaretti's high-profile launch of the Corviale formalization project appears part of a wider attempt to regain support in peripheries (see www.partitodemocratico.it/primo-piano/per-le-periferie-bandi-pluriennali-e-voto-nelle-citta-metropolitane-la-proposta-del-pd/).

40 https://laboratoriocorviale.it/.

41 See https://laboratoriocorviale.it/attivita/accompagnamento-sociale/progetto-delle-memorie/. The photographs of squatted homes taken just before their demolition underscore the investments made over the decades, both financial – in terms of the quality of the furniture and materials – and affective.

42 Many residents pay rent as low as ten euro per month, based on their income. Utility bills, however, are calculated differently and can be as high as 300 euro. For those with a social pension of around 500 euro, this is unaffordable.

References

AdnKronos. (2017). Emergenza casa, Raggi: "Ho chiesto disponibilità caserme". *AdnKronos*, 1 September. www.adnkronos.com/fatti/cronaca/2017/09/01/emergenza-casa-oggi–vertice-minniti-raggi_SrvwcUQdrTFvWtisx7wv7M.html.

AdnKronos. (2019). Condono edilizio, oltre 4 mln pratiche inevase da 35 anni: Pa perde 19 mld. *AdnKronos*, 6 November. www.adnkronos.com/soldi/economia/2019/11/06/condono-edilizio-mln-pratiche-inevase-anni-perde-mld_EprkS4QwL3CSWznMLPFLVK.html?refresh_ce.

AGI. (2019). Quante case occupate ci sono in Italia? *AGI*, 26 July. www.agi.it/fact-checking/occupazioni_abusive_italia_dati-5917522/news/2019-07-26/.

Allen, J., Barlow, J., Leal, J., Maloutas, T., & Padovani, L. (eds). (2004). *Housing and welfare in Southern Europe.* Blackwell. https://doi.org/10.1002/9780470757536.

Altrock, U. (2016). Conceptualising informality: Some thoughts on the way towards generalisation. In C. McFarlane & M. Waibel (eds), *Urban informalities: Reflections on the formal and informal* (pp. 171–193). Ashgate. https://doi.org/10.4324/9781315548814.

Angeli, F. (2016). Alloggi popolari a Roma, ecco il tariffario del mercato nero. *La Repubblica*, 7 February. https://roma.repubblica.it/cronaca/2016/02/07/news/alloggi_popolari_ecco_il_tariffario_del_mercato_nero-132889524/.

Angeli, F. (2017). Roma, Corviale tra abusivi e droga: il chilometro di cemento dove detta legge "er Palletta". *La Repubblica*, 10 October. https://roma.repubblica.it/cronaca/2017/10/10/news/roma_corviale_tra_abusivi_e_droga_il_chilometro_di_cemento_dove_detta_legge_er_palletta_-177844389/.

Arzilli, A. (2019a). La Regione: "Ora stop agli sgomberi, a cominciare da viale del Caravaggio". *Corriere della Sera*, 22 August. https://roma.corriere.it/notizie/politica/19_agosto_22/regione-ora-stop-sgomberi-cominciare-viale-caravaggio-cb4a72a0-c43b-11e9-b4f3-f200f033f7a0.shtml.

Arzilli, A. (2019b). Case popolari, 25 anni d'attesa. *Corriere della Sera*, 10 May. https://roma.corriere.it/notizie/politica/19_maggio_10/case-popolari-25-anni-d-attesa-l-ultima-sara-assegnata-2044-615fa044-728e-11e9-861b-d938f88a2d19.shtml.

Associazione 21 luglio. (2015). *Rapporto annuale 2015.* www.21luglio.org/2018/wp-content/uploads/2019/05/Rapporto_annuale_2015_def_web-1.pdf.

Associazione 21 luglio. (2018). *Rapporto annuale 2018.* www.21luglio.org/2018/wp-content/uploads/2019/04/rapporto-annuale-2018.pdf.

Associazione 21 luglio. (2020). *Dove restano le briciole.* www.21luglio.org/2018/wp-content/uploads/2020/01/drlb-integrale.pdf.

ATER. (2015). *Concorso internazionale di progettazione: Rigenerare Corviale.* https://presstletter.com/wp-content/uploads/2015/05/rigenerare-Corviale.pdf.

Belloni, M., Fravega, E., & Giudici, D. (2020). Fuori dall'accoglienza: Insediamenti informali di rifugiati tra marginalità e autonomia. *Politiche Sociali*, 2, 225–244.

Belotti, E., & Annunziata, S. (2018). Governare l'abitare informale: Considerazioni a partire dai casi di Milano e Roma. In A. Balducci, O. de Leonardis, & V. Fedeli (eds), *Terzo rapporto sulle città. Mind the gap: Il distacco tra politiche e città.* Il Mulino.

Berdini, P. (2010). *Breve storia dell'abusivismo edilizio.* Donzelli.

Berdini, P., & Nalbone, D. (2011). *Le mani sulla città.* Alegre.

Bisbiglia, V. (2017). Roma, Raggi chiama in causa il Governo sull'emergenza abitativa: "200mila case vuote, uno scandalo. Porre rimedio". *Il Fatto Quotidiano*, 29 August. www.ilfattoquotidiano.it/2017/08/29/roma-raggi-chiama-in-causa-il-governo-sullemergenza-abitativa-200mila-case-vuote-uno-scandalo-porre-rimedio/3824860/.

Bisbiglia, V. (2018). Roma, sgombero del campo rom Camping River: famiglie separate, alloggi solo per una decina. Così molte hanno rinunciato. *Il Fatto Quotidiano*, 26 July. www.ilfattoquotidiano.it/2018/07/26/roma-sgombero-del-campo-rom-camping-river-famiglie-separate-alloggi-solo-per-una-decina-cosi-molte-hanno-rinunciato/4519135/.

Bisbiglia, V. (2019). Roma, la beffa delle case popolari: troppo grandi per famiglie di 1–2 persone. *Il Fatto Quotidiano*, 26 May. www.ilfattoquotidiano.it/2019/05/26/roma

-la-beffa-delle-case-popolari-troppo-grandi-per-famiglie-di-1-2-persone-che-sono-la-maggior-parte-di-quelle-in-attesa/5208555/.
Busby, M. (2017). Italian police use water cannon against refugees occupying Rome square. *The Guardian*, 24 August. www.theguardian.com/world/2017/aug/24/italian-police-water-cannon-refugees-rome-square.
Campanella, N. (1995). *Roma. Nuovo Corviale: Miti, utopie, valutazioni*. Bulzoni.
Cellamare, C. (2014). The self-made city. In I. Clough Marinaro & B. Thomassen (eds), *Global Rome: Changing faces of the eternal city* (pp. 205–218). Indiana University Press.
Chianese, S. (2017). The baraccati of Rome: Internal migration, housing, and poverty in fascist Italy (1924–1933). CEIS Tor Vergata Research Paper Series, no. 395.
Chiodelli, F., Coppola, A., Belotti, E., Berruti, G., Clough Marinaro, I., Curci, F., & Zanfi, F. (2020). The production of informal space: A critical atlas of housing informalities in Italy between public institutions and political strategies. *Progress in Planning*. Advanced online publication. https://doi.org/10.1016/j.progress.2020.100495.
Chiodelli, F., Hall, T., Hudson, R., & Moroni, S. (2017). Grey governance and the development of cities and regions: The variable relationship between (il)legal and (il)licit. In F. Chiodelli, T. Hall, & R. Hudson (eds), *The illicit and illegal in regional and urban governance and development: Corrupt places* (1st ed., pp. 1–16). Routledge. https://doi.org/10.4324/9781315317663-1.
Chiodelli, F., & Moroni, S. (2014). The complex nexus between informality and the law: Reconsidering unauthorised settlements in light of the concept of nomotropism. *Geoforum*, 51, 161–169. https://doi.org/10.1016/j.geoforum.2013.11.004.
Chiodelli, F., & Tzfadia, E. (2016). The multifaceted relation between formal institutions and the production of informal urban spaces: An editorial introduction. *Geography Research Forum*, 36, 1–14.
Clough Marinaro, I. (2014). Rome's 'legal' camps for Roma: The construction of new spaces of informality. *Journal of Modern Italian Studies*, 19(5), 541–555. https://doi.org/10.1080/1354571X.2014.962254.
CNEL (Consiglio nazionale economia e lavoro). (2018). Osservazioni e proposte sul tema"povertà, disuguaglianze e inclusione". http://europa.basilicata.it/2021-27/wp-content/uploads/2020/02/CNEL_Contributo_III_20190708.pdf.
Comune di Roma. (2004). Popolazione romana. www.comune.roma.it/PCR/resources/cms/documents/02mosaico2_04_04.pdf.
Coppola, A. (2017). Roma: La metropolizzazione parassitaria e i suoi modi informali. In C. Cellamare (ed.), *Fuori raccordo: Abitare l'altra Roma* (pp. 223–238). Donzelli.
Coppola, A. (2018). A very old neo-liberalism: The changing politics and policy of urban informality in the Roman borgate. In L. Caldwell & F. Camilletti (eds), *Rome: Modernity, postmodernity and beyond* (pp. 83–98). Legenda.
Cubeddu, F., & Puccini, E. (2020) Indagine sulla povertà a Tor Bella Monaca. *Osservatorio Casa Roma*. https://osservatoriocasaroma.com/2020/05/02/indagine-sulla-poverta-a-tor-bella-monaca/.
D'Albergo, E., & Moini, G. (2015). *Il regime dell'Urbe: Politica, economia e potere a Roma*. Carocci.
D'Albergo, L. (2019). Capitale abbandonata: tra palazzi, cinema e vecchie fabbriche 161 edifici dimenticati. *La Repubblica*, 14 May. https://roma.repubblica.it/cronaca/2019/05/14/news/capitale_abbandonata_tra_palazzi_cinema_e_vecchie_fabbriche_161_edifici_dimenticati-226246361/.

Davoli, C. (2018). Le occupazioni abitative a Roma: Una "pratica di movimento" per il diritto all'abitare. In A. Coppola & G. Punziano (eds), *Roma in transizione: Governo, strategie, metabolismi e quadri di vita di una metropoli* (pp. 303–316). Planum.

De Ghantuz Cubbe, M. (2020). Sos casa a Roma: 200 mila in emergenza. Ma la risposta del Comune è lenta. *La Repubblica*, 1 June. https://roma.repubblica.it/cronaca/2020/06/01/news/sos_casa_a_roma_200_mila_in_emergenza_ma_la_risposta_del_comune_e_lenta-258141585/.

Dellapasqua, E. (2015). Ponte Mammolo, amianto e detriti. E tornano gli immigrati. *Corriere della Sera*, July 3. https://roma.corriere.it/notizie/cronaca/15_luglio_02/ponte-mammolo-amianto-detriti-tornano-immigrati-a216fe82-20e6-11e5-b510-55e71b40db58.shtml.

Del Monaco, A. (2006). Corviale accomplished. www.luciobarbera.it/Writings/Corviale%20Accomplished_fw.pdf.

De Santis, S. (2020). Roma, sgomberate da baraccopoli 30 famiglie di filippini. *La 7*, August 12. https://tg.la7.it/cronaca/roma-sgomberate-da-baraccopoli-30-famiglie-di-filippini-12-08-2020-152627.

Di Feliciantonio, C. (2017). Spaces of the expelled as spaces of the urban commons? Analysing the re-emergence of squatting initiatives in Rome. *International Journal of Urban and Regional Research*, 41(5), 708–725. https://doi.org/10.1111/1468-2427.12513.

Erbani, F. (2013). *Roma: Il tramonto della città pubblica*. Editori Laterza.

Esposito, E., & Chiodelli, F. (2020). Juggling the formal and the informal: The regulatory environment of the illegal access to public housing in Naples. *Geoforum*, 113, 50–59. https://doi.org/10.1016/j.geoforum.2020.05.002.

Favale, M. (2018). Roma, per liberare il campo rom il Comune fa distruggere i container di sua proprietà. *La Repubblica*, 24 June. https://roma.repubblica.it/cronaca/2018/06/24/news/roma_per_liberare_il_campo_rom_il_comune_fa_distruggere_i_container_di_sua_proprieta_-199900093/.

FEANTSA. (2020). Fifth overview of housing exclusion in Europe. www.feantsa.org/public/user/Resources/OHEE/2020/Fifth_Overview_of_Housing_Exclusion_in_Europe.pdf.

FEANTSA. (n.d.). ETHOS: European typology of homelessness and housing exclusion. www.feantsa.org/download/ethos2484215748748239888.pdf.

Federcasa-Nomisma. (2016). Dimensione e caratteristiche del disagio abitativo in Italia. www.istitutodegasperi-emilia-romagna.it/pdf-mail/290_11052016a3.pdf.

Fiorentino, M. (1985). *La casa: Progetti 1946–1981*. Edizioni Kappa.

Floris, F. (2019). In Italia 1,6 miliardi mai spesi per le politiche abitative. *Redattore sociale*, 4 September. www.redattoresociale.it/article/news/la_roma_degli_sgomberi_e_dell_invenduto_in_italia_1_6_miliardi_mai_spesi_per_le_politiche_abitative.

Gennari Santori, F., & Pietromarchi, B. (2006). *Osservatorio nomade: Immaginare Corviale*. Mondadori.

Gentili, M., & Hoekstra, J. (2019). Houses without people and people without houses: A cultural and institutional exploration of an Italian paradox. *Housing Studies*, 34 (3), 425–447.

Giudice, S. (2018). Dentro le baraccopoli nascoste nel cuore di *Roma* [Video]. *YouTube*. www.youtube.com/watch?v=6O7IiakkS6o.

Grazioli, M. (2017). From citizens to citadins? Rethinking right to the city inside housing squats in Rome, Italy. *Citizenship Studies*, 21(4), 393–408. https://doi.org/10.1080/13621025.2017.1307607.

Grazioli, M. (2021). *Housing, urban commons and the right to the city in post-crisis Rome: Metropoliz, the squatted Città Meticcia.* Palgrave.

Hung, C. (2019). Sanctuary squats: The political contestations of Piazza Indipendenza Refugee occupiers. *Radical History Review*, 135, 119–137. https://doi.org/10.1215/01636545-7607872.

ISTAT. (2015). Le persone senza dimora. www.istat.it/it/files/2015/12/Persone_senza_dimora.pdf.

ISTAT. (2019a). Il benessere equo e sostenibile in Italia. www.istat.it/it/files/2019/12/Bes_2019.pdf.

ISTAT. (2019b). Le statistiche dell'ISTAT sulla povertà. www.istat.it/it/files//2020/06/REPORT_POVERTA_2019.pdf.

La Repubblica. (2015). Ponte Mammolo, sgomberato campo abusivo che fu visitato da Papa Francesco. *La Repubblica*, 11 May. https://roma.repubblica.it/cronaca/2015/05/11/news/tensioni_a_ponte_mammolo_sgomberato_campo_abusivo_ferita_una_vigilessa-114088113/.

La Stampa. (2021). Unimpresa: oltre 10 milioni di italiani a rischio povertà per colpa del Covid. *La Stampa*, 4 April. www.lastampa.it/economia/2021/04/04/news/unimpresa-oltre-10-milioni-di-italiani-a-rischio-poverta-per-colpa-del-covid-1.40111413.

Legambiente. (2019). *Ecomafia 2019: Le storie e i numeri della criminalità ambientale in Italia.* Edizioni Ambiente.

Magliaro, F. M. (2018). Vertice Salvini-Raggi: "Ripristinare la legalità. Nei campi rom 30mila parassiti. *Il Tempo*, 29 July. www.iltempo.it/roma-capitale/2018/07/25/news/vertice-salvini-raggi-ripristinare-la-legalita-nei-campi-rom-30mila-parassiti-1080140/.

Manna, E., & Esposito, R. (eds). (2019). La povertà a Roma: Un punto di vista. *Caritas Roma.* www.caritasroma.it/wp-content/uploads/2019/11/Rapporto_2019.pdf.

Maranghi, E. (2016). Geografie abitative a Tor Bella Monaca: Uno spaccato sulla domanda di abitare e il significato della casa pubblica oggi. *Territorio*, 78, 63–68. https://doi.org/10.3280/tr2016-078007.

Marchini, R., & Sotgia, A. (2017). *Roma, alla conquista del West: Dalla fornace al mattone finanziario.* DeriveApprodi.

Médecins sans Frontières. (2018). Fuori campo: Insediamenti informali, marginalità sociale, ostacoli all'accesso alle cure e ai beni essenziali per migranti e rifugiati. *Medici Senza Frontiere.* www.medicisenzafrontiere.it/wp-content/uploads/2018/06/Fuoricampo2018.pdf.

Moatasim, F. (2019). Entitled urbanism: Elite informality and the reimagining of a planned modern city. *Urban Studies*, 56(5), 1009–1025. https://doi.org/10.1177/0042098018767011.

Montagna, N., & Grazioli, M. (2019). Urban commons and freedom of movement: The housing struggles of recently arrived migrants in Rome. *Citizenship Studies*, 23 (6), 577–592. https://doi.org/10.1080/13621025.2019.1634375.

Mudu, P. (2014). Housing and homelessness in contemporary Rome. In I. Clough Marinaro & B. Thomassen (eds), *Global Rome: Changing faces of the Eternal City* (pp. 62–78). Indiana University Press.

Mudu, P., & Chattopadhyay, S. (eds). (2016). *Migration, squatting and radical autonomy.* Routledge. https://doi.org/10.4324/9781315673301.

OHCHR. (2009). The right to adequate housing. UN-Habitat. www.ohchr.org/Documents/Publications/FS21_rev_1_Housing_en.pdf.

Palma, E. (2019). Casalotti, protesta di Casapound e cittadini contro i rom: "Non li vogliamo". *Corriere della Sera*, 10 April. https://roma.corriere.it/notizie/cronaca/19_ap

rile_10/casalotti-protesta-casapound-cittadini-contro-rom-non-li-vogliamo-00987474-5bba-11e9-ba57-a3df5eacbd16.shtml.
Pizzo, B., & Altavilla, E. (2018). Embedding illegality, or when the illegal becomes licit: Planning cases and urban transformations in Rome. In F. Chiodelli, T. Hall, & R. Hudson (eds), *The illicit and illegal in regional and urban governance and development: Corrupt places* (1st ed., pp. 164–180). Routledge. https://doi.org/10.4324/9781315317663.
Pow, C. (2017). Elite informality, spaces of exception and the super-rich in Singapore. In R. Forrest, S. Y. Koh & B. Wissink (eds), *Cities and the super-rich: Real estate, elite practices and urban political economies* (pp. 209–228). Palgrave. https://doi.org/10.1057/978-1-137-54834-4_11.
Puccini, E. (2016). *Verso una politica della casa*. Ediesse.
Puccini, E. (2019). L'integrazione fra le politiche del welfare è possibile? Roma, stranieri e case popolari. In E. Manna & R. Esposito (eds), *La povertà a Roma: Un punto di vista* (pp. 152–167). Caritas Roma. www.caritasroma.it/wp-content/uploads/2019/11/Rapporto_2019.pdf.
Rhodes, J. D. (2008). Collective anxiety: Corviale, Rome, and the legacy of '68. *Log*, 13(14), 75–86.
Rigucci, P. (2019). Abitare difficile: La casa a Roma tra squilibri e criticità, desideri e risorse. In E. Manna & R. Esposito (eds), *La povertà a Roma: Un punto di vista* (pp. 168–179). Caritas Roma. www.caritasroma.it/wp-content/uploads/2019/11/Rapporto_2019.pdf.
Roma Capitale. (2017). Commissione capitolina permanente VII: Verbale 16. 19 May. www.comune.roma.it/resources/cms/documents/ccppatrimonio_19052017.pdf.
Roy, A. (2005). Urban informality: Toward an epistemology of planning. *Journal of the American Planning Association*, 71(2), 147–158. https://doi.org/10.1080/01944360508976689.
Roy, A. (2009). Why India cannot plan its cities: Informality, insurgence and the idiom of urbanization. *Planning Theory*, 8(1), 76–87. https://doi.org/10.1177/1473095208099299.
Roy, A. (2018). The potency of the state: Logics of informality and subalternity. *Journal of Development Studies*, 54(12), 2243–2246. https://doi.org/10.1080/00220388.2018.1460470.
Roy, A., & AlSayyad, N. (eds). (2004). *Urban informality: Transnational perspectives from the Middle East, Latin America, and South Asia*. Lexington Books.
Solimene, M. (2018). Zingari buoni e zingari cattivi: Breve storia delle politiche delle amministrazioni capitoline alle prese con gli zingari/nomadi/rom. In S. Pontrandolfo (ed.), *Politiche locali per Rom e Sinti in Italia* (pp. 155–179). CISU.
Storto, G. (2018). *La casa abbandonata*. Officina Edizioni.
Szakolczai, A. (2009). Liminality and experience: Structuring transitory situations and transformative events. *International Political Anthropology*, 2(1), 141–172.
Thomassen, B. (2015). Thinking with liminality: To the boundaries of an anthropological concept. In A. Horváth, B. Thomassen, & H. Wydra (eds), *Breaking boundaries: Varieties of liminality* (1st ed., pp. 39–60). Berghahn.
Turner, V. (1967). *The forest of symbols: Aspects of Ndembu ritual*. Cornell University Press.
UN-Habitat. (n.d.). Concepts and definitions. https://unstats.un.org/sdgs/metadata/files/Metadata-11-01-01.pdf.
UNAR (Ufficio Nazionale Antidiscriminazioni Razziali). (2012). Strategia nazionale d'inclusione dei rom, dei sinti e dei caminanti. www.lavoro.gov.it/temi-e-priorita/infa

nzia-e-adolescenza/focus-on/integrazione-rom-sinti-e-caminanti/Documents/Strategia%20Nazionale.pdf.

Unione Inquilini. (2019). Provvedimenti esecutivi di sfratto, richieste di esecuzione, sfratti eseguiti per provincia. www.unioneinquilini.it/index.php?id=8763.

Vasudevan, A. (2021). Between illegality and insurgency. Notes on the history of urban informality in the Global North. [Conference presentation] Houses of Cards? The Rules and Institutions of Housing Illegality in Western Countries. Cambridge University. Online, 19–21 April. [Video]. *Youtube*. https://youtu.be/UXKhgujsoqE.

Vidotto, V. (2017). Corviale, Rome: An architectural and social utopia of the seventies. In M. Baumeister, B. Bonomo, & D. Schott (eds), *Cities contested: Urban politics, heritage and social movements in Italy and West Germany in the 1970s* (pp. 97–120). Campus.

Watson, V. (2009). Seeing from the South: Refocusing urban planning on the globe's central urban issues. *Urban Studies*, 46(11), 2259–2275. https://doi.org/10.1177/0042098009342598.

3 Liminality on the street

The shifting rules of (in)formal vending

Introduction

Informal street vending is commonly understood as encompassing all types of legal goods and services sold in urban public spaces through practices that defy some element of official regulation (Cross, 2000). This vastly diverse domain spans from trading in historical neighbourhood markets to fleeting, individualized transactions. Vendors may be fully unlicensed, or they may be authorized but violate specific terms of their permits. The sector's social and economic complexity is evident in the immense variety of goods sold and in the varying levels of income that sellers can earn. Long assumed to be a residual, low-profit and barely productive sector, recent international studies instead highlight both its economic dynamism (Chen & Carré, 2020; Cupers, 2015; Rogan & Cichello, 2020) and the multiple actors that it brings together: national and regional authorities, street-level bureaucrats, consumers, residents, transnational and local traders, artisans and tourists (Crossa, 2020). Some types of informal street commerce are celebrated for their traditional role in urban life, for their social vitality and diversity, and their ability to connect consumers to local artistic and agricultural products. Others are instead stigmatized, considered an uncontrolled invasion of public space, a threat to hygiene and governance which must be repressed.

Rome, like many other Italian cities, has a lengthy history of such informal economic activity. The flexibility and diversification of street trading offer crucial opportunities for income generation, especially to actors excluded from more regulated employment sectors that require high financial capital and bureaucratic conformity. In this environment, migrants, minorities, and other under-protected agents can assert their entrepreneurial capacity and build economic autonomy. At the same time, the sector is an important reflection of Italy's undeclared and precarious labour market more broadly. As in many other advanced economies (Boels, 2014; Breman, 2020; Chen and Carré, 2020; Graaf & Ha, 2015; Lund, 2020), formal and stable working conditions are becoming the preserve of a shrinking and privileged population, as many previously waged jobs become casualized and the "gig economy" expands. With its estimated 3,652,000 informal workers, Italy's

DOI: 10.4324/9780429353321-4

unobserved economy amounted to about 211 billion euro in 2018: almost 12% of national GDP (ISTAT, 2020).[1] Informal vending is a structural feature of that labour market, providing livelihoods to countless households and an essential means of reducing poverty. However, the exclusion of unregistered workers from Italy's primarily wage-based social protections exposes them and their families to conditions of extreme vulnerability. Indeed, the COVID-19 pandemic has highlighted all too vividly the lack of welfare support available to this large segment of the workforce (Johnson & Ghiglione, 2020; The Economist, 2020).

The expansiveness and visibility of informal street vending in Rome makes it a core sphere for exploring how practices of informality connect to the urban political economy. The heterogeneous legal and social profiles of its traders produce power dynamics that are highly unbalanced and result in notable inequalities of opportunity. The sector is in fact structured around hierarchies that have been reinforced in recent years through a combination of ambiguous public policies and the monopolistic tactics of established vendors. In mapping the positions of informal traders within Rome's broader field of street commerce, this chapter highlights how local and national policies have made it difficult for newcomers to acquire formal vending licences, resulting in the frequent penalization of non-Italians. When political pressures have pushed the municipal authorities to repress informal trades, immigrants and ethnic minorities have often been those most visibly targeted. This performance of law and order has been selectively enacted, allowing other actors to continue their informal and illegal practices freely. The analysis shows that this grey governance mechanism of oscillating toleration and repression has not occurred haphazardly. The interests of many Italian vendors, who constitute an important reservoir of votes, have repeatedly been prioritized, most notably at election time. Concurrently, neoliberal pressures to valorize real estate in the city centre have triggered drives to "order" and aestheticize its public spaces by reducing the apparent unruliness associated with street vending. These initiatives have taken on explicitly ethnic connotations, with the stigmatizing label of *abusivi* ("informals") wielded selectively to expel minority traders – especially Roma – while legitimizing Italian vendors' claims to exclusive rights to the city.

The analysis begins with a brief overview of the history of street vending in Rome and the sector's contemporary size and social importance. Since the forms and spaces of street vending today are so diversified, the subsequent mapping of the field is organized by typologies. It starts with the most regulated and politically exalted manifestation – the food and household goods markets found in most neighborhoods (*mercati rionali*) –, progressing then to single stalls positioned in economically strategic locations, followed by itinerant vendors. Although informal practices are shown to exist at every level of the field, unlicensed and precarious traders are particularly concentrated in this third category, balancing visibility and invisibility, toleration and hostility, on a daily basis. The fourth typology is that of flea markets, where vendors with a variety of different legal statuses operate side by side within the same space. It is here that the tensions and power relations between multiple institutional and commercial actors are most evident. The analysis brings to the fore how sellers' various levels of social and temporal capital condition how the authorities treat them. Some are able to continue selling their wares at the same stalls each week, building long-term networks with clients and other vendors thanks to their visibility and spatial continuity; others must operate transiently and furtively, subject to much greater obstacles in establishing predictable sales relations and strategies. The spectrum of fixedness/evanescence which emerges across the field produces multiple gradations of liminality, where relative clarity or insecurity of status has far-reaching repercussions on actors' commercial and corporeal freedoms in public space.

The final section homes in on the tangible effects of these forces in the working lives of Roma street traders. The case study traces a 25-year process through which Roma vendors have been forced out of commercial hubs that are crucial to attracting a clientele, relegated – step by step – to the most isolated and peripheral areas of the city. The analysis ties this trajectory to revanchist dynamics in high value neighbourhoods and to processes of "urban cleansing" (Smith, 1996), whereby notions of dirt and purity have been mobilized by politicians, media, residents, and other traders to expel them from the urban centre. Many Roma vendors, however, hold out against the fleetingness and liminality – the forced mobility and insecurity – that these pressures engender. Many now congregate in semi-authorized markets on private land, where the risk of expulsion is less immediate than on public property. There they stake a claim to the city and its trade circuits, insisting on permanence and visibility and resisting the dominant construction of them as nomads and criminals, reaching for whatever clarity of status they can despite the obstacles.

Given the broad time frame covered, the social and spatial fragmentation of street vending, and the plurality of actors involved, the chapter draws on mixed data collection methods aiming to triangulate between perspectives and compensate for often partial experiences, memories, and materials. Archival sources furnish the basis for the historical discussion and the media analysis, as well as the institutions' evolving approaches to street trade. Primary documents produced by vendor associations and representatives provide examples of their discourses and their engagements with licencing regulations. The ethnographic focus on Roma traders draws on oral history accounts by vendors who have experienced the various phases of their expulsion first from institutionally tolerated informal markets, then from the Porta Portese flea market, and their ensuing dispersal into precarious micro markets of varying levels of authorization. The analysis of the most recent phase is based on participant observation in one semi-authorized market, integrated with visits to a similar one, as well as various illegal trade venues between early 2018 and March 2020, when the first COVID-19 lockdowns dramatically disrupted sales. Interviews with vendors in both types of markets provide crucial depth and context to my own observations.

History and social role of street vending in Rome

Rome's position as a crossroads of trade stems back to its very origins as a settlement. The importance of its commercial life grew alongside its urban and political expansion until the collapse of the Western Roman Empire in the 5th century. Little is known about what followed in the early Middle Ages, but a clear picture emerges from the 12th century onwards of a city bustling with street commerce of all types. In addition to its officially designated markets and its many unauthorized stalls, a large population of itinerant vendors moved through crowds selling from their baskets of goods (Sanfilippo, 2006). Throughout much of the city's history, street trade was the primary means by which every layer of society provisioned foodstuffs and household items. The papal authorities tried hard to tax the sector and to regulate it through hygiene and quality assurance policies, but theirs was a largely unsuccessful struggle. Indeed, the frequency with which edicts had to be reasserted between the 16th and 18th centuries (Palumbo, 2006) underlines how frequently these decrees were violated. Despite plans to rationalize the system first under Napoleonic rule and then by the post-unification Italian authorities, the situation changed little in practice until well into the 20th century (Francescangeli, 2006). Transient vending and informal clusters of stalls remained the norm and regulations were rarely enforced.

Although an organic system of rules for market trading was introduced in 1891, unofficial intermediaries continued to inflate food prices and moneylenders exploited customers' difficulties in affording basic goods until the Fascist period. Only then were clear measuring, accounting, and payment processes enforced. With its focus on social control and urban planning, the regime also began to develop purpose-built markets located throughout the city's residential districts. The projects interrupted by World War II were taken up and expanded further in the post-war years, so that by the 1960 Olympics, the city had 109 official markets (Francescangeli, 2006). Paradoxically, though, this achievement coincided with Italy's economic boom, which reduced the centrality of street trade as consumers took their new wealth to more prestigious sales outlets. Thus, while in 1951 almost 29% of trade occurred through street vending, by 1971 it had fallen to 12%. This decline then continued, reaching an all-time low of 9% in 2001 (Confesercenti, 2018).

Italy's economic stagnation in the 21st century has, however, revitalized the sector as many entrepreneurs have found themselves unable to cover the overheads involved in bricks-and-mortar outlets. In 2007 – just before the global financial crisis – there were around 100,000 registered itinerant businesses (La Repubblica, 2018). By 2018 the number had almost doubled to 188,988 (La Stampa, 2018).[2] They now make up 22% of all official companies in Italy, most of them micro-businesses run by a single individual (Unioncamere, 2019). More than half these traders are foreign nationals (around 100,000) and their membership is getting younger. It has become a highly dynamic sector that produces an estimated annual revenue of 11 billion euro

(Confesercenti, 2018) and has the versatility to provide a livelihood to a wide range of actors, many of whom would otherwise be excluded from legal entrepreneurship. In fact, its high concentration in Southern Italy, where obstacles to traditional enterprise are most acute, reflects this important poverty-mitigating role (Confesercenti, 2018). Moreover, the impoverishment of many Italian families has matched demand to supply: approximately 25 million consumers shop weekly from street vendors, especially in the lowest income areas.

Official and informal street markets therefore continue to be central features of neighbourhood life, bringing together a wide range of customers and sellers and producing spaces for mutual engagement in sharp contrast to social divisions mirrored in mainstream commercial areas. It is in markets that embodied skills of craftsmanship and knowledge are valorized and transmitted. Here, low-income actors can build security and community, compensating for gaps in services and opportunities encountered elsewhere. When such markets are spontaneous and unauthorized, they become counter-hegemonic spaces (Mikola, 2015), escaping top-down ordering and evading some of the logics of contemporary capitalist consumption. Indeed, much of the literature celebrates the sociality that is produced within those contexts. It underlines their role in enabling citizens to make and remake the city in ways that meet their needs, and fostering belonging and inclusion, irrespective of planning policies and official rhetorics (Evers & Seale, 2015). In some Global Southern cities there is now growing recognition that informal markets are essential to local economies and poverty reduction. Punitive policies are gradually being replaced by ones that enhance traders' stability and formality (Meneses-Reyes, 2018; WIEGO, 2020). In Italy, however, responses have not evolved beyond repression or blind-eye-turning, apart from some isolated exceptions in a few Northern cities (Clough Marinaro, 2018). In Rome, drives to "cleanse," "civilize," and "reorder" public spaces in areas of rising real-estate value have instead partially forced informal economies out of central areas, as the case study section illustrates. These policies of poverty displacement have been accompanied, however, by selective toleration when the survival activities of poor urbanites occur within their "rightful" place (Douglas, 2015): in the city's hidden or low-value interstices and peripheral zones.

Rome's long history of street trade has thus involved a gradual but determined and escalating push towards rationalization and formalization. Parts of the sector have nonetheless strongly resisted these forces. A Manichean public discourse has accompanied the process, with the less controlled forms of trade consistently vilified as disorderly, dirty, and dangerous. At the same time, official neighbourhood markets are widely celebrated as a "strong component of Rome's economic and social identity [...] an integral part of [its] cultural heritage, to be protected and valorized" (Giulioli, 2006, p. 7). Yet, the distinctions between formal and informal trading are far less clear-cut than such portrayals would suggest. Among registered traders, for example, there is high tax evasion and non-payment of social security contributions (Confesercenti,

2018; Guano, 2010). The following sections demonstrate that informality is entrenched throughout the entire sector, although its manifestations vary depending on the groups involved. Street trading therefore reflects the modalities of informal employment generally in Italy (De Gregorio & Giordano, 2016), where much irregular work is symbiotically integrated within formal businesses, large and small, across multiple economic sectors.

Becoming informal: paradoxes in regulating Rome's street vending

On the surface, today's system of street trade licensing appears straightforward. Municipalities are responsible for designating and policing the areas in which vending is and is not permitted, implementing a calendar of markets, and monitoring the rotation of stalls. They issue two types of authorizations. Type A is for fixed stalls in markets or fairs, or isolated stands in designated locations. Type B is specifically for itinerant vendors, who may trade for up to two hours in any public space except specified vending-free zones (Decreto Legislativo 31 marzo, 1998, n. 118).[3] In theory, the costs involved in obtaining a licence are low. Aspiring vendors must pay a tax (*marca da bollo*) of around 15 euro plus a municipal fee of between 80 and 100 euro to make their application. They are also required to establish Value Added Tax status (*partita IVA*) and register with the local chamber of commerce for an annual fee of 120 euro (Camera di Commercio Roma, 2020). In practice, though, the situation in Rome is far less accessible and transparent. In 2017, the municipality delegated the task of issuing licences to the individual boroughs, although it retains various coordinating responsibilities. The result is confusion about the respective functions of these levels of government, as well as bureaucratic overlaps that further hamper an application process that was very slow to begin with (Torresan, 2019). Traders complain of overly burdensome red tape and high taxation rates (Confesercenti, 2018), coupled with a lack of institutional overview of the situation. Indeed, the municipality has not updated its licensing records since 2015 (Panié, 2018).

*Neighbourhood markets (*mercati rionali*)*

Neighbourhood markets are the most formalized and regulated of street-trading environments. Yet, even in this sub-sector, the failure of Rome's authorities to maintain a transparent system for managing them in recent decades has forced many traders to devise compensatory informal mechanisms. Over a thousand market stalls (about 25% of the total) are currently closed and have not been reassigned (Roma Capitale, 2020). Although individual boroughs do occasionally issue new licences for specific locations, "nobody knows exactly how many outlets are active and how many are not" (Panié, 2018, p. 13). In the last major drive to reanimate the sector with new stalls in 2013, it took four years for the municipality to process the licence applications, by which time many traders had given up or found alternative solutions. This institutional inertia obstructing potential newcomers has fostered a parallel informal system whereby licence-holders sublet their spots to others. While this has created opportunities for some commercial renewal, it has also enabled established traders to take over more stalls than the law allows, effectively creating semi-monopolistic domination of some venues. Outlets are also sold informally but expensively: licensed stalls on neighbourhood food markets, for example, are traded for between ten and twenty thousand euro depending on their infrastructure.[4] In addition to this initial outlay, stallholders must then be able to pay monthly rental and service charges to the municipality. Thus, although the sector is widely extolled for providing a low-investment route to running a business, the costs in Rome can be prohibitive. Acquiring a stall through formal means is only possible for those with the temporal capital to wait through the long bureaucratic processes. Obtaining one informally requires significant financial capital and extensive social networks. The informal practices that have emerged to compensate for institutional inadequacies have not resulted, therefore, in any subversion of established hierarchies. Prospective traders who lack those forms of capital are instead obliged to turn to the sectors discussed next, where the municipality's even more pronounced and long-standing withdrawal has created greater spaces for action but also more glaring inequalities.

(Un)licensed pavement vending

Vendors operating outside the circuit of markets, as itinerant sellers or running single pavement stalls, face a bureaucratic situation that is even more static. The city authorities stopped issuing new licences of these types in 2006 (Deliberazione del Consiglio Comunale 6 febbraio 2006, n. 35, Art. 30), and it has become extremely difficult for street traders to work legally in the commercial and touristic hub of the historic centre (Piazzoni, 2020). Here too, significant capital investments are required to take over existing licences, as Piazzoni (2020, p. 5) explains:

> (only a few sellers with a special "121" *Type B* permit for "artisans" are allowed to work in the historic core) (Comune di Roma 2006, 2011). These measures led people who could afford it to buy licenses from retiring artisan vendors, which today can cost between 50,000 and 60,000 euros. Poor immigrants were – and continue to be – forced to sell irregularly. Moreover, unlike Italians who continue to sell informally, most immigrants lack the means and connections to bribe the city employees, patrollers, and established sellers who unofficially regulate street activities (Liguori and Orlando 2012).

An investigation in 2017 found that about 80% of Rome's 12,000 street-vending licences were irregular in that they were issued by unauthorized entities or they violated new traffic codes or cultural heritage protection rules (Custodero, 2017). Since 2004, in fact, no street trade is allowed within 200 metres of institutional, religious and heritage sites (Decreto Legislativo 22 gennaio 2004, n. 42). A series of broader "pro-decorum" initiatives have also been introduced in recent years to facilitate the expulsion of unlicensed vendors and others considered a threat to local order and aesthetics.[5] Although an attempt was made by the city council to distance some stalls from the monuments in 2014 (Marino, 2017; Serloni, 2015) and again in late 2019, many others remain undisturbed (Garrone, 2020). The implementation of these regulations has, in fact, been very selective. As the above quotation suggests, having the financial and social capital to bribe local officials to turn a blind eye or otherwise influence decision-making processes is crucial in determining whether one may continue to sell or not. Many pavement stalls have also remained in place because the municipality has not identified enough commercially viable alternative sites in less obstructive locations (Corriere della Sera, 2020). Here the authorities' forbearance towards unauthorized trading has been motivated by a reluctance to penalize vendors for the consequences of institutional slowness and ambiguity. Systematically fining them would trigger protests that would heighten public attention to the contradiction between the administration's rhetorical claims to fight "urban blight" and its actual inertia, especially in anticipation of the 2021 municipal elections.

An additional element in the opacity of this sector is a decades-long system of semi-monopolistic control of Rome's pavement vending sites by a single family: the Tredicine. Since the 1980s, this family has gradually taken over hundreds of licences. By 2012 its members and allied groups were estimated to control over three hundred stalls: approximately 22% of authorized street vending. Among these were 42 of the 68 lucrative food and beverage vans parked near the city's historic monuments (Angeli & Tonacci, 2012). The municipality had by then ceased to dispense new licences, simply renewing those of established vendors. Any newcomer seeking to penetrate the sector would have to pay around 650,000 euro on the informal market to acquire a van and its licence (Angeli & Tonacci, 2012). Meanwhile, other vendors reported being forced to pay kickbacks of 4,000 to 5,000 euro to rent monthly sales spots, on top of the official rental fee of 500–600 euro. To whom these bribes were paid was not specified, although recent judicial inquiries have started to shed light on a complex city-wide system of corruption. In February 2019, Rome's public prosecutor's office announced an ongoing investigation into 16 individuals believed to constitute a criminal organization involved in extortion and bribery (Allegri, 2019; Sacchettoni, 2019). Among the suspects were two employees of the municipal Department for Economic Development, Productive Activities and Agriculture responsible for managing the rotation of stalls and licences. The charges involved taking bribes to influence the rotations, failing to sanction irregularities, and reserving the most lucrative spots for allied vendors. Moreover, high-ranking members of two street vendors' unions – among them the brothers Dino and Mario Tredicine – were investigated for bribery and for using one of the unions' headquarters as the logistical base for the shadow management of licences and vending shifts. A third layer of suspects involved six stallholders acting as bribe and debt collectors, often employing violence and intimidation, on behalf of the group's upper echelons. The investigation led to 18 people being arrested in September 2020 (Izzo, 2020; Vincenzi, 2020). They are currently awaiting trial and the inquiry has expanded to include forty other individuals and 240 stalls. Further allegations concern traders being forced to turn to the organization's loan-sharks if they cannot afford the bribes of up to 60,000 euro a year required to access sales spots. Members of the group have additionally been accused of coercing vendors to give them a cut of the COVID-19 relief payments received from the state (Vincenzi, 2020). Should these actors be found guilty in court, this would indicate that the paralysis in managing this segment of Rome's street-trading economy has been orchestrated, at least in part, by criminal actors who have penetrated the political system. The municipality's top-down informalities would thus have been to the direct benefit of illegal interests. Whether systemically coordinated or not, the impossibility of less resource-rich actors formally accessing permits and vending spots has presented them with two alternatives: accept extortive informal arrangements or face the vulnerability of operating with no permits at all.

Itinerant vending

Mobile vending is the sub-sector in which most unauthorized street sales are carried out in Rome.[6] Traders who cannot acquire an official licence to work in the high-consumption areas of the city centre must often turn to this solution. Moreover, it offers essential income-generating opportunities to undocumented immigrants and asylum-seekers, but also to many legally resident foreigners struggling to find employment in other sectors. Rome is thus no different from the numerous cities globally where informal sales provide a fundamental means for marginalized residents to survive and build up social networks when official rights and avenues to integration are closed off (Recchi, 2020). In circumstances where these vendors must juggle disappearing from the view of law enforcement officers while still remaining visible to potential buyers – and hyper-visible when they need protection from the police if their safety is endangered (Piazzoni, 2020) – mobility is a core asset. It enables them to follow the temporal rhythms of the city, moving with the flows of clientele as they change neighbourhoods in key moments of the day and night (Cupers, 2015). Elasticity is also essential for managing potential conflicts, avoiding excessive proximity to competitors with more established claims to good sales spots, while ensuring that other vendors are near enough in moments of need. The importance of sociality among such traders is becoming ever more evident as scholars underline the alliances that they weave, often across different ethnic groups, to alert each other if police begin patrolling the area, and with local shopkeepers and business owners who provide them with facilities to safely store their merchandise (Cancellieri &

Ostanel, 2015; Piazzoni, 2020). Social ties expand beyond these logistical concerns, though, as vendors build relations within the neighbourhoods in which they live and work. Locals often support them against evictions and police actions, buy their goods out of solidarity (Clough Marinaro & Panella, 2021), and recognize them as rightful members of an increasingly cosmopolitan urban community (Piazzoni, 2020). This type of vending is founded, furthermore, on strong commercial rationales: it permits nimble adjustments in the typologies of goods sold as supply and demand opportunities change. It involves no infrastructural investment, no overhead costs, no obligation to remain in the city if better markets open up elsewhere.

Mobility is thus fundamental to a multitude of agentive tactics through which vendors negotiate daily arrangements with the law and with their economic and social networks. Despite their evident integration in the city's commercial flows and value chains, however, their status as illegal actors places them in a condition of permanent liminality. Their safety and possibilities for action are contingent on the variable moods and attentions of external actors: police officers, hierarchically more powerful vendors, or the criminal actors discussed above that appear to manage part of this sector. Fleetingness, though essential for survival, is burdensome in many ways. It conditions the types of goods that can be sold – making it impossible to sell bulky and heavy merchandise, for example – and exposes vendors to everyday violence and the risk of confiscation of their assets. They are constantly vulnerable to the punitive arm of the state while being afforded none of its protections (Chen & Carré, 2020). Consequently, some unauthorized vendors operate on the margins of Rome's official markets, especially those in working-class neighbourhoods where policing tends to be more sporadic. Sociality, safety in numbers, and a steady flow of clientele are thereby guaranteed, allowing them to grasp some spatial and commercial stability while maintaining the possibility of a quick escape if the authorities choose to crack down.

Institutional responses to these activities have been as mutable in Rome as they are in many Global Southern cities. On the one hand, police are selective in their enforcement, often turning a blind eye to Italians while penalizing foreigners and minorities (Piazzoni, 2020). With the latter group too they employ discretionary favouritisms, facilitating escape routes for vendors they know well (Piazzoni, 2020), or letting them off with warnings rather than fining them (Clough Marinaro, 2018). There is therefore an implicit recognition that such vending is critical to the survival of many low-income groups. On the other hand, this toleration is always retractable and conditional on macro-level political forces and temporalities. Piazzoni (2020), for example, reports the escalation of anti-immigrant clampdowns in the centre of Rome in 2018, shortly after the success in national elections of the securitarian League party, with Matteo Salvini at its head. Equally, the repeated activation of "pro-decorum" ordinances by the municipal government have appeared to strategically signal a commitment to urban management in the face of complaints of low-quality public services in the city (ACOS, 2018, 2020; Il Messaggero, 2019; Il Sole 24

Ore, 2019). In such cases, political actors discursively construct informal street vending as the primary threat to urban beauty and public order, using it to redirect attention from institutional responsibilities underlying social tensions and problematic urban management. Central to this portrayal is the accusation that traders undermine legality and compete unfairly with local businesses. This message was clearly conveyed, for example, in a flyer and posters distributed by the city council to accompany the introduction of new municipal police regulations in June 2019. One image shows a street vendor happily counting their earnings in front of a shopkeeper who has had to cut prices and looks upset. Another shows an unkempt person running away from a super-hero-type police officer, carrying sunglasses, watches, crates of mineral water, and fireworks.[7] These images create a narrative of hostility and economic incompatibility between street vendors and shopkeepers that offer no recognition of the much more nuanced relations and commercial intertwinements that were highlighted above.[8] They also send the implicit message that street vendors primarily offer counterfeit goods. At the same time, they negate any state role in generating an environment where legal alternatives are obstructed and where responses of law-enforcement officials are deeply equivocal.

Flea markets: Porta Portese

Rome's flea markets bring together vendors of all types and levels of authorization, providing a unique vantage point from which to explore hierarchies between them and their differential treatment by municipal authorities. Although the city has various such markets, the historic Porta Portese flea market – one of the largest in Europe, located in the central and touristic neighbourhood of Trastevere – is emblematic of the multi-layered mechanisms of informality that have evolved over time. Moreover, some of its vendors have been active in discursively differentiating between traders to lobby for specific group interests with the municipal authorities. This section underlines the long-standing institutional ambiguities in regulating the market and explores how vendors have been able to influence policy and enforcement in ways that perpetuate informalities and distinctions of legality, precarity, and power. It also provides part of the historical and social context within which the later case study, focusing on Roma vendors, is situated.

Porta Portese originated as a hub for exchanging black market goods during World War II and remained predominantly informal and self-organized for much of its subsequent history. "Informally legitimized by the city as a free trade zone" (Ya-Chih Yang, 2009, p. 18), it was untaxed and unregulated, allowing urban poor to buy necessities and make a living with small trades. In the post-war economic boom years, it attracted internal migrants and, from the 1980s, foreign ones. It thus grew tenfold, from 246 stalls in 1949 to approximately 2,400 in 2000, with authorities mostly ignoring its activities and growth, apart from occasional haphazard attempts to register some stalls. For over 65 years, Porta Portese was a highly integrative "heterarchical" public space

(Wiley, 2008, p. 77), fluidly connecting people of all classes, cultural backgrounds, and legal statuses: a microcosm of the globalizing city. However, in 2007 its location in one of Rome's most rapidly gentrifying areas caused it to be targeted by a major "requalification" and "rationalization" drive by the centre-left municipal administration. This followed a re-election campaign that had confirmed the incumbent mayor's agenda of rebranding Rome as an attractive hub for international financial investment. The market's layers of informality and its apparent disorder were no longer compatible with the city's global aspirations. Consequently, the municipality declared that it would be halved in size: licences for 970 stalls would be approved and the remaining approximately one thousand stallholders would be relocated to four peripheral markets. A census of stalls was thus initiated in 2008 but, rather than clarifying sellers' legal statuses as intended, it exposed a complex and historically consolidated system of informalities. Half the vendors were found to be fully unlicensed, while many others had been pragmatically allowed to run stalls for years with the wrong permits, such as mobile vendor licences that in theory ban sellers for staying on the same spot for more than two hours. As Ya-Chih Yang (2009, p. 20) explained at the time of the "formalization":

> the mythical "Porta Portese license" that never existed, determined who could stay and who had to go. The city demands operational licenses that can only be obtained through nearly impossible bureaucratic processes that had been continuously revised over the years to the point where it is so complex, it becomes a Catch 22. [...] In the ecology of the market, ownership of vending space is claimed through time. A vendor who has been at the same spot for thirty years has the right to continue his or her occupation. Like the bloodline of a family, the entitlement to vending spaces are passed down through immediate families and friends or otherwise leased and sold to third parties in the same manner as property. In the particular culture of informal trades, business contracts are bounded by verbal promises rather than written proof. Therefore, the notion of a valid "Porta Portese license" is considered a joke for the people who have been in the trade long enough to know the legal loopholes.

In the face of lack of regulatory clarity and consistency, therefore, alternative methods for ordering Porta Portese's spaces had emerged, the most legitimized of which was temporal capital. Simple protracted presence afforded traders the right, uncontested for decades, to remain in the market. Indeed, one of the documents most commonly accepted by the municipal police in lieu of a formal licence was – paradoxically – a past fine proving that the trader had been working there without authorization for a significant amount of time. A demonstrated history of rule-bending thus conferred the right to stay, much like the recognition of long-term squatting during the formalization process in Corviale (chapter 2).

When the Porta Portese "requalification" plan was set in motion, in September 2007, police officers blocked all the market's entrance points, checking licences and refusing access to unregistered traders. The long-term – mainly Italian – vendors reacted furiously, deploying alleged "urban guerrilla" tactics: blocking traffic, overturning vehicles, burning garbage (Frignani & Sacchettoni, 2007). The violence achieved the goal of delaying their eviction indefinitely, with only the "totally irregular" ones subsequently removed "to guarantee propriety and security." Six hundred "habitual traders" were instead regularized, conferring official legitimacy to their temporal capital. The municipality thereby enacted discretionary distinctions between the gradations of informality, attributing rights to some while denying them to others.

This forbearance towards some informal vendors was implemented in highly ethnicized ways. Since foreign nationals tended to be the most recent arrivals in the market, they were often unable to demonstrate a continuous long-term presence there, making them the category most frequently barred by the police. Moreover, they were systematically targeted for checks and expulsion in the run-up to the "formalization" drive, often on the basis of immigration status rather than sales permits. A series of night-time police raids were carried out specifically aiming to remove such groups as they waited to set up their stalls at dawn.[9] These actions were clearly motivated by pressures from locals who portrayed immigrants and Roma as the source of the neighbourhood's alleged unruliness:

> inhabitants … put up banners on buildings: "Roma and illegal immigrants out" […], "get off our pavements."
>
> (Salvatori, 2007)

> to try to send the nomads away, last Sunday residents of via Federico Rosazza and Via Ippolito Nievo attached hoses to taps and poured water from their balconies onto the Roma on the street.
>
> (Coletti, 2007)

> "It's all the fault of Gypsies and crooks who don't respect the rules and create unrest," adds another street vendor, "we can't all be blamed."
>
> (Martelli, 2007)

> "I come here every week" – says one lady – "and I don't think it's right to take it out on these people. Yes, they are unauthorized but they're not dangerous like others. You just need to walk around, go deeper into the market, to see who should really be removed. It's full of Gypsies and lowlifes who commit crimes and create dirt, those are the people who should be banned."
>
> (Martelli, 2007)

> "Porta Portese has been scourged for years by thefts, blight, dirt, and Gypsies."
>
> (Quirito, 2007)

By pushing minority vendors out of the area without comprehensively enforcing regulations on trade, the municipal authorities successfully placated two apparently contrasting blocks of voters: local residents who demanded increased controls in the market and many of its irregular Italian stallholders. In doing so, informalities were hierarchically ordered, and inequalities of ethnicity and citizenship reinforced.

These public narratives hinged on a rhetoric of cleansing in which Roma, especially, were conflated with physical dirt and lack of hygiene, and portrayed as bearers of a more generalized symbolic pollution. At the same time, elite discourses accompanying the formalization policy produced a sanitized and nostalgic account of Porta Portese's history which whitewashed its origins as a black market and its decades-long unregulated existence. Local politicians claimed the formalization would "preserve the market's historic identity" and return it to "its ancient splendour," its "role sculpted in tradition."[10] Some even lobbied, unsuccessfully, to restrict the merchandise traded there to reflect this rewriting of the past: "the House of Freedoms party proposes putting a brake on the typologies of goods to be sold there, privileging antiques, old books, and artisanal goods from Rome and its province" (Il Giornale, 2008). The market's history as a hub of illegal trades and its constant adaptation to the needs and tastes of the city's evolving population were thereby discursively erased, replaced with ethnically loaded claims to ownership of its physical space and cultural identity.[11] With the expulsion of numerous foreigners from its confines, Italians – many of them former internal migrants themselves – were established as the legitimate bearers of history and allowed to stay. Porta Portese was thus transformed from a heterarchical to a hierarchical public space defined by "roots." Herzfeld's notion of "spatial cleansing" (2006) was clearly at work: a fictitious past was monumentalized and a homogeneous "national" heritage invented through eliminating groups now classified as "out of place." Apparently neutral discourses concerning public safety regulations and sanitation were harnessed to remove the market's "messiness" embodied in migrants and minorities, while leaving other informalities intact.

Since then, many migrant vendors have been forced into perpetual mobility to avoid being targeted by the authorities. This has limited their possibility of acquiring the stability that would enable them to build a long-term client base, thus directly impinging on their income levels. Informality intersects here with multiple other dimensions of inequality: of wealth, of political and citizenship rights, of visibility and the right to difference (Chen and Carré, 2020; Crossa, 2020; Shepherd, 2012). The discriminatory implementation of the formalization initiative has since been repeated in the application of more recent "pro-decorum" policies on street vending. "That racial constructions determine how these laws are enforced becomes apparent any time police appear on the street. While all vendors of color run away, white sellers stay put, knowing that patrollers will ignore them" (Piazzoni 2020, pp. 5–6). These discretionary applications of "urban cleansing" policies have further racialized the right to public space and made the livelihoods of non-Italian vendors more insecure, displacing them from the city's high-revenue areas.

This fight against diversity, against "globalization from below," has been part of a broader attempt to transform Rome's central neighbourhoods into elite hubs of consumption. Yet, while enacting similar methods to other Western cities such as New York (Shepherd, 2012), this "globalization from above" has not been fully effective. Projects to improve Porta Portese's infrastructure, for example, have not been activated. In 2012, the Lazio region was allocated 3.5 million euro of EU funds to restructure the market and surrounding areas, but the money was not spent (Roma Today, 2013). Moreover, municipal rhetorics claiming a determination to impose legality and end tax evasion have not translated into transparent and equitable systems for managing vending rights. Five years after the formalization drive, approximately one-third of traders remained "tolerated," not paying fees or taxes (Parisi, 2012). By 2016, around nine hundred vendors were working there without licences (ANSA, 2016). At the same time, the patchy and selective methods of institutional oversight have done little to deter illegal activities within the market's confines, with stallholders periodically complaining of criminal or exploitative practices (Paglino, 2011), and media emphasizing the presence of stolen and counterfeit goods (La7, 2015; Nicolini, 2017). In July 2020, seven people were arrested for usury and extortion, using the market as a base of operations (La Repubblica, 2020). The selective wielding of regulations as a tool of grey governance has not, therefore, achieved full neoliberal development and commodification of the space. Nonetheless, it has advanced localized electoral interests, and property prices have continued to rise in the area (Notiziario immobiliare, 2020; Pagliuca, 2021).[12] It has thus been coherent with a more general tendency in Rome's urban management to focus on self-referential and minimally productive development strategies that perpetuate a rentier economy, reinforcing income inequalities and financial precarity in its bottom layers (Roma Ricerca Roma, 2021).

The politics of temporal capital

The historic accumulation of layers of informality among Porta Portese vendors has not only fostered segmentation between regularized traders and unauthorized ones. It has also cemented different degrees of informality among the latter group. In the absence of clear rights, an unofficial hierarchy has emerged where the most valorized form of capital is temporal. While all the irregular traders there are liminal – suspended between prolonged institutional forbearance and the constant risk of a sudden eviction order – those with higher temporal capital have obtained greater scope for negotiating with the authorities. The social capital built among long-term vendors has enabled them to act collectively and claim a right to stay, whereas the individualized and fragmented situations of many migrant sellers has made it almost impossible to similarly voice demands for stability and security of income.

Unlike in many cities of the Global South, where informal vendors have created associations to represent their needs and, in many cases, successfully lobby for permits and rights (Alba Vega, 2012; Carré, Horn & Bonner, 2018; Meneses-Reyes, 2018; Recchi, 2020), traders' organizations in Rome speak predominantly for licensed sellers. Like the municipal authorities discussed previously, they stigmatize informal vendors as a source of unfair competition and crime, and actively contribute to the semantic conflation of immigration with informality. For example, the Italian merchants' association Confesercenti (2018, p. 32) states that "Italian markets are increasingly besieged by unlicensed vendors, largely foreigners," and claims that 83.2% of these non-nationals evade taxes and social security contributions. It asserts that for every hundred legal traders working in markets, there are 15 "outlaws" (*fuori legge*) who unfairly intercept their customers by selling nearby and who can undercut their prices by up to 20% on some goods. The accusations go further, asserting that "there is a network of front men of foreign origin [...] who are 'controlled' by organized crime" (Confesercenti, 2018, p. 31). Another traders' organization has called for legislation to facilitate confiscation of goods and "in case of recidivism in unauthorized vending, revoking residency permits for non-EU citizens" (FIVA Confcommercio, 2018, p. 6). This juxtaposition of law-abiding Italian traders and informal or criminal foreign ones does not reflect the reality that many nationals, including licensed ones, participate in various types of rule-bending, as previous sections have shown. It also glosses over the fact that Italians predominate where organized criminal activity is involved, such as the networks between traders and municipal employees in Rome currently under investigation. In equating migrants with a threat to security and order, these vendors participate – alongside residents and politicians across the ideological spectrum – in urban revanchism (Smith, 1996), contributing to the racialized hierarchy of rights to public space.

The mobilization of temporal capital has extended politically far beyond the specific case of Porta Portese, though. In fact, struggles over this type of capital have conditioned the management of street vending across the entire city for a decade and a half. In 2006, the EU Parliament and Council passed Directive 2006/123/EC (*Services in the Internal Market Directive*, widely known as the Bolkestein Directive). Its aim was to promote fair competition, simplification, and transparency in the European services sector. Among its requirements was that national legislation protecting certain categories of service providers be abolished. It banned states from including discriminatory criteria in allocating authorizations to trade, such as having previously exercised the activity for a given period. The Directive was transposed into Italian law in 2010 (Decreto Legislativo 26 marzo 2010, n. 59), but its application to street vending has since been repeatedly postponed. The national budget passed in 2017 (Legge 27 dicembre 2017, n. 205) prolonged existing licences to the end of 2020. Subsequent coronavirus relief legislation (Legge 17 luglio 2020, n. 77) then extended them until 2032. This ongoing non-application of EU law at the national level has been determined by intensive lobbying on the part of vendors' associations since the Directive was passed (Bizzotto, 2017).[13] Indeed, demonstrations and sit-ins by traders have been very vocal, particularly in Rome (Il Post, 2017; La Repubblica, 2017; Monaco, 2016; Vendemiale, 2016). Vendors fear that the introduction of a tender process with competitive criteria for authorization, in place of automatic renewal, will lead to them losing their stalls and consequently their incomes. The Confesercenti group articulated these concerns by demanding that temporal capital be explicitly built into Italian legislation to ensure that it "recognizes and unequivocally valorizes the professionalism accrued on stalls as an essential criterion for reassigning licences" (FIVA Confcommercio, 2018, p. 2).

Although such changes have not been inserted into national law, they have been explicitly integrated into Rome's municipal legislation. The city council introduced new regulations governing street trade in July 2017 (Delibera Assemblea Capitolina, 1 giugno 2017, n. 30). Licences would thenceforth be put out to tender, but applicants with the longest demonstrable history of street vending, and those already holding a licence, would be prioritized in the allocation process. In the case of new licences being issued – rather than existing ones renewed – various other aspects would be emphasized: youth, social disadvantage, local production of goods, and innovation. In principle, therefore, the regulations opened up possibilities for newcomers to enter the sector. In practice, very few new licences have been issued since 2017. Consequently, the vending population remains much the same as before. This stasis is aggravated by the fact that the regulations allow a single family to own up to ten stalls, and a single individual to hold six licences at once. The monopolistic power of established groups in the field, such as the Tredicine (Panié, 2018), is thereby perpetuated, to the detriment of those who lack similarly high social and temporal capital. While these regulations do protect jobs and reward expertise, hopes that the EU Directive would promote equality of opportunity, generational change, and revitalization of the sector (Torresan 2019) have not been met so far. However, in a dramatic reversal of her earlier support for the vendors' protests, in March 2021 mayor Virginia Raggi announced that the extensions to licences were suspended and that the municipality would soon put them out to tender. A new wave of demonstrations immediately followed (Frignani, 2021), and the Confcommercio association began legal proceedings, accusing the city council of violating national law (Confcommercio, 2021). The municipality postponed the suspension for three months, until June 2021, to temporarily placate the protesters (Spadaccino, 2021), but the struggle between the two camps is likely to endure for much longer.

This mapping of the street-vending field underlines how central the actions of Rome's authorities have been in creating a system of symbiosis between official and informal trading. Its unauthorized forms are largely a consequence of the municipality's failure to manage licensing and create functional ways for new actors to enter the field legally. This has penalized all types of traders by forcing them to rely on high financial and social capital to survive in a sector that could instead offer innovative and equalizing opportunities for entrepreneurship among resource-poor actors. In part this is the outcome of decades of institutional neglect: the low prioritization of the sector for policy development and spending by a municipality facing many other urban dysfunctionalities. Yet, the authorities have not fully withdrawn, leaving traders to rule the field themselves. The selectivity with which different arms of local government have intervened on some occasions, only to then disappear again, indicates that the temporalities and targets of its actions have been politically motivated. Performances of "tough on illegalities" agendas have occurred in critical moments when the authorities' legitimacy has been in question and their sovereignty has needed reasserting. By visibly focusing their repressive power on immigrants and Roma, they have signalled their "potency" (Roy, 2018) to part of the electorate, while barely disturbing the informal and criminal interests of other parts.

The kaleidoscopic informalities of Roma street vendors

This section focuses on the specific repercussions that these exclusionary processes have had on many of the city's Roma residents. By virtue of their centuries-old stigmatization and the poverty that such discrimination has fuelled, the economic survival of many households depends heavily on street trading. The discussion traces a 25-year trajectory through which these traders have been relegated to Rome's most hidden and peripheral zones and further unpacks how those processes have reflected evolutions in the city's neoliberal governance.

"Degypsifying" Rome's street markets

In the post-war period, a vast unauthorized settlement developed along the Via Casilina, in a working-class district of eastern Rome. At its peak, in the 1990s, it was home to around 1,200 Roma and other poor residents. Despite repeated evictions, part of its population stayed until 2010, when remaining homes were definitively bulldozed. Its residents were stable features of the neighbourhood for six decades and integrated into its multiple informal economies. Their marginalization from mainstream housing (see chapters 2 and 5) thus tightly intersected with their economic livelihoods. Although living conditions in the camp were dire, they did provide external space that facilitated such work, allowing them to accumulate, repair, and clean goods before selling them. A predominant source of income was the collection and sale of metals, household goods, and clothing from dumpsters or sourced through personal contacts with businesses, parishes, and households. Each family had their preferred route and schedule for gleaning, and supply was generally plentiful. The goods were primarily sold to Roma wholesalers who then traded them in city-centre flea markets such as Porta Portese. In 1991, however, some Casilina residents decided to bypass these intermediaries and set up their own stalls, creating an informal market along the neighbourhood's main road every Sunday morning. Initially, traders placed sheets on the pavement before dawn to occupy spaces. With time, tables and beach umbrellas appeared, with vendors claiming the same spots every week. These informal arrangements were strikingly efficient. As one interviewee, a long-time seller on the market, explained:

> It was all self-managed and there was no extortive racket behind it. You could earn as much as 500,000 lire [250 euro] a week; about 600 people lived well from that income. The market provided financial security, stability, and well-being for many families [...]. There were very few stolen goods and for a long time the authorities tolerated the situation because Roma traders left the place clean. We paid about 10,000 lire [5 euro] each to someone who cleaned the whole road – it may even have been a municipal employee. The market was so tolerated that we could organize ourselves like that. The police came by to check there were no stolen goods but that was all.

The market's successful functioning depended on four key factors: traders' ability to self-organize equitably, a significant demand for second-hand goods among the area's low-income residents, the establishment of long-term trust and acceptance between Roma and other neighbourhood inhabitants. The fourth crucial element was the authorities' active acceptance of its informality, while dissuading illegality.

However, between 1995 and 1996, the municipality began to require stallholders to show a formal licence and some vendors started to drift away, unable or unwilling to pay the required fees. Over the following two years, police checks on unregistered stalls intensified, culminating in the market's total formalization in 1998. For most Roma, trading there ceased to be economically viable, although some continued to sell informally at its margins, ready to run if police patrols arrived. According to one of the stallholders I interviewed, "the end of that market created a real economic crisis for us. If the authorities had somehow regulated it in its original form, it would have continued to provide work for a lot of people." Instead, by subjecting it to ordinary licensing systems, the market was opened up to traders with permits and more capital, while the Roma who lacked the necessary residency and work documents were excluded. In order to enable some to continue trading, an NGO began opening Roma-specific markets – emphasizing "ethnic" craftwork – around the city. One was positioned inside the Casilino 700 settlement; however, it only survived for three Sundays (Rossi, 2006). Customers who had been happy to shop along the road were far less comfortable entering the encampment and thus stayed away.

The Casilina market's formalization must be contextualized within broader political developments of the time. In 1993, with the arrival of the city's first directly elected mayor, Francesco Rutelli, Rome began a period of neoliberalization which affected multiple sectors of urban governance. This involved branding the capital as a global, efficient, formal city – making rhetorical claims of fighting corruption in urban management – while simultaneously reaffirming "conservative social and cultural values" (D'Albergo & Moini, 2013, p. 12). Roma were explicitly targeted by policies to include them in formal labour markets through training courses in work "typical of Gypsy culture," while informal trades were repressed (Clough Marinaro, 2003). In practice, though, their rising exclusion from city markets was not matched by a similar zeal in helping them access legal employment. Vending therefore remained central to the economic survival of many Roma households, who continued to work in various small ethnic-specific markets located in areas much more isolated and less lucrative than the Casilina. The bureaucratic statuses of these sites were precarious, dependent on erratic and often informal consent of local boroughs or even single officials. One interviewee described these grey agreements in terms reminiscent of colonial relations:

> Typically, a zealous local official looks for a boss, a representative who, while not necessarily a crook, seizes the opportunity and says, "Don't worry, I'll handle this. The piazza will be full, I'll organize the cleaning, you just deal with me." That is how the system works [...]. Officials should not deal with a "boss," they should regulate. But the "boss" is functional to the system: he guarantees Roma's links to power and he guarantees to the institutions that there will be no stolen goods, the area will be clean, while providing Roma the certainty of a secure place to work.

This statement underlines the role that selective institutional toleration played in managing power relations on the street. In areas of the city with a historically established Roma presence, street-level bureaucrats often tacitly allowed the trades to continue, recognizing that many families had no alternative sources of income; that informal vending was preferable to worsening poverty or crime. This toleration, however, was channelled through individuals who had built up local social capital, acting as brokers between the institutions and other Roma traders. Vendors I interviewed repeatedly spoke of inequalities within such markets. Some were forced to pay extortive kickbacks to be allowed to trade there or to be positioned in the most lucrative sections, while others paid no fees. Harassment of sellers who belonged to Roma groups not related or allied to the organizers was also common. Despite such problems, these venues often survived for decades. When I asked a trader to explain why the authorities continued to ignore one such market despite the internal abuses and the frequent complaints by nearby residents, she argued: "the police are happy: we used to sell in front of the metro station, now we're hidden and don't bother anyone." Forbearance was thus contingent on inconspicuousness.

With the new millennium, the public visibility of Roma poverty became a rising concern for the municipality and an increasingly important driver of urban policy. By pushing traders out of the Casilina market, the city authorities had inadvertently forced many to join Porta Portese, where a primarily Roma section had already developed as a thriving node of business and socialization. It appealed to many non-Roma clients attracted by the cheap goods and "exotic atmosphere" (Solimene, 2016, p. 125). Roma traders had become integrated within the market's economy, generally accepted by other stallholders, and sought after by antiquarians, collectors, and wholesalers

(Clough Marinaro & Daniele, 2014; De Angelis, 2007). Although their presence was unregistered, "law enforcement officers turned a blind eye" (Solimene, 2016, p. 125), as they did with the many other irregular vendors and informal/illegal activities. However, the apparent disorderliness of the Roma's presence there – the messy heterogeneity of the wares, the noisy sociality of the vendors – clashed with the administration's escalating neoliberal agenda of commercializing the city centre, as we saw in the previous section. Despite Mayor Veltroni's attempt to advance a hybridized, "social" form of neoliberalism (D'Albergo & Moini, 2013, 13), emphasizing social justice and community-building in his 2006 re-election campaign, 2007 witnessed his administration's amplification of explicitly anti-Roma securitizing discourses and practices. Roma were labelled an "emergency" to be managed through intensive policing and housing policies that pushed them into ever more isolated peripheries (Clough Marinaro & Solimene, 2019). This practice of simultaneously making them highly visible to the state and concealed from urban residents aimed to alleviate widespread perceptions that living conditions and security in the city were deteriorating as a consequence of neoliberal policies (Berdini & Nalbone, 2011; De Lucia & Erbani, 2016; Ilardi & Scandurra, 2009). The displacement of Roma's poverty from central areas enabled the municipality to claim it was actively tackling the causes of urban "insecurity" while neglecting the macro-level forces underlying rising economic and social precarity.

The eviction from Porta Portese had a major destabilizing effect on the entire panorama of Roma street trade. As one interviewee recalled, "the almost 700 traders kicked out of Porta Portese poured into the [other] Roma markets in the following weeks. This – combined with the general 'security crisis' – resulted in the cancellation of all authorizations as officials became concerned about these markets' increased size and visibility." Roma thereby lost all access to formalized trading spaces and were forced to fragment into interstitial locations for their now illegal vending. Many went on to set up unlicensed stalls on the fringes of neighbourhood markets, such as on Fridays near the Great Mosque and Sundays at the Porta Portese II flea market in the eastern periphery. Some entirely illegal sporadic markets also appeared in vacant lots in the Ostiense and Garbatella neighbourhoods. However, their lack of garbage collection and hygiene facilities aggravated the hostility of local residents and made them continually subject to police raids. In both situations, the likelihood of fines and confiscations forced traders to sell low-value goods to minimize their possible losses, adding to the paucity of their revenues.

Polarizing shades of grey

In reaction to this intensified precariousness, two semi-formal markets have emerged in recent years as traders have sought ways to build greater financial and spatial stability. These sites diverge from previous typologies in various ways: both are on private land, on the city's peri-urban fringes, far from commercial and public transport networks. They are both run by non-Roma organizations registered as cultural associations, making them subject to less rigid and onerous licences than mainstream markets. This means that institutional intervention is less intense, although here too there is a police presence, both uniformed and plain-clothed. Nevertheless, one market has received multiple orders to close due to contestations about permits, and appeals processes are ongoing. The other is an offshoot of a previous market that was shut down in 2017 because of bureaucratic irregularities. In both cases, regulatory issues have been harnessed by nearby residents and local political parties objecting to the presence of Roma vendors. Thus, traders' economic precariousness and legal uncertainty persist here too, although both markets did manage to achieve some continuity from 2014 until the 2020/21 coronavirus-related lockdowns forced them to close for long periods.

Despite no coordination between them, both markets operate similarly, with a transparent system of regulations, membership, and fees. Internal inequalities are visible nevertheless: more established and wealthy vendors position themselves near the entrance, displaying their wares on tables, while others tend to be at the margins, often on muddy terrain with only a sheet to display their lower-value goods. For some Roma, the fees and fuel costs exceed typical earnings, making these markets economically unviable. For others, though, the financial outlay pays off in commercial stability. As occurred in the past at Porta Portese, traders have developed extensive business networks with antiquarians, designers, and collectors who ask them to look out for specific types of goods and often buy in bulk: crate-loads of small toys, comics, vintage cameras, sewing machines, electronic parts, construction tools. While most merchandise brings in little cash, the relative predictability of demand allows traders to strategize how they display and rotate goods targeting the tastes of their habitual clientele (Figure 3.1).

Figure 3.1 Semi-formal street market in Rome's periphery

The term most often repeated by traders describing these environments is their relative *tranquillità*: a sense of normalcy, of notably reduced vulnerability and tension compared to other, more precarious, markets. In both locations, a food and drinks van provides an excuse for conversations over coffee, and children can run around safely. Consequently, both have the feel of a day's outing, with multiple generations arriving to spend time together. As is typical of street markets (Brown, 2017; Evers & Seale, 2014; Graaf & Ha, 2015; Seale, 2016), there is also a clear celebration of salesmanship skills and sociality. Vocal competitiveness, humour, cultural exchange, and solidarity merge together in a heterogeneously inclusive setting. The day-to-day business of sharing news and negotiating social relations also creates opportunities for building more extensive commercial networks. In fact, the centrality to these markets in Roma's economic life became evident when both were temporarily shut down for bureaucratic irregularities during the summer of 2017, and then due to the pandemic in spring 2020 and 2021. Sellers expressed their deep anxiety over the sudden disappearance of their primary income source, and their desperate attempts to find alternatives. Many stated that if such closures persisted, they would be forced into illegal trades to survive. Consequently, when the markets have been able to operate, vendors have carefully monitored that their own and others' behaviours conform to non-Roma ideas about "order." They often become alarmed when vendors spread goods outside their designated spaces, when merchandise starts to look "messy," and stolen objects appear. Their fears that these could trigger the markets' closure generate a strong sense of personal self-regulation, of individualization in the neoliberal sense, which combines forced self-reliance with a felt duty to police – or "govern" (Rose, 2000) – the community from within.

The contemporary polarization between the two semi-formal markets and the only alternative – selling illegally and fleetingly in interstitial locations – can be viewed as the completion of a neoliberal trajectory for managing Roma's street trades that began in the mid-1990s. Presented and implemented in various ways, the drives to remove these vendors from public spaces and view have resulted in their survival economies becoming increasingly hidden, separated from mainstream social and consumption hubs. Circularly, this distancing has perpetuated poverty by artificially isolating them from the commercial crossroads where trade most naturally thrives (Seale, 2016). Such trades cannot be fully eliminated, however, because they provide goods and services difficult for the city's expanding impoverished population to otherwise access. These are not superfluous economies, therefore: they are the inevitable and essential contrapositive to the neoliberal system. They are economic spaces in which a precarious and undervalued labour force activates skills and offers goods no longer valorized within mass production and consumption markets. Relegated but not removed, they are the outcome of urban ordering processes aimed at concealing the "'confusion of categories'" (Herzfeld, 2006, p. 144) inherent to city life.

The use of formalization drives as technologies for "cleansing" high-value districts as part of their commodification and place-image transformation has been observed in many metropolises, especially in emerging economies (Duru, 2015; Graaf & Ha, 2015: Green, 2015; Mital, 2015; Evers & Seale, 2015). What is particularly striking about Rome is the explicitly racialized forms that this cleansing-through-(in)formalization has taken. Roma street traders have been especially targeted through regulatory manoeuvres that have pushed them into ever more acute conditions of irregularity and vulnerability. The municipal authorities have thereby constructed an essentialized, ethnicized Romani "difference" as somehow more problematic, more threatening, than a wide array of other urban informalities that remain intact. This process has been inextricably tied to the escalation in Roma's city-wide (and nation-wide) securitization, which has projected them as the cause of rising urban tensions and fear. By uprooting Roma traders from long-established neighbourhood economies in Casilina, obstructing their access to Porta Portese, pushing their trades into ethnically concentrated and marginal locations, their construction as the city's deviant Other has been affirmed. Progressive municipal withdrawal from planning and funding social inclusion programmes for them has accompanied this trajectory. The treatment of Roma's street trades is thus symptomatic of the city's evolving neoliberal regime: it has combined institutional retrenchment, the increased necessity for weak economic actors to compete and become entrepreneurs of the self, and the intensified surveillance of the securitizing arm of the state.

Conclusion

Informal street trade has been a defining feature of Rome's public life and commerce for centuries. Attempts to stifle it have generally failed because they have not been accompanied by a real ability to resolve its foundational causes: high levels of poverty and precarity among traders and customers, and the lack of spaces and regulatory frameworks for such commerce to be carried out in equitable and secure ways. Rather than following many other global cities in recognizing the importance of these trades to social life and the mitigation of hardship, Rome has remained firmly rooted in its modernist vision of urban management, predicated on implementing order and preserving aesthetics in its monumental centre. The neoliberal rebranding techniques of recent years have simply raised the monetary stakes of this approach. The resounding narrative advanced by politicians, media, and licensed vendors divides traders into two artificially distinct categories of legal and illegal subjects that mask a far more complex reality. Not only do they obscure the innumerable ways in which sellers of all types navigate around tax and planning codes, permits and licensing restrictions which constitute the sector's myriad shades of grey. They also cloak the interdependency between the state's claims to uphold a legal and normative order and "the hidden sacrifices" that are forced on "the 'poorest of the poor'" (Panella, 2021, p. 7). In continuously defining and redefining what constitutes legality, and then failing to make that legality accessible in practice, the various layers of the state have produced a political and social order where rights are scarce and must be fought over. It has then acted as arbiter, determining which documents, which actors' claims, it is temporarily willing to recognize, and which not.

Couched in terms of neutral urban planning, of the impartial language of law, Rome's selective modulation of regulatory definitions and of their practical enforcement is the quintessence of grey governance in action. It constitutes a technology whereby the authorities can selectively repress economic activity "when it is politically convenient to get rid of vendors, and relax enforcement when it is politically convenient to allow them to work" (Roever, 2020, pp. 173–174). However, it goes far beyond the pragmatic, tactical manoeuvres suggested in this quote. It produces and reproduces cultural and social dynamics that are hierarchical and systemic, its politics defining ideologies of value in the city and materializing power in public space. As the size of the street-vending sector has spread, fuelled by growing precarity and welfare retrenchment, competition for space and customers has become increasingly fierce. In a field where that competition is not managed around transparent, univocal rights, legitimacy must be asserted in other ways. Vendors who can mobilize financial or social capital to acquire and maintain their positions in the field do so. Where such resources are lacking, temporal capital becomes a core vector for asserting cultural authenticity and, with it, ownership of public space. The urban revanchist rhetoric of individual vendors at Porta Portese, and of associations representing traders more widely, contribute to defining a clear hierarchy that is both symbolic and economic. This jockeying over positions does nothing, however, to subvert the neoliberal order which relegates street trades – with all the knowledge, skill, and bodily labour that they draw on – to residual, marginal economic positions. At this bottom end of the economic system, the two resources that hold political weight – the ability to mobilize votes at election time and a claim to embodying the city's heritage – are wielded against those who lack even those assets: migrant and minority vendors.

At once deeply integrated in the fabric of social life – interwoven on a daily basis with residents, shopkeepers, buyers, even individual police officers (Clough Marinaro & Panella, 2021; Piazzoni, 2020) – these informal traders are continuously exposed to risk. To avoid arrests, fines, or losing their goods, they must juggle visibility and invisibility, fleetingness and rootedness. Their condition of being at once within and without is not just bureaucratic; it is deeply corporeal. Their liminality is embodied through anxiety, loneliness, fatigue (Panella, 2021). Roma's congregation on the two semi-formal markets is a way to escape that existential precarity, to lessen the intensity of that liminality. It enables them to forge some security not just at the individual level but for entire communities who have been accorded the status of Italy's "internal 'Other'" (Clough Marinaro & Sigona, 2011). Theirs is one of the many ways that marginalized traders make a claim to the city. It is a means not just to survive but to build autonomy and organize their lives on their own terms, a resolve that they share with informalized and vulnerable groups in the Middle East (Bayat, 2013; Yiftachel, 2009), Vietnam, Ghana (Gillespie, 2017; Kurfürst, 2016), and other contexts where alternative collective action is obstructed.

Notes

1 This statistic combines the illegal economy (worth approximately 19 billion euro) and the submerged economy (undeclared and underdeclared earnings, worth 192 billion euro).
2 Note that the number peaked in 2015, with 195,000 firms registered, and has fallen somewhat since (FIVA Confcommercio, n.d.).
3 They can also sell at markets and fairs if there are remaining spaces not allocated to Type A traders. The latter may sell in an itinerant capacity when they are not occupying their designated market stand.
4 www.annunciambulanti.it/mercato/mercati-compro-vendo-affitto/mercati-lazio/
5 Legge 18 aprile 2017, n. 48 and Delibera Assemblea Capitolina 6 giugno 2019, n. 43. See Piazzoni (2020) for further discussion of these regulations.
6 The merchants' association, Confesercenti (2018) estimates that there are about 105,000 fully unlicensed vendors in Italy, 75% of whom are believed to be non-nationals.
7 These two posters/pages of the flyer can be viewed at www.facebook.com/virginia.raggi.m5sroma/posts/1409586139223831/ and https://twitter.com/virginiaraggi/status/1199040607794212869/photo/1. Unfortunately, I am not able to reproduce them in this book because the municipal authorities failed to provide me with information about their procedure for obtaining copyright permissions, despite my repeated requests.
8 Clough Marinaro and Panella (2021) discuss in greater depth processes whereby informally and illegally sourced goods can make their way into formal shops.
9 Media reports of the time convey the centrality of ethnicity in these crackdowns: "Porta Portese, anti-Roma raid by the municipal police" (Martelli, 2007); "the outcome of the anti-informal trading blitz in the capital's historic market was 104 foreigners – many Roma, some Poles and Senegalese, all lacking documents – all stopped and identified" (Rida, 2007).
10 Gaetano Rizzo, Municipal Councillor for Commerce (La Repubblica, 2007); Casa delle Libertà Party (Il Giornale, 2008).
11 A 2012 radio interview with Maurizio Cavalieri, President of the Porta Portese vendors' association provides a powerful example of the discursive strategies used to portray Roma and other unlicensed vendors at the market as spoiling its economy and reputation – and by extension that of the entire city – while glorifying the informal trades of the past (www.youtube.com/watch?v=e9h1WJBppcU).
12 See Lelo et al. (2019) for an excellent collection of maps providing multifaceted indicators of Rome's spatialized inequalities. The residents of Trastevere are shown to be among the most privileged in the city in terms of human capital, education and employment levels, the availability of public services, and stability of house prices. Households are generally small and the population is young and often unmarried, reflecting the area's gentrification.
13 Italy's complaints against the Directive were thus different from those of various other countries, such as France, whose resistance was based on fears that the legislation would promote "social dumping" by eroding labour protections and encouraging intra-EU migration of workers.

References

ACOS (Agenzia per il controllo e la qualità dei servizi pubblici locali di Roma Capitale). (2018). Relazione annuale 2018. www.agenzia.roma.it/it-schede-19-relazione_annuale_2018.

ACOS (Agenzia per il controllo e la qualità dei servizi pubblici locali di Roma Capitale). (2020). Relazione annuale 2020. www.agenzia.roma.it/it-schede-850-relazione_annuale_2020.

Alba Vega, C. (2012). Local politics and globalization from below: The peddler leaders of Mexico City's historic center streets. In G. Mathews, G. L. Ribeiro, & V. C. Alba, (eds), *Globalization from below: The world's other economy* (pp. 203–220). Routledge. https://doi.org/10.4324/9780203106006-20.

Allegri, M. (2019). Tredicine e il racket bancarelle: "Sulle licenze comandiamo noi". *Il Messaggero*, 10 April. www.ilmessaggero.it/roma/news/tredicine_ambulanti_bancarelle_roma-4419396.html.

Angeli, F., & Tonacci, F. (2012). L'impero milionario dei Tredicine, i caldarrostai padroni dei mercati di Roma. *La Repubblica*, 12 April. https://inchieste.repubblica.it/it/repubblica/rep-it/inchiesta-italiana/2012/04/12/news/i_signori_delle_caldarroste-33192162/.

ANSA. (2016). Marchini a P.Portese, illegalità legale. *ANSA*, 20 March. www.ansa.it/lazio/notizie/2016/03/20/marchini-a-p.portese-illegalita-legale_5330566a-7c3e-4109-8398-7a6dfecae891.html.

Bayat, A. (2013). *Life as politics: How ordinary people change the Middle East*. Stanford University Press.

Berdini, P., & Nalbone, D. (2011). *Le mani sulla città: Da Veltroni ad Alemanno storia di una capitale in vendita*. Alegre.

Bizzotto, M. (2017). Interrogazione con richiesta di risposta scritta E-001962–17 alla Commissione. Commercio ambulante: esclusione del settore dalla direttiva Bolkestein in Italia. European Parliament, 23 March. www.europarl.europa.eu/doceo/document/E-8-2017-001962_IT.html.

Boels, D. (2014). It's better than stealing: Informal street selling in Brussels. *International Journal of Sociology and Social Policy*, 34, 670–693. https://doi.org/10.1108/ijssp-04-2013-0049.

Breman J. (2020). Informality. The bane of the labouring poor under globalised capitalism. In M. A. Chen & F. Carré (eds), *The informal economy revisited: Examining the past, envisioning the future* (pp. 31–37). Routledge. https://doi.org/10.4324/9780429200724-3.

Brown, A. (2017). *Rebel streets and the informal economy*. Routledge.

Camera di Commercio Roma. (2020). Diritto annuale 2020. www.rm.camcom.it/pagina3540_diritto-annuale-2020.html.

Cancellieri, A., & Ostanel, E. (2015). The struggle for public space: The hypervisibility of migrants in the Italian urban landscape. *Cities*, 19(4): 499–509. https://doi.org/10.1080/13604813.2015.1051740.

Carré, F., Horn, P., & Bonner, C. (2018). Collective bargaining by informal workers in the Global South: Where and how it takes place. WIEGO (Women in Informal Employment: Globalizing and Organizing) Working Paper no. 38. www.wiego.org/sites/default/files/migrated/publications/files/Carre_Collective_Bargaining_Informal_Workers_WIEGO_WP38.pdf.

Chen, M. A., & Carré, F. (2020). Introduction. In M. A. Chen & F. Carré (eds), *The informal economy revisited: Examining the past, envisioning the future* (pp. 1–27). Routledge. https://doi.org/10.4324/9780429200724-1.
Clough Marinaro, I. (2003). Integration or marginalization? The failures of social policy for the Roma in Rome. *Modern Italy*, 8(2), 203–218. https://doi.org/10.1080/1353294032000131247.
Clough Marinaro, I. (2018). Salvaging Rome: Roma Waste traders and the city's "garbage crisis". *Etnografia e ricerca qualitativa*, 9(1), 11–31.
Clough Marinaro, I., & Daniele, U. (2014). Evicting Rome's undesirables. Two short tales. In I. Clough Marinaro & B. Thomassen (eds), *Global Rome: Changing faces of the eternal city* (pp. 114–128). Indiana University Press.
Clough Marinaro, I., & Panella, C. (2021). Informal economies, illegal subjects: Roma and Senegalese traders in Rome. In C. Panella & W. E. Little (eds), *Norms and illegality: Intimate ethnographies and politics* (pp. 111–135). Lexington Books.
Clough Marinaro, I., & Sigona, N. (2011). Introduction. Anti-Gypsyism and the politics of exclusion: Roma and Sinti in contemporary Italy. *Journal of Modern Italian Studies*, 16(5), 583–589. https://doi.org/10.1080/1354571x.2011.622467.
Clough Marinaro, I., & Solimene, M. (2019). Navigating the (In)formal city: Roma, urban life and governance in Rome. *Cities*, 95. https://doi.org/10.1016/j.cities.2019.102402.
Coletti, G. M. (2007). Porta Portese, blitz dei vigili anti-rom. *Il Tempo*, 23 September, p. 29.
Corriere della Sera. (2020). Roma, "Commissariare il I Municipio. Via le bancarelle da Prati": Raggi contro Alfonsi. *Corriere della Sera*, 19 November. https://roma.corriere.it/notizie/cronaca/20_novembre_19/roma-commissariare-municipio-via-bancarelle-prati-raggi-contro-alfonsi-35aa186c-2a7a-11eb-a3fb-78126c23822f.shtml.
Confcommercio. (2021). Ambulanti, Fiva-Confcommercio: Giusta la protesta odierna ma sbagliata nelle modalità. https://confcommercioroma.it/ambulanti-fiva-confcommercio-giusta-la-protesta-odierna-ma-sbagliata-nelle-modalita-comunicato-stampa/.
Confesercenti. (2018). Il commercio su aree pubbliche in Italia. www.confesercenti.it/wp-content/uploads/2018/07/IL-COMMERCIO-SU-AREE-PUBBLICHE-IN-ITALIA.pdf.
Cross, J. (2000). Street vendors, and postmodernity: Conflict and compromise in the global economy. *International Journal of Sociology and Social Policy*, 20, 29–51. https://doi.org/10.1108/01443330010789061.
Crossa, V. (2020). Street vending and the state. Challenging theory, changing research. In M. A. Chen & F. Carré (eds), *The informal economy revisited: Examining the past, envisioning the future* (pp. 167–172). Routledge. https://doi.org/10.4324/9780429200724-29.
Cupers, K. (2015). The urbanism of Los Angeles street vending. In K. Graaff & N. Ha (eds), *Street vending in the neoliberal city: A global perspective on the practices and policies of a marginalized economy* (pp.139–163). Berghahn.
Custodero, A. (2017). Roma, otto bancarelle su 10 con licenze irregolari: "Fermiamo l'assedio". *La Repubblica*, 4 October. https://roma.repubblica.it/cronaca/2017/10/04/news/roma_otto_bancarelle_su_10_con_licenze_irregolari_fermiamo_l_assedio_-177312313/.
D'Albergo, E., & Moini, G. (2013). Politics, power and the economy in Rome: Continuity and change in an urban regime. *Métropoles*, 12, 1–29. https://doi.org/10.4000/metropoles.4626.

De Angelis, R. (2007). Uomini e pulci. In A. Criconia (ed.), *Architetture dello shopping. Modelli del consumo a Roma* (pp. 153–168). Meltemi.

De Gregorio, C., & Giordano, A. (2016). The heterogeneity of undeclared work in Italy: Some results from the statistical integration of survey and administrative sources. Rivista di statistica ufficiale, no. 2/2016, 99–129. www.istat.it/it/files/2018/09/Articolo-5.pdf.

De Lucia, V., & Erbani, F. (2016). *Roma disfatta: Perché la capitale non è più una città e cosa fare per ridarle una dimensione pubblica.* Castelvecchi.

Douglas, M. (2015). *Purity and danger: An analysis of concepts of pollution and taboo.* Routledge.

Duru, A. (2015). The politics of space in the marketplace: Re-placing periodic markets in Istanbul. In C. Evers & K. Seale (eds), *Informal urban street markets: International perspectives* (pp. 149–157). Routledge.

Evers, C., & Seale, K. (eds). (2015). *Informal urban street markets: International perspectives.* Routledge. https://doi.org/10.4324/9781315756431.

FIVA Confcommercio. (2018). Quattro proposte per il rilancio del commercio su aree pubbliche. www.fiva.it/uploads/file/1519732745969.pdf.

FIVA Confcommercio. (n.d.). Cifre e numeri. Il profilo sintetico del settore. www.fiva.it/stats.html.

Francescangeli, L. (2006). Luoghi e regole del mercato dall'Ottocento al Novecento: Una storia comunale. In L. Francescangeli & O. Rispoli (eds), *La memoria dei mercati. Fonti e documenti sulla storia dell'annona e dei mercati di Roma* (pp. 107–114.) Nuove Tendenze.

Frignani, R. (2020). Roma, piazza Venezia bloccata dai furgoni dei venditori ambulanti contro la Raggi. *Corriere della Sera,* 8 March. https://roma.corriere.it/notizie/cronaca/21_marzo_08/protesta-ambulanti-furgoni-piazza-venezia-manifestante-si-sente-male-2caa19d4-7fec-11eb-a06c-fddde4eb7de2.shtml.

Frignani, R., & Sacchettoni, I. (2007). Ambulanti, rivolta a Porta Portese. *Corriere della Sera,* 24 September, p. 1.

Garrone, L. (2020). Roma, centro storico: Il Comune li sposta, gli ambulanti restano. *Corriere della Sera,* 3 January. https://roma.corriere.it/notizie/cronaca/20_gennaio_03/comune-li-sposta-ambulanti-restano-0eae6b20-2d94-11ea-af94-9dcececd831c.shtml.

Gillespie, T. (2017). From quiet to bold encroachment: Contesting dispossession in Accra's informal sector. *Urban Geography,* 38(7), 974–992. https://doi.org/10.1080/02723638.2016.1191792.

Giulioli, R. (2006). Prefazione. In L. Francescangeli & O. Rispoli (eds), *La memoria dei mercati. Fonti e documenti sulla storia dell'annona e dei mercati di Roma* (p. 7). Nuove Tendenze.

Graaff, K., & Ha, N. (eds) (2015). *Street vending in the neoliberal city: A global perspective on the practices and policies of a marginalized economy.* Berghahn.

Green, L. (2015). "People have to find their own way of making a living": The sale of food in an informal Ha Noi street market. In C. Evers & K. Seale (eds), *Informal urban street markets: International perspectives* (pp. 17–27). Routledge.

Guano. E. (2010). Taxpayers, thieves, and the state: Fiscal citizenship in contemporary Italy. *Ethnos,* 75(4), 377–401. https://doi.org/10.1080/00141844.2010.522246.

Herzfeld, M. (2006). Spatial cleansing: Monumental vacuity and the idea of the West. *Journal of Material Culture,* 11(1/2),127–149. https://doi.org/10.1177/1359183506063016.

Ilardi, M., & Scandurra, E. (2009). *Ricominciamo dalle periferie.* Manifestolibri.

Il Giornale. (2008). Il futuro già vecchio. *Il Giornale*, 19 January. www.ilgiornale.it/news/porta-portese-futuro-gi-vecchio.html.

Il Messaggero. (2019). La Capitale è più vivibile? Quella classifica che sconcerta i romani. *Il Messaggero*, 17 December. www.ilmessaggero.it/roma/news/roma_capitale_vivibile_romani-4930877.html.

Il Post. (2017). Perché gli ambulanti protestano. *Il Post*, 16 March. www.ilpost.it/2017/03/16/ambulanti-bolkestein/.

Il Sole 24 Ore. (2019). Qualità della vita 2019. https://lab24.ilsole24ore.com/qualita-della-vita/.

ISTAT. (2020). L'economia non osservata nei conti nazionali. Anni 2015–20. www.istat.it/it/files/2020/10/Economia-non-osservata-nei-conti-nazionali.pdf.

Izzo, E. (2020). Racket delle bancarelle a Roma,18 arresti. Favori in cambio di cene, vestiti firmati e abbonamenti allo stadio. *La Stampa*, 23 September. www.lastampa.it/cronaca/2020/09/23/news/racket-delle-bancarelle-a-roma-18-arresti-favori-in-cambio-di-cene-vestiti-firmati-e-abbonamenti-allo-stadio-1.39339580.

Johnson, M. & Ghiglione, D. (2020). "Pasta and beans." Italy's shadow workers are out of the safety net. *The Financial Times*, 30 March. www.ft.com/content/08847c08-9582-4c48-9d2d-319f8593da19.

Kurfürst, S. (2016). Informality as a strategy: Street traders in Hanoi facing constant insecurity. In C. McFarlane & M. Waibel (eds), *Urban informalities: Reflections on the formal and informal* (pp. 89–110). Routledge. https://doi.org/10.4324/9781315548814.

La 7. (2015). Il mercato del rubato a Porta Portese. *La 7*, 21 July. [Video]. www.la7.it/lariadestate/video/il-mercato-del-rubato-a-porta-portese-21-07-2015-159458.

La Repubblica. (2007). L'assessore Gaetano Rizzo: "Entro il 20087 riqualificheremo il mercato". *La Repubblica*, Cronaca di Roma, 24 September, p. 3.

La Repubblica. (2017). Protesta Bolkestein a Roma, furgoni ambulanti rallentano il traffico. *La Repubblica*, 14 November. https://roma.repubblica.it/cronaca/2017/11/14/news/protesta_contro_riforma_bolkestein_ambulanti_con_300_furgoni_rallentano_traffico_roma-181075331/.

La Repubblica. (2018). Il boom delle bancarelle. *La Repubblica*, August 30, p. 27. www.unioncamere.gov.it/uploaded/Generale/Comunicazione/Dicono%20di%20noi/2018/Agosto/rep30agosto.pdf.

La Repubblica. (2020). Usura, estorsione e riciclaggio a Roma: Scoperta la banda di Porta Portese. Sette arresti. *La Repubblica*, 3 July. https://roma.repubblica.it/cronaca/2020/07/03/news/usura_estorsione_e_riciclaggio_a_roma_scoperta_la_banda_di_porta_portese_sei_arresti-260857003/.

La Stampa. (2018). Il numero del giorno. 188,998 le imprese di commercio ambulante in Italia. *La Stampa*, 30 August, p. 26. www.unioncamere.gov.it/uploaded/Generale/Comunicazione/Dicono%20di%20noi/2018/Agosto/lastampa30ago.pdf.

Lelo, K., Monni, S., & Tomassi, F. (2019). *Le mappe della disuguaglianza: Una geografia sociale metropolitana*. Donzelli.

Lund, F. (2020). The place of informal workers in different approaches to social protection. In M. A. Chen & F. Carré (eds), *The informal economy revisited: Examining the past, envisioning the future* (pp. 203–209). Routledge. https://doi.org/10.4324/9780429200724-36.

Marino, I. (2017). Camion bar: Una battaglia vinta. 1 April. www.ignaziomarino.it/tribunale-roma-giusta-la-decisione-della-giunta-marino-sui-camion-bar/.

Martelli, G. (2007). Maxi retata a Porta Portese. *Il Tempo*, 24 September, p. 1.

Meneses-Reyes, R. (2018). (Un)authorized: A study on the regulation of street vending in Latin America. *Law and Policy*, 40(3), 286–315. https://doi.org/10.1111/lapo.12106.

Mikola, M. (2015). On being and becoming in Melbourne's marketplaces. In C. Evers & K. Seale (eds), *Informal urban street markets: International perspectives* (pp. 28–36). Routledge. https://doi.org/10.4324/9781315756431.

Mital, R. (2015). The importance and necessity of the informal market as public place in Delhi. In C. Evers & K. Seale (eds), *Informal urban street markets: International perspectives* (pp. 176–186). Routledge.

Monaco, L. (2016). Roma, gli ambulanti in piazza contro la Bolkestein: "Non siamo tutti Tredicine". *La Repubblica*, 29 November. https://roma.repubblica.it/cronaca/2016/11/29/news/roma_gli_ambulanti_in_piazza_contro_la_bolkestein_non_siamo_tutti_tredicine_-153074001/.

Nicolini, L. (2017). Strumenti musicali rubati venduti al mercato di Porta Portese. *Roma Today*, 25 December. www.romatoday.it/cronaca/strumenti-musicali-rubati-venduti-porta-portese.html.

Notiziario immobiliare. (2020). Mercato immobiliare Roma: Un leggero incremento ma significativo. 29 August. www.notiziarioimmobiliare.it/mercato-immobiliare-roma-5596.

Paglino, G. (2011). "Porta portese è un mercato totalmente abusivo, verso la chiusura". *Il Fatto Quotidiano*, 4 December. www.ilfattoquotidiano.it/2011/12/04/porta-portese-mercatototalmente-abusivo-verso-chiusura/175177/.

Pagliuca, G. (2021). Case a prova di pandemia: I quartieri dove i prezzi salgono del 20% (da Milano a Roma). *Corriere della Sera*, 3 March. www.corriere.it/economia/casa/cards/casa-prezzi-fino-20percento-ecco-zone-che-hanno-retto-meglio-pandemia-covid/roma1-trastevere-del-5percento.shtml.

Palumbo, M. (2006). "Le piazza dove si vendono robbe". La normativa sui mercati romani nei bandi dei secoli XVI-XVIII. In L. Francescangeli & O. Rispoli (eds), *La memoria dei mercati. Fonti e documenti sulla storia dell'annona e dei mercati di Roma* (pp. 27–53). Nuove Tendenze.

Panella, C. (2021). Preface. In C. Panella & W. E. Little (eds), *Norms and illegality: Intimate ethnographies and politics* (pp. 1–9). Lexington Books.

Rogan, M., & Cichello, P. (2020). (Re)conceptualising poverty and informal employment. In M. A. Chen & F. Carré (eds), *The informal economy revisited: Examining the past, envisioning the future* (pp. 98–102). Routledge. https://doi.org/10.4324/9780429200724-15.

Rossi, M. (2006). Rom a Roma. Pratiche di integrazione e controllo: Il campo di via Casilina 700. In R. De Angelis & F. Mignella Calvosa (eds), *La periferia perfetta: Migrazioni, istituzioni e relazioni etniche nell'area metropolitana romana* (pp. 221–243). FrancoAngeli.

Panié, F. (2018). *Magna Roma. Perché nel comune agricolo più grande d'Italia i mercati rionali stanno morendo*. Terra. www.terraonlus.it/wp-content/uploads/2018/12/Magna-Roma_web.pdf.

Parisi, L. (2012). Porta Portese, viaggio nel mercato romano senza regole. *Il Fatto Quotidiano*, 24 January. www.ilfattoquotidiano.it/2012/01/24/porta-portese-terra-nessuno/186154/.

Piazzoni, F. (2020). Visibility as justice: Immigrant street vendors and the right to difference in Rome. *Journal of Planning Education and Research*, 1–16. https://doi.org/10.1177/0739456x20956387.

Quirito, A. M. (2007). Blitz dei vigili a Porta Portese: "Stop a ricettazione e abusivi". *E Polis*, 24 September, p. 1.

Recchi, S. (2020). Informal street vending: A comparative literature review. *International Journal of Sociology and Social Policy*. https://doi.org/10.1108/ijssp-07-2020-0285.

Rida, O. (2007). Porta Portese, un blitz anti-abusivi "annunciato". *Il Giornale*, Cronaca di Roma, 24 September.

Roever, S. (2020). Street vendors and regulations. In M. A. Chen & F. Carré (eds), *The informal economy revisited: Examining the past, envisioning the future* (pp. 173–177). Routledge. https://doi.org/10.4324/9780429200724-30.

Roma Capitale. (2020). I numeri di Roma Capitale. Mercati rionali. Anno 2020. www.comune.roma.it/web-resources/cms/documents/Mercati_rionali2020.pdf.

Roma Ricerca Roma. (2021). Un manifesto per Roma. Il diritto a una città giusta. Percorsi per uscire dalla crisi del valore. www.ricercaroma.it/economia/.

Roma Today. (2013). Restyling per Porta Portese: Roma Capitale si aggiudica il bando da 3 milioni e mezzo. *Roma Today*, 8 May. www.romatoday.it/zone/monteverde/monteverde/lavori-mercato-porta-portese.html.

Rose, N. (2000). Community, citizenship, and the Third Way. *American Behavioral Scientist, 43*(9), 1395–1411. https://doi.org/10.1177/00027640021955955.

Roy, A. (2018). The potency of the state: Logics of informality and subalternity. *Journal of Development Studies*, 54(12), 2243–2246. https://doi.org/10.1080/00220388.2018.1460470.

Sacchettoni, I. (2019). Roma, il clan delle bancarelle: 16 indagati, i soldi anche nella cyclette. *Corriere della Sera*, 14 February. https://roma.corriere.it/notizie/cronaca/19_febbraio_14/clan-bancarelle-soldi-nascostianche-cyclette-6a3939a0-2fc7-11e9-9db5-c6e1c6b28b3d.shtml.

Salvatori, G. (2007). Porta Portese, presidio di residenti e vigili. *L'Unità*, Cronaca di Roma, 23 September, p. 1.

Sanfilippo, I. L. (2006). Roma nel Medioevo: Luoghi ed economia del mercato tra XI and XV secolo. In L. Francescangeli & O. Rispoli (eds), *La memoria dei mercati. Fonti e documenti sulla storia dell'annona e dei mercati di Roma* (pp. 13–26). Nuove Tendenze.

Seale, K. (2016). *Markets, places, cities*. Routledge.

Serloni, L. (2015). Colosseo, Fori, Pantheon e piazza di Spagna: Monumenti liberi da camion bar. *La Repubblica*, 9 July. https://roma.repubblica.it/cronaca/2015/07/09/news/colosseo_fori_pantheon_e_piazza_di_spagna_monumenti_liberi_da_camion_bar-118716898/.

Shepherd, R. (2012). Localism meets globalization at an American street market. In G. Mathews, G. L. Ribeiro, & V. C. Alba (eds), *Globalization from below: The world's other economy* (pp. 186–202). Routledge. https://doi.org/10.4324/9780203106006-19.

Smith, N. (1996). *The new urban frontier: Gentrification and the revanchist city*. Routledge. https://doi.org/10.4324/9780203975640.

Solimene, M. (2016). Intrecci. Alcune note etnografiche sulla migrazione dei rom romeni a Roma attraverso lo sguardo dei rom bosniaci. In S. Pontrandolfo & L. Piasere (eds), *Italia romaní*. Vol. 6, *Le migrazioni dei rom romeni in Italia* (pp. 109–140). CISU.

Spadaccino, M. R. (2021). Campidoglio, Coia: "Basta monopoli, ora i bandi. Licenze prorogate fino a giugno." *Corriere della Sera*, 10 March. https://roma.corriere.it/notizie/cronaca/21_marzo_10/campidoglio-coia-basta-monopoli-ora-bandi-licenze-prorogate-fino-giugno-a85b2274-810b-11eb-b4d9-f9ad19747109.shtml.

The Economist. (2020). Hitting the poorest hardest. Italy's informal workers fall back on charity. *The Economist*, June 6. www.economist.com/europe/2020/06/06/italys-informal-workers-fall-back-on-charity.

Torresan, M. (2019). I mercati rionali, tradizionalmente in evoluzione. Dinamiche di una formula storica ancora attuale. In D. Patti, L. Polyak, & M. Torresan (eds), *Il rilancio dei mercati. Spazio pubblico, servizi comunitari ed economia circolare* (pp. 14–27). https://cooperativecity.org/product/il-rilancio-dei-mercati-spazio-pubblico-servizi-comunitari-ed-economia-circolare/.

Unioncamere. (2019). Italia "itinerante": Oltre 180mila operatori nel commercio ambulante. Il 56% parla straniero ma in alcuni comuni i banchi italiani sono oltre il 90%. www.unioncamere.gov.it/P42A4251C160S123/-italia–itinerante—oltre-180mila-operatori-nel-commercio-ambulante–il-56–parla-straniero-ma-in-alcuni-comuni-i-banchi-italiani-sono-oltre-il-90-.htm.

Vendemiale, L. (2016). Roma, ok a mozione anti-Bolkestein: Il Campi doglio sta con gli ambulanti. Che minacciano Onorato: "Te sfonnamo". *Il Fatto Quotidiano*, 3 November. www.ilfattoquotidiano.it/2016/11/03/roma-ok-mozione-anti-bolkestein-il-campidoglio-sta-con-gli-ambulanti-che-minacciano-onorato-te-sfonnamo/3166540/.

Vincenzi, M. E. (2020). Roma, mazzette per camion bar e banchi della Befana: 18 arresti. Ci sono anche due Tredicine. *La Repubblica*, September 23. https://roma.repubblica.it/cronaca/2020/09/23/news/roma_corruzione_per_le_licenze_agli_ambulanti_18_arresti_favori_in_cambio_di_cene_vestiti_firmati_e_abbonamenti_allo_sta-268241716/.

WIEGO (Women in Informal Employment: Globalizing and Organizing). (2020). Street vendors and public Space: Essential insights on key trends and solutions. www.wiego.org/sites/default/files/resources/file/Street%20Vendors%20and%20Public%20Space%20-%20An%20EBook.pdf.

Wiley, D. (2008). The urban square: Remediating public space. *Stream: Interdisciplinary Journal of Communication*, 1(1). https://doi.org/10.21810/strm.v1i1.6.

Ya-Chih Yang, A. (2009). A portrait of Porta Portese. [Unpublished masters dissertation]. University of Waterloo, Canada. https://uwspace.uwaterloo.ca/handle/10012/4361.

Yiftachel, O. (2009). Critical theory and "gray space": Mobilization of the colonized. *City*, 13(2/3),246–263. https://doi.org/10.1080/13604810902982227.

4 Informal lending

The challenges of financial liminality

Introduction

Lending and borrowing money outside the official financial sector is a globally widespread informal practice. In many low-income countries, it offers fundamental support for small-scale enterprises.[1] In most advanced economies, it is instead a function of chronic financial precarity. Gamblers or workers whose income does not meet immediate consumption needs must often turn to predatory credit suppliers, such as legal payday lenders or illegal loan-sharks (Ellison et al., 2006). Informal borrowing in Italy manifests both these realities. It has a much more extensive cash economy than most developed countries (Dell'Oste & Parente, 2018; Esselink & Hernandez, 2017) and, as the previous chapter underlined, a large segment of the labour force is highly precarious or working undeclared jobs. Many actors are thus often unable to access formal bank loans. Consumption-oriented informal lending appears to have risen in recent years, offering a rare source of liquidity to tide households over during periods of financial instability. Strikingly for a developed economy, many small entrepreneurs in Italy also depend on unauthorized loans to maintain their production, indicating that there is a structural need not satisfied by the existing formal credit market. This phenomenon has deep historical roots, but the country's stagnation and economic rigidities of recent decades have caused it to flourish. Rome's difficulties in overcoming the impacts of the 2008 financial crisis have expanded it (Unioncamere, 2014) and there is now concern that undercapitalized small and medium-sized enterprises (SMEs) are borrowing heavily from illegal lenders to cover overhead costs in the face of dramatically depleted revenues resulting from the COVID-19 pandemic.

In the last decade, Rome has been repeatedly dubbed Italy's "loan-sharking capital" (*capitale dell'usura*) (Busà & La Rocca, 2011; Favale & Tonacci, 2012; Lanzara, 2020). Although informal loans have long been a core element of the local economy, there are indications that the profiles, goals, and methods of its unofficial lenders are changing. In particular, the city appears affected by a growing trend among criminal organizations in expanding their lending power throughout the country, far beyond their traditional

DOI: 10.4324/9780429353321-5

territories.[2] Mafia groups are widely reported to be exploiting high demand for liquidity to augment their assets in the formal economy or to launder illegal earnings (CNEL, 2008; Libera, 2015; Saviano, 2021; Savona & Riccardi, 2015). However, the sector is much more nuanced than is acknowledged in most mainstream accounts, which consider only two categories of lending: the fully legal and the fully illegal. I demonstrate in this chapter that a large hybrid sector has evolved in Rome as supplementary to the formal market, stretching across multiple gradations between the informal and the illegal, the mutually beneficial and the highly exploitative. Since Italy's restrictive legislation on lending has made it difficult for banks to accommodate firms' need for financial flexibility, borrowing from informal and illegal sources has become a logical and often effective response to the normal pressures of doing business. However, the presence in the field of criminals with recourse to violence means that an initially productive credit relationship can evolve into one of predation. As the chapter's ethnographic discussion highlights, conflicting temporal demands often underlie this transition, as institutional timeframes prove too slow or too pressing to be manageable for many precarious economic actors. Informal/illegal lending is thus shown to be predicated on a fundamental disjuncture between the temporalities of banks and state agencies and those of actors with a shortage of financial buffers. When the ensuing gaps are filled by predatory lenders, the borrowers enter a situation of protracted liminality, suspended in a dependent debt relationship from which there are few protections and limited avenues for escape. This is therefore probably the most dangerous of the liminal spaces examined in this book. In this sphere of Rome's informal economies, time is monetized; temporal flexibility is bought and sold, and economic survival is often dependent on it. The power inequalities that it generates are at their most extreme, though; potentially even deadly.

Powerful taboos associated with unofficial lending create even greater methodological challenges to data gathering than most other informal practices. Widespread under-reporting causes this field to be "characterized by high dark numbers" (Savona & Riccardi, 2015, p. 81). The cases that do come to public attention are often the most extreme, in which borrowers have no alternative but to seek help from the state. Much informal lending operates far more ambiguously, though, and its full dimensions cannot be quantified with any accuracy. Some large-scale profiles of the sector and estimates of its size have been attempted and are useful in tracing its contours. Lenders' and borrowers' common resistance to discussing the topic, however, makes qualitative accounts especially rare.[3] This chapter takes a multi-method approach, integrating available institutional reports and statistical evaluations with in-depth interviews carried out with three Roman entrepreneurs who have borrowed informally or illegally in recent years. The small size of the sample reflects the vulnerability that many borrowers feel and the taboos that accompany this practice. Nevertheless, these first-person accounts provide insights into borrowers' decision-making processes and the affective experiences of operating in such a normatively equivocal sphere. The analysis also draws from interviews and discussions with members of four NGOs that support debt-trapped people in Rome. These informants have long-term experience in the field, are exposed to a broad range of debt situations, and serve numerous people, enabling them to identify patterns in the relationships between their clients and illegal lenders and to provide detailed accounts of the dynamics involved in individual cases. As the main interface between such borrowers and state institutions, they are also crucial sources of first-hand knowledge of the efficacy of legal and institutional protections.

The chapter thus explores how the exigencies of day-to-day business practice on a micro scale are tightly interwoven with the macro-level effects of legislation, practices within the formal credit sector, and the capacity of institutions mandated to fight illegal lending. The first section outlines Italian legislation regarding lending for interest and discusses some of the terminological ambiguities that plague the field. This is followed by an overview of existing data on the phenomenon nationally, regionally, and in Rome, and reports of organized crime group expansions into this market in Lazio. The third section focuses on the suppliers of unofficial credit and on the demand, highlighting how the need for informal loans frequently intertwines with other engagements in the informal economy. The subsequent ethnographic discussion explores borrowers' relations with their lenders and their accounts of operating in the liminal space between their legal business activities and dependency on illegal actors. It investigates how both temporal demands and the ambiguous moralities around debt relations shape their calculations, practices, and experiences. The final section explores why borrowers rarely turn to the authorities even when their lenders become oppressive or violent, and analyzes whether the policies aiming to disincentivize informal and illegal borrowing adequately address the real causes of demand.

Legal clarity, conceptual ambiguities

In 1993, Italy introduced a new Consolidated Law on Banking (Decreto Legislativo 1 settembre 1993, n. 385: *Testo unico bancario*), which reformed the entire credit sector. Under this law, only registered banks and financial intermediaries that are approved, monitored, and listed by the Bank of Italy may lend for interest. They therefore dominate the formal credit supply. Private individuals may also provide loans for interest, as long as they do not do so systematically or professionally. These private sources are mostly undeclared and unmonitored, making up an important – and largely invisible – part of the informal market. Irrespective of the provider, all interest rates must remain below those stipulated in anti-usury legislation which was introduced in 1996 (Legge 7 marzo 1996, n. 108), in response to a series of suicides by debt-trapped individuals. This law defines any loan as usurious and illegal if the interest rate and other costs supersede 50% of the average interest rate set by legally registered credit institutions. Much of the law focuses on capping the charges imposed by legal credit providers, but it also indirectly acknowledges the existence of a parallel market. For example, it deems interest rates to be usurious if "disproportionate" to the loan, even if the interest is below the legal threshold, and if the recipient is in a "condition of economic or financial difficulty." It also considers various aggravating circumstances: if the lender is operating within a financial institution or in a professional capacity; if they require company shares or property deeds as collateral; if the loan fees harm someone in "a state of need," an entrepreneur, professional, or artisan. These provisions recognize an empirical reality in Italy: predatory lending often involves members of the formal financial sector, it particularly targets struggling businesses, and can entail systematically stripping firms of their assets.

The law does not explicitly distinguish between a bank that temporarily exceeds the interest-rate threshold and a loan shark who traps a borrower in a cycle of ever-increasing debt. In recent years, most legal complaints of usury have in fact concerned bank charges (Commissario, 2019), while the far more dangerous predatory lending continues to be largely hidden from institutional view. Moreover, a wide range of informal credit agreements exist between these two extremes that are often conflated with loan-sharking. Indeed, debate in Italy is plagued by a lack of clear and differentiated terminology. The term most widely used to refer to informal or illegal lending, across all registers, is *usura*. Those who provide the credit are generally called *usurai*. Irrespective of its definition in law, most dictionaries characterize *usura* both as lending money for *any* interest and for *excessive* interest, reflecting the historical condemnation of interest-based lending in Ancient Greek and Jewish traditions and in subsequent Catholic teaching (Filotto, 1997). Although the Church gradually accepted formal banking from the late Middle Ages, it continued to censure informal lending (Herzfeld, 2009). A moral ambiguity thereby emerged which remains strong to this day. While unofficial lending is widespread, the connotations of parasitism and greed associated with the label *usura* cause the practice to remain heavily stigmatized.[4] In its everyday use, therefore, *usuraio* generally conveys the same meaning as the English word "loan shark" despite the fact that not all informal or illegal lending involves predatory behaviour. The scientific literature tends to further perpetuate the binary assumption that all such lending is extortionate, and that legal credit is instead manageable (Benvenuti et al., 2017; Dugato 2013; Mugellini, 2012). Little attention is paid to the fact that not all illegally high interest rates are perceived as difficult to repay or, conversely, that legal loans can trap borrowers in inescapable cycles of debt. To distinguish more clearly between the dualistic legal definitions and the more nuanced gradations of borrowers' experiences, here I use the terms *usury* and *illegal lending* to refer to loans whose interest rates clearly exceed the legal threshold defined in Italian law or when private actors lend professionally and systematically. Instead, I term *informal* those loans that are provided privately and unsystematically and where interest rates are low, non-existent, or not highlighted as a concern. I reserve the term *loan-sharking* for cases of clear exploitation, in line with Mayer's definition:

> loan-sharking is not the annual percentage rate lenders charge, but the length of time expensive debt endures. Loan-sharking is debt-trapping; it is a predatory practice that consists in renewing short-term loans again and again in order to maximize fee income.
>
> (2012, p. 828)

This enables us to distinguish between high interest loans that bleed the borrower dry or appropriate their assets and those that instead enable economic survival.

Mapping an invisible market

Given this dichotomous perspective on lending in Italy, very few studies explore its real gradations. Part of the problem lies in the fact that only an estimated 5% of people who borrow outside the formal system ever turn to the authorities (Giuffrida, 2019). Its underreported nature makes it impossible to gauge the number of people and sums involved. Several studies claim that about 40,000 *usurai* are operating in the country (Confesercenti, 2017; Unioncamere, 2014). Estimates of the illegal sector's annual turnover vary widely, from 24 billion euro (Confesercenti, 2017), to 82 billion euro (Eurispes, 2016). Two distinct markets for illegal loans are usually identified: private households and small businesses. Demand for personal loans has risen notably since the 2008 crisis; almost two million households are over-indebted to legal credit providers (53% higher than in 2006) and may turn to unauthorized lenders to help pay interest on their legal debts and meet other consumption needs (Fiasco, 2019). Eurispes (2016) calculated that in 2015 around 12% of families borrowed from illegal sources and that the average size loan was above 20,000 euro; one anti-usury NGO instead claims it has risen to 40–45,000 euro (Giuffrida, 2019). Overall, it is likely that such lenders provided at least 30 billion euro in capital to families (Eurispes, 2016). Although no similarly detailed estimates exist for more recent years, these patterns are unlikely to have diminished as many households continue to struggle in the face of structurally high unemployment, high taxation, and restricted bank lending. Moreover, although demand from the business world is generally calculated as a separate category from personal borrowing, domestic and company finances are often tightly interwoven in Italy's many family-owned small businesses. In such cases personal savings often constitute the company's very limited capital, production is frequently located in the home, and members' employment income is directly tied to the firm's profits. Losing assets in one sphere can have devastating repercussions for the other.

It is estimated that 10% of all Italy's entrepreneurs turned to illegal lenders in 2015, with a total of over 400,000 companies affected (Eurispes, 2016). The numbers are widely assumed to have risen significantly since then. Wholesale and retail traders, construction companies, and agricultural producers are those most involved (Commissario, 2019). Small and medium-sized firms are particularly susceptible to such borrowing because they have narrow profit margins and often lack financial buffers to withstand shocks such as abrupt revenue slumps, a rise in overhead costs, or unexpected expenses.[5] A sudden inspection by the tax authorities, a pressing payment order from suppliers, tight repayment instalments on equipment, or a bank's refusal to extend a loan can all force otherwise legal entrepreneurs to turn to unofficial sources (Bosio, 2017; Confesercenti, 2017). This type of credit often provides the only means for businesses faced with strictures to continue operating legally and paying employees. Rather than a separate economic sector, therefore, it is functional to – and deeply embedded within – Italy's legal business world.

For many small firms, survival has proved extremely difficult since the economic crisis of 2008, which caused over 1.6 million businesses to close in the following five years (CENSIS, 2013). Despite gradual gains in parts of the Italian economy from 2015 until early 2020,[6] the recovery was weak even before the 2020 COVID-19 crisis.[7] A critically low supply of legal credit to SMEs has made this situation harder still. Between 2011 and 2018, bank lending to small and medium-sized firms fell by 27%: a reduction of 252.8 billion euro (Il Giornale delle PMI, 2019). Although businesses with fewer than twenty employees make up 98% of Italian companies, they receive only 18% of bank credit (Il Giornale delle PMI, 2019). All observers concur that it is this intense restriction of bank lending that feeds the demand for unofficial credit. Since 2008, in fact, Italian banks have become even more cautious about allocating high-risk loans, since usury law prohibits them from covering the risk by charging interest much above the average rate. The intensification of international banking regulations brought in with the Basel III accord in 2010 have exacerbated the situation by requiring more stringent credit risk assessment mechanisms for evaluating loan applications, leaving little space for personalized negotiations between banks and entrepreneurs. A fundamental factor in the formal sector's ongoing prudence is Italy's high proportion of bad loans, which remain a cause of concern and vulnerability for banks (Crow, 2020; Legorano, 2019). A systemic problem underlies this extreme caution: Italy's slow and inefficient judiciary results in weak enforcement of credit contracts and protection of lenders' rights (Casolaro et al., 2006; Spina & Stefanizzi, 2007).[8] Rather than face years of delay before they can recover their capital if a borrower defaults on the loan, many banks simply prefer to avoid the risk. Deep reform of Italy's judicial system is therefore indispensable to address widespread mistrust in the state's ability to safeguard property rights.

The COVID-19 pandemic has further aggravated many of these factors. Over 456,000 jobs were lost during 2020 and many employees had their hours reduced (Il Sole 24 Ore, 2021). As the government's bans on firing workers are gradually lifted, these numbers will inevitably worsen. This is likely to trigger a major increase in undeclared employment, adding to the 3.2 million people estimated to have been working informally before the pandemic began (CGI Mestre, 2021). Around 240,000 of the companies that closed in 2020 are believed to have done so exclusively because of the pandemic (Confcommercio, 2020a), and a further 292,000 were struggling to survive in early 2021 (CGI Mestre, 2021). While consumption rates fell by 10.9% in 2020 (Confcommercio, 2021), companies' overhead expenses remained. At the same time, 290,000 firms saw their requests for official loans rejected in 2020 and financial support from the state was slow to arrive (Confcommercio, 2020b, 2020c). All these elements have fuelled a dramatic rise in the need for liquidity, which has been accompanied by widespread alarm about the opportunities that this has presented to the country's criminal organizations (Commissario, 2021; Domani, 2021). Direct lending is only one of the ways such organizations benefit. There are also strong signals that they are buying up struggling firms and using them to undercut surviving ones, generating a competitive pressure that is likely to force others to sell and thereby allow the crime groups to further expand their market control (Saviano, 2021).

Lazio ranks immediately behind the southern regions in many assessments of vulnerability to illegal lending (Eurispes, 2016; Fiasco, 2011; Scaglione, 2014; Unioncamere, 2014). The indicators generally used to measure this exposure merge economic data (e.g. unemployment and bankruptcy rates) with crime statistics (reports of extortion, threats of violence, arson, etc). Lazio's high position in these studies reflects two important issues. Economically, although the region has some internationally competitive sectors, it is less industrially developed than most other central and northern regions of the country and contributes only 11% of national GDP (EC, 2019). Its SMEs continued to struggle even before the COVID-19 crisis (Federlazio, 2020). The region has high levels of short-term labour contracts and average declared incomes are low (around 22,000 euro p.a.) (UPI, 2018). Although Rome tends to perform better than the rest of the region, it has nonetheless attracted concern about its vulnerability to illegal lending. A significant rise in over-indebted people turning to support organizations was noted in the capital between 2012 and 2014 (FAI, 2014; Unioncamere, 2014) and again in 2019, when one NGO announced that predatory lending had risen by 20% over a decade (Giuffrida, 2019). This trend has been matched by an apparent growth in mafia-type loan-sharking in the capital (Regione Lazio, 2019). Indeed, a second core factor that contributes to Lazio's high exposure to predatory lending is its growing vulnerability to organized crime. There is now a consolidated presence of mafias in southern parts of the region, with a strong tendency towards infiltration into the legal economy (Martone, 2017). As we will see below, concerns are rising that Rome is also increasingly being targeted as mafias' modi operandi and financial strategies evolve.

A multitiered supply side

Paradoxically, while the illegal lending sector has expanded, official reports to the authorities have plummeted. In 1996, 1,436 complaints of usury were made to the police (Confesercenti, 2017). In 2010, the number had fallen to

374; by 2018 it was down to 189 (ISTAT, 2020b). Annually, around 10% of these reports have originated in Lazio. Clearly, official data provide little basis for understanding the spread of this market or its typologies. These dark numbers partly reflect a lack of trust in the efficacy of the authorities and the judicial system, which we return to in later sections. However, they also raise questions about the accuracy of prevailing narratives that all illegal lending exploits and dispossesses the borrowers. It is generally assumed that fear of violent retaliation from loan sharks motivates under-reporting. As the rest of this chapter argues, though, other calculations are also at play which reflect a spectrum of credit relations that range from exploitative to supportive. These relational dynamics are determined by how the specific needs of the borrowers intersect with the strategic interests of the lenders. Here, I trace various categories of illegal/informal loan providers in Rome, from more to less organizationally structured ones, outlining how differences in their long-term goals influence whether they are likely to resort to violent and rapacious means.

The primary explanation offered for under-reporting relates to the expansion of organized criminal groups in this sector (Commissario, 2019; Eurispes, 2016). It is likely that in areas of Italy where powerful organizations are known to dominate the credit market, reports to the police will be disproportionately low as the deterrents of intimidation or loyalty are much stronger than in contexts where lenders operate individually or lack such a pervasive reputation. How OCGs manage the loans and the interest rates they charge depends, however, on their strategic objectives. When the intention is to forcibly acquire legal assets, the common approach is to charge high interest rates and then, when the entrepreneur is no longer able to sustain repayments, require them to transfer part or entire ownership of the business to the lender. The firm can continue to operate at a loss and the original proprietor often maintains an income, acting as a straw person for the organization's legal transactions. While the threat of violence remains an option to ensure compliance, in many cases this is not necessary as business owners who have no other employment opportunities may consider this preferable to closing. If, on the other hand, the criminal group's goal is to cultivate support from businesspeople in its areas of operation, it may use its extensive liquidity to provide loans at rates of interest that are close to or even below those of the legal banking sector. This strategy has clearly been employed during the COVID-19 crisis (Saviano, 2020). Such loans are likely to be perceived by borrowers as supportive, at least in the short and medium term, rather than oppressive. Gratitude may serve as a stronger disincentive to report than fear, therefore. In either case, the source of financial help, although unofficial, may be considered more productive and immediate – shorn of bureaucratic requirements and lengthy procedures – than the limited formal services available to struggling firms. Borrowers may engage with such lenders not exclusively out of desperation but as part of a cost-benefit calculation that weighs the loan as a preferable alternative to insolvency in a period of financial turbulence.

To what extent Rome's credit market has been penetrated by OCGs in this way is, of course, unknown. Judicial investigations since 2012 have revealed rising investments in the capital's legal businesses by all traditional mafias, especially Camorra and 'Ndrangheta groups originating in Campania and Calabria respectively (Pignatone & Prestipino, 2015). Anti-mafia agencies report that 'Ndrangheta clans are financing illegal credit, often through local intermediaries (Regione Lazio, 2019). Their predominant strategy is to maintain minimal visibility, making financial investments through the "grey area" of collusive legal actors, rather than seeking to acquire territorial power.[9] Nevertheless, there is also evidence of 'Ndrangheta members operating as violent debt collectors for local criminal groups (Fiano, 2017). Camorra networks are instead those most visibly involved in the city's street crime sectors, combining drug-dealing with other territorially based activities such as illegal gambling and extortion (Clough Marinaro & Borselli, 2019). In these cases, illegal lending aims to instil fear and assert local supremacy, particularly in low-income neighbourhoods on the south-eastern side of the city. Here it takes the form of traditional loan-sharking, using violence as a technique for maximizing criminal reputations in a highly competitive environment.

Rome is, in fact, home to a fragmented and heterogenous panorama of criminal organizations, many of them deeply embedded autochthonous groups. Among these, the Fasciani and Spada families, both based in Ostia, have been declared full-fledged mafia-type associations, capable of using their intimidatory power to produce widespread submission and *omertà* (conspiracy of silence). Both organizations are actively involved in *usura* (Regione Lazio, 2018, 2019). The Casamonica clan has an even wider geographical reach and is possibly the most powerful and brutal mafia in the city. This family's contemporary wealth is rooted in their history as providers of illegal credit and violent debt collection since the 1970s (Cimmarusti, 2019; Regione Lazio, 2019; Trocchia, 2019). Wire taps and witness testimonies show that they specialize in aggressive debt-trapping, charging monthly interest rates that start at 20% and rise with every late payment. If not resolved quickly, debts can grow for decades without the borrower managing to repay the principal loan. All these groups appear to use loan-sharking for the triple purpose of diversifying income sources, co-opting local businesses, and maximizing criminal "brand" reputations. Recent investigations have also revealed that smaller independent criminal groups copy those same methods to assert dominance in their districts (Bianconi, 2018).[10]

The credit market is so large as to accommodate a variety of actors with diverse goals and operational strategies, who weave often temporary and fluid alliances across social groups normally considered distinct. The Luna Nera probe of 2017 is paradigmatic of such convergences. It revealed that partners in a legal car dealership in Rome were providing illegal credit and using violent and extortive debt collection methods. Though operating independently, they were backed up by 'Ndrangheta and Camorra connections, while benefitting from the professional skills of collusive lawyers, accountants, bankers, corrupt tax and law enforcement agents (Fiano, 2017). The *Mafia Capitale* investigations into corrupt relations between criminal actors, entrepreneurs, and members of Rome city government indicated that some of the actors involved also participated in loan-sharking (Savatteri & Grignetti, 2015).[11] In a city where no one group can achieve a criminal monopoly, organized but flexible multi-scalar networks of different types have thus become widespread (Regione Lazio, 2019).

Violent criminal organizations are an important, but by no means exclusive, feature of Rome's illegal or informal credit supply. Individual lenders, widely labelled "neighbourhood usurers," have historically been the most common category. These are often small business owners who sell cash to other local traders or families, sometimes at usurious interest rates, but often at levels that are in line with legal rates and that avoid predation. Some observers claim that these actors are in decline, struggling to provide the large sums increasingly being requested (Confesercenti, 2017). Others argue that they are used by mafias as a bridge into local communities, using their relations of trust with borrowers to provide an inconspicuous avenue for laundering criminal incomes (Busà & La Rocca, 2011; Eurispes, 2016). In my interviews it emerged that autonomous neighbourhood lenders remain a source of credit to businesses and are often not reported because they are perceived to be supplying an essential service. Here, lenders' close knowledge of the local economic environment and strong social networks serve as an informal means of risk assessment and peer pressure, much like in microfinance systems in less developed economies (Ito, 2003). Borrowers must repay promptly if they hope to borrow again in the future and preserve their reputation. Social and temporal capital are assets that support such lending. This is rarely rapacious or violent and shifts along the informal-illegal spectrum, depending on whether loans are provided systematically or sporadically, and how their costs compare to official rates. Similar forms of mutual benefit characterize part of the growing phenomenon of employees who offer loans to co-workers, often dubbed the "usurer in the office next door" (Eurispes 2016, p. 3). They too are routinely depicted as predatory loan sharks. However, debt-trapping requires some form of implicit or explicit threat to ensure continued payment of extortionate interest. Employees of the same organization arguably have mutual leverage: the borrower and lender are equally able to expose each other, with the risk for the lender of endangering their job or permanently damaging their workplace reputation by being stigmatized as an *usuraio*. While there have been reported cases of predation in such relationships (Eurispes 2016), it is probable that many white-collar lenders simply seek to gain a second income from the interest. In such environments, it is a more secure business strategy to operate as a trusted informal credit-supplier, earning limited interest over extended periods, than to demand extortionate rates that will eventually financially destroy their borrowers.

Rome also features highly organized "parabanking" networks (Busà & La Rocca, 2011): actors working in financial services, accounting, and commerce who use the expertise and contacts built in their legitimate businesses to offer informal or illegal loans to clients and colleagues. In some cases, bank employees themselves bridge the formal and unofficial sectors, directly referring clients to informal lenders after denying them a loan (Pardo, 2000; Eurispes, 2016) or giving lists of their rejected loan applicants to such lenders, enabling the latter to proactively offer their services (Monizzi, 2018). An additional blurring occurs when private individuals act as guarantors for bank loan applications on the part of actors who would otherwise be refused. The guarantor charges a fee without having disbursed any capital. Alternatively, they take out the loan themselves and then pass the funds on to the real borrower, demanding interest on top of that of the bank (Eurispes, 2016). It seems clear that many of these relations are founded on trust and social proximity. Indeed "victims and perpetrators frequent the same economic and social environments and share other common characteristics: age, profession, they frequent the same leisure venues and have identical cultural backgrounds" (Confesercenti, 2017). Formal and informal actors and practices thus interweave in a zone of ambiguity, meeting a demand that originates primarily in the "legal city" (Spina & Stefanizzi, 2007). The supply is multitiered, socially fluid, and has adapted to a wide variety of contexts, producing a spectrum of debt relations. Some of these become unmanageable and exploitative, but not all of them do.

The demand side: precarity and informalities

As in every developed economy, a core demand for informal/illegal loans originates in highly vulnerable groups: drug-users, prostitutes, gambling addicts, and others who struggle to balance income and expenditures (Eurispes, 2016; Fiasco, 2019; Spina & Stefanizzi, 2007). Where entrepreneurs are concerned, dominant narratives identify three main causes: the shortage of bank loans discussed above, pre-existing over-indebtedness to legal lenders, and a lack of financial expertise that hinders many small business owners from anticipating and shielding against future shocks (Della Bella, 1997). These explanations are partly borne out in my fieldwork and are explored further in the next section. Here I focus instead on an additional, and arguably crucial, set of factors underpinning demand: how other informal business practices produce a need for unofficial loans, making such borrowing inseparable from Italy's large undeclared economy.

Abenante's (2018) research on informal loans among migrants in Italy has found that such borrowing, especially from family, friends, or other community networks, is widespread. Almost half the respondents (49%) have exclusively contracted informal loans; 62% have instead merged formal and informal ones. A small proportion referred to accessing loans from "informal systems outside the community" (1.4%) and from their employers (1.5%). Despite not specifying what kind of interest, if any, is charged for these loans, the findings provide important insights into the sector. They belie the prevailing assumption that such borrowing is limited to marginal economic actors excluded from the formal credit system, showing instead that informal and formal loans are often complementary and contracted for distinct reasons. Informal ones most commonly serve short-term needs and unexpected expenses, while bank loans enable longer-term investment strategies in housing, vehicles etc. Those who most frequently use informal credit – more often even than undocumented migrants – are registered self-employed workers. This confirms that such borrowing is not an indicator of financial exclusion but an operational necessity for many small business actors. A strong signal that systemic, rather than cultural, imperatives are at play is that migrants turn to informal financing more frequently in Italy than they did in their home countries. A case study of Bangladeshis in Rome provides a partial explanation: many of them avoid formal banking because they fear exposing their finances to official scrutiny, particularly when their business practices occur within the informal economy (Abenante, 2018). The many reasons to elude institutional attention explored in the previous chapter – a lack of sales licences, inability to pay Italy's high bureaucratic costs, etc. – are thus deeply intertwined with this sphere. The survey also highlights that such loans often set the foundations for economic and social inclusion in the country. Undocumented migrants may need to borrow to pay for fictitious or real employment and housing contracts, for example, to become eligible for residency and other permits (Spina & Stefanizzi, 2007). Informal credit can thus be essential to completing a migratory project and is not always perceived as exploitative, even when interest rates are high (Becucci, 2019).

Similarly detailed investigations of informal lending among Italian citizens are not available, although statistical analyses by the Bank of Italy corroborate the finding that informal and formal credit are often complementary: 28% of informal borrowers also have bank loans. In many cases, informal credit serves to furnish the down-payments on formal loans or to avoid defaulting on the latter if repayment becomes difficult. While 20% of informal borrowers are credit-constrained, confirming that banking restrictions do play a part, a much larger proportion (50%) are not interested in official loans at all, and half of those "do not even hold a bank account" (Benvenuti et al., 2017, p. 11). This indicates that, just like many migrants, a sizable proportion of Italians are not attracted to the formal sector, preferring to turn to actors they personally trust and to avoid the slow and bureaucratically complicated procedures with which banks are associated.[12]

The relationship between the official and informal economy thus warrants deeper discussion. Italy has one of the largest non-observed economies (NOE) among developed countries (Medina & Schneider, 2018), accounting for approximately 211 billion euro, or 12% of GDP (ISTAT, 2020c).[13] Only about 10% of this concerns criminal trades. The rest is made up of undeclared work (37.3%), under-reporting of value added (46.1%), and other sources of income such as off-the-book rents and tips. This shadow economy is a consolidated phenomenon within which transactions are carried out in cash to avoid the country's high taxes and social security contributions as well as its inefficient bureaucracy. The causes of the phenomenon are multiple, but a core element is the heavy fiscal burden on businesses and personal income (Confcommercio, 2017), aggravated by the fact that this taxation does not significantly affect social equality through welfare redistribution mechanisms (Williams, 2014). Moreover, despite attempts to simplify bureaucratic procedures in recent years, opening and managing businesses legally continues to be much more onerous and administratively complex than in most other advanced economies (World Bank 2019a, 2019b). There is consequently an ongoing and widespread perception that the state is hyper-invasive, proliferating laws and bureaucratic requirements that constrain freedom of action while doing little to protect the needs and interests of precarious economic actors. Many consider that the social contract is not being fulfilled, as high tax contributions are not met by guaranteed rights and public services (Boni, 2014; Guano, 2010). Citizens' distrust in the political and legal institutions of the state thus remains an unresolved problem (Demos, 2019; Eurispes, 2020), with privatized and informal solutions often appearing more effective than state provisions.

As studies of informal economies around the globe have amply demonstrated, informal economic practices are symbiotically intertwined with the formal economy. Italy is no exception. Hybrid strategies take on many forms; legal entrepreneurs may officially declare only a portion of their revenue, employers may register workers for part of their effective working hours and pay the remaining wage under the table, places of work may be squatted or unregistered, or not conform to safety and licencing regulations. In many such cases, the economic actor's declared assets are greatly inferior to their real value. Not only does this mean that they may lack enough legal collateral for a bank loan; they may also have no interest in exposing their real assets to official scrutiny. In these circumstances, contracting an illegal loan with high interest rates is financially more advantageous than the taxes, possible fines, and back-payments that would be incurred in the legal system. Moreover, as Masciandaro's (2001) economic model underlines, the real value of undeclared assets not usable as collateral for a bank loan is instead factored into the illegal debt relationship. The high interest rate must therefore be understood as an illegality cost that reflects the benefits offered over those of a bank: greater speed, discretion, a valuation of real wealth, and a higher tolerance of risk (Masciandaro, 2001, p. 200). Illegal creditors hold a further competitive advantage by virtue of their willingness to renegotiate loans even when the project for which the capital was invested does not return the expected results quickly. While a bank will seize the collateral if repayment is not forthcoming, the illegal creditor will be more prone to extend the debt since the risk is compensated by the high interest rate and the knowledge that illegal means, such as violence, can be used if necessary. The illegal lender can therefore be understood as selling a temporal service: while the bank will be unlikely to give the elastic deadlines the borrower may need to balance costs and revenues, the illegal lender provides the flexibility that may be essential to the business' survival while not threatening the collateral, at least in the short term. The illegal sector thus furnishes a crucial resource – time – that is scarce in the legal market.

Masciandaro further underlines that actors are more willing to turn to illegal creditors if they have a low sensitivity to illegality. This appears supported by Spina & Stefanizzi's (2007) study of recorded usury cases in Milan which found that a third of borrowers had themselves been previously reported for crimes, mostly white-collar ones such as tax evasion. In environments where rule-breaking is widespread and normatively licit, and where trust in formal institutions is scant, the psychological barriers to resorting to illegal loans will be relatively low. This is particularly evident where organized crime groups have broad legitimacy. However, it extends to other contexts where actors perceive an absence of state support, either because operating in the formal economy is considered financially crippling (Pardo, 2000), or because their condition of precarity excludes them from accessing formal safety nets. The official financial sector has been slow in adapting to an increasingly unstable labour force dependent on short-term, sporadic employment contracts, especially among young people in particular need of mortgages and other loans (Spina & Stefanizzi, 2007).[14] The potential for such unprotected workers – Italians and migrants – to turn to alternative sources of credit is therefore high.

The debates outlined here complicate the assumption enshrined in law and advanced by most policymakers that a clear line distinguishes a legal, beneficial loan from an illegal, exploitative one. They show, instead, that informal or illegal credit is often unavoidable and essential in permitting many actors to continue operating within the legal economy. Italy's large non-declared economy and the many ways in which legal and illegal practices merge within it, produces a vast grey area in which money and financial services are bought and sold away from the gaze of the state.

Ambiguities, time, and stigma: the liminality of informal borrowing

Informal or illegal debt relations are affectively charged experiences imbued with complex moral and practical calculations. This section explores my ethnographic research with Roman entrepreneurs who have entered such relations, and with members of associations working with debt-trapped people. Their voices confirm that many of the national-level patterns discussed above are indeed in place in Rome. But they also draw out the normative and emotional nuances that these dynamics often engender, such as perceiving the state as a source of danger rather than protection, and the burden of shame that is often placed on those who borrow. These affective experiences are expressions of the intense social vulnerability that comes with the liminal condition of borrowing outside legally sanctioned circuits. On the one hand, contracting informal and illegal credit is a way for businesses to "buy time": fast access to cash is essential to maintaining control of a business that is subject to exogenous constraints and delays. On the other, when borrowing becomes protracted it places "debtors at the mercy of events that they often cannot control – injects a viscerally painful temporality, of real time with all its uncertainty and unpredictability, into social experience" (Herzfeld, 2009: 57). It can be very difficult for a borrower to discern at what moment the loan transitions from being a functional support to one where the cost of temporal latitude – the interest – entraps them in new and overwhelming time constraints. This is liminality at its most perilous; when people become stuck, suspended outside social protections and clearly defined statuses with few avenues of escape, pilloried and isolated for entering such a symbolically charged state.

The most persistent theme brought up by my interviewees concerned the need to borrow informally to maintain regularity in their tax, social security, and other payments to the state. One entrepreneur recounted that she had borrowed illegally to continue paying her employees' social security contributions when business slowed because she was unwilling to make them redundant, partly out of loyalty and partly anticipating that sales would soon pick up again. Others, in times of economic difficulty, have paid employees' wages but postponed social security payments. This, however, results in the accumulation of onerous fines; when payment is due, rather than risk the state's confiscation of their assets, they turn to unofficial lenders for help. One NGO representative spoke of the sometimes devastating experience of being targeted by the tax collection company, Equitalia: "we have seen cases where the initial demand for a tax repayment of 5,000 euro has grown to 20,000 in the space of six months." These are technically fines, not interest payments, and thus do not come under Italy's usury law. However, when costs rise by 300–400% per annum, far outstripping the interest rates charged by many illegal lenders, it becomes financially advantageous to borrow from unauthorized sources and close one's debts with the state. Fear of becoming entangled in a state bureaucracy perceived as rigid and unreasonable can outweigh the apprehension that businesspeople feel in turning to such a lender. Their choice is not founded on naivety but on a calculated need to avoid the state's protracted timeframes for resolving disputes and the perception that it is easier to maintain control in dealings with an individual lender than with multiple impersonal institutions. This lack of trust in the state is further aggravated when businesspeople contracted to provide services to the public sector must wait, sometimes for years, to be paid.[15] The legal procedures for forcing prompt payment are themselves slow and costly and thus often not worth embarking on. The state's own inefficiency thus directly incentivizes the informal/illegal sector.

The phenomenon, discussed previously, of actors combining legal and illegal loans was confirmed in the fieldwork. One interviewee turned to a loan shark in an attempt to pay back interest on over a dozen legal loans. NGOs reported numerous similar cases of clients who had become over-indebted to formal lenders – one had accumulated 26 such loans, another 17 – and had borrowed illegally to juggle the continuous demands for repayment. Many businesspeople instead obtain illegal credit to avoid their bills of exchange and cheques bouncing, which can lead them to be formally protested by the bank, incurring high costs and affecting their future access to cheques and other essential banking tools. Many interviewees mentioned the fear of being listed on the banking system's shared databases of uncreditworthy actors, viewing this as an insurmountable obstacle to continuing to operate in the legal economy. They also spoke of bank personnel advising their clients to take out loans with legal private credit agencies (*finanziarie*) rather than endanger their banking privileges. These *finanziarie* are widely perceived, however, as unpredictable and potentially dangerous, their contracts and products far less transparent than those of banks. They often operate on the margins of the law, charging interest rates as high as the legal threshold permits but adding an array of processing fees and insurance costs, and then using strategies to force repayment that my informants have experienced as psychologically violent, such as continuous harassing phone calls and visits. When debts accumulate with these institutions, some borrowers prefer to try to extinguish them through an informal loan which appears, at least at the outset, cheaper and less suffocating. Various informants stressed, however, that this intermediary step is often skipped, with bank employees directly connecting customers to unofficial lenders, as well as tax consultants and lawyers offering their clients unauthorized loans. This confirms that chains linking the legal, informal, and illegal sectors are an important element of the Roman credit market.[16] The anthropological literature underlines that borrowers accord creditors degrees of licitness that do not directly correspond to the actual legality of the institution or the interest rate charged. Their moral evaluations are instead based on whether lenders charge excessive or manageable interest: "In this culture strozzini [usurers] are socially differentiated and, in the description of ordinary people and some observers, include many finanziarie, quite regardless of their official (legal) status" (Pardo, 2000, pp. 70–71). Herzfeld's study of Roman artisans similarly found that banks are perceived as obstructive or exploitative and are frequently accused of practising "legalized usury" (2009, p. 319).

Debt relations become even more multi-layered when retailers find themselves having to buy stock from wholesalers on credit. Interviewees report a widespread practice of suppliers in Rome exploiting shopkeepers' financial weakness to force them to take on more inventory than they can realistically trade, or to oblige them to sell specific brands and products. When revenues prove too low to pay back the credit, a new loan must be contracted, often from those same wholesalers. In such situations, the business may continue for years in a condition of debt dependency. Indeed, in the current economic climate, some entrepreneurs borrow from unofficial lenders to maintain an enterprise that they know is failing, because they do not perceive any viable economic alternatives. In Italy's system of low labour mobility, high unemployment, and limited welfare support, an artisan or small business owner faces grave obstacles to finding new sources of income. As one interviewee stated: "I'm 55. If I close my shop, who's going to give me another job? Where else can I use the professional knowledge I've developed over a lifetime?" The problem becomes intergenerational when entrepreneurs view their business as the main legacy and source of job security to pass on to their children. My interviewees also spoke of the high financial costs and bureaucratic obstacles to winding up a company in Italy that act as a strong deterrent to closing a business, even when it is unproductive. Again, in such cases, an illegal loan serves to postpone an emotionally and objectively difficult decision.

Many lenders do not conform to the stereotypical image of rapacious loan-sharks. One interviewee borrowed from an acquaintance in her eighties whose fees only became suffocating after several years. Her methods for extracting repayment were based on threatening to publicly shame the borrower, rather than through physical violence. Similar mechanisms are at work among stallholders in markets and neighbourhood shops. Lenders, often traders themselves, are deeply embedded in those communities and must walk a fine line between presenting themselves as honest and reliable to mitigate the stigma associated with their lending, while also conveying an implicit threat that failure to repay is not an option. Hinting that they have connections with organizations that practise violent debt collection, such as the Camorra or Casamonica clans, is an effective means of sending the message. The extent to which individual neighbourhood lenders are in fact creating alliances with, or being replaced by, OCGs in Rome is unclear, however. One NGO member stated, "roughly a third of usury victims we work with have borrowed from neighbourhood lenders, a third from white-collar lenders – lawyers, tax consultants, people connected to banks –, and the last third borrow directly from criminal gangs." As argued in earlier sections, these categories are in fact blurred as networks weave across these typologies. The danger for many borrowers lies in the impossibility of knowing whether an apparently trustworthy contact is operating individually and motivated by personal profit, or whether they are working towards predatory debt-trapping. It is here that the historically established and functional practice of informal lending can mutate into a criminal one with potentially devastating consequences for the borrower.

The moral status of borrowers is as complex as that of illegal lenders, merging notions of passive victimhood with deep-rooted stigmas concerning a shared guilt for participating in a debt relationship. One interviewee resisted telling her family about her loan shark because "my mother lived in the same building as the usurer and I was ashamed; they saw each other every day. As the debt got worse it became harder to tell my husband too. I couldn't tell him I had lost all that money" – and indeed, when forced to inform her family, she was repeatedly shamed and ostracized. She equated the stigma with the often equally ambiguous status of sex crime victims: "when a person is raped, it is they who feel shame, not the rapist." Another interviewee declared "debt is like leprosy: once it attaches itself to you it is difficult to get rid of it," confirming Herzfeld's finding that "the taint of having fallen into the usurer's hands is [...] treated as an incurable disease" (2009, p. 147). The bodily metaphors used to express this shame are extended to notions of its inevitable contagion. It was described by all my interviewees as an illness that affects the entire family: "it produces enormous scars. Loan-shark victims are like drug addicts. They need money at all costs because the next day they have to pay up, so they ask everybody: parents, relatives, friends. But when the money does not come back, people stop helping and the family's cohesion breaks down." Thus, the dishonour is often accompanied by isolation and feelings of failure, especially in terms of the ability to support the household: "how do you admit to your family that you have failed, that you cannot maintain the standard of living that they expect?" The age-old Catholic condemnation of borrowers as complicit in the sin of usury therefore merges with contemporary expectations of reliability, financial dexterity, and the ability to avoid "spending beyond one's means."

This tendency to treat debt-trapped borrowers as polluting, to distance and denigrate them, is perpetuated by many NGO actors who attribute blame to them while simultaneously constructing them as hapless victims. As one interviewee declared, "those who borrow illegally are never saints and some are often quite arrogant, thinking that they can fix their problems themselves. But if they get themselves into that situation, it's their own fault." Another claimed, "these are people who don't know how to handle money. There's something wrong with them, a pathological relationship with money and an inability to say no to the things they want." Thus, borrowing is frequently portrayed as a corollary of consumerism and the need for social affirmation through status symbols. Such accusations of lacking critical judgment are also used to explain why many feel gratitude to their lenders: "they don't realize that the lender is their torturer. They think he is a friend and they are grateful that 'he helped me in my hour of need'. But what kind of friend charges you 10% interest per month?"

None of these explanations for borrowers' ambivalent attitudes do justice to the multiplicity of debt relations and the exogenous situations that push people into them. When lacking legal financial solutions, gratitude may not be misplaced or naïve but instead reflect the absence of safe and efficient institutional alternatives. Borrowers are often aware that informal or illegal credit places them in a liminal state of indeterminacy, where uncontrollable and dangerous outcomes are constantly possible. They hope to extinguish the debt quickly, but if they find themselves unable to, they become stuck, long term, in that liminality. It is here that their vulnerability escalates, as does the acute anxiety that accompanies it. Not only is the borrower's economic survival endangered; where organized criminal groups are involved, so is their physical welfare. This suspension outside any "jurally sanctioned relationships" (Turner, 1967, p. 101), combined with the existential peril, is what exposes borrowers to the symbolic violence of shame and blame that serves to keep the danger they represent at a safe distance from the rest of the community. The power of this stigma means that, unlike the other informal practices studied in this book, the borrower is deprived of social support networks: they are left to navigate the uncertainty alone. This extended liminal condition may never be fully resolved. If it is, termination often occurs through destruction: the loss of one's business, one's home and family, suicide. Borrowers may, however, seek help to exit the liminal zone, turning to NGOs and state institutions to support them in restructuring and closing their debts. These entities act as masters of ceremonies, guiding the borrower through a process of transition towards a cleansed, post-liminal state. As the next section shows, though, this journey is arduous and not always successful.

Challenges to transitioning out of financial liminality

The anti-usury law of 1996 introduced a range of measures to prevent people becoming over-indebted and entering the liminal sphere of illegal borrowing. These include a Fund for the Prevention of Usury, which finances non-profit associations to carry out awareness-raising campaigns, help individuals restructure loans, and support them in reporting illegal lenders. Much of the Fund is earmarked for organizations authorized to negotiate and guarantee bank loans with high-risk borrowers whose requests would normally be rejected. It thus addresses the banking restrictions that push so many borrowers towards informal and illegal lenders. Nevertheless, embarking on this credit restructuring process is often traumatic for borrowers who are forced to acknowledge that they have lost control of their finances and must cede much of their autonomy to tutors and counsellors who impose stringent schedules for repaying their debts. This can be experienced as deeply humiliating. Two borrowers have spoken of feeling infantilized and condemned, while facing years of financial austerity. As one stated, "now I am paying back loans to three banks instead of six and I will be for the next ten years. The suffocation continues, it's just of a different type." This protracted rite of passage, during which the liminal actor is accompanied by a team of experts towards ultimate liberation, must be endured with tenacity for it to succeed. Such a ritual should be entirely secure, yet an element of externally imposed precarity remains. The state has repeatedly failed to finance the Prevention Fund, whose budget is therefore minimal and uncertain (Commissario, 2015). The associations consequently struggle to offer continuous services essential in supporting debtors through the long procedures. While many psychologists and lawyers work for these organizations on a voluntary basis, lack of funding has forced them to pay court fees and other operating costs out of their own pockets. One organization underlined the irony that the state had obliged it to accrue debts of over 100,000 euro.

A second entity, the Solidarity Fund for Usury Victims was also created to enable entrepreneurs to rebuild their business or develop a new one. Accessing these funds is conditional on the borrower pressing charges against the usurer and concretely contributing to a conviction. In such cases, the fund provides a ten-year interest-free loan to cover damages and losses incurred through usury. These provisions are in striking contrast to those for victims of extortion who do not have to repay the state funds, because – as one interviewee put it – "they didn't ask to be extorted." Here a moral distinction is once again made, with usury victims perceived as complicit in a crime. The stigma exposes them to potential new dimensions of liminality even in this phase of reintegration into formal business life. The loan is only activated once the public prosecutor decides there are adequate grounds to build a criminal case. If the court case is not successful, though, or if the usurer dies during the proceedings, the loan can be revoked, returning the victim to insolvency. An additional problem is that such funds are only available to entrepreneurs and self-employed professionals, not other borrowers with immediate expenses to cover. The practical result is that such actors have few real alternatives to continuing to borrow illegally. Without financial benefits for reporting, there is no real incentive to embark on the drawn-out process which will eventually oblige them to face the lender in a courtroom. As one interviewee stated, "why would I go through all that hassle and inform everyone I know that I ended up in the hands of a loan shark, that I broke the law too?"

Myriad other disincentives aggravate the problem. Few of the loans negotiated exceed 25,000 euro, which is rarely adequate to cover business debts. They also require private guarantors such as family members, reinforcing the psychological pressures discussed earlier. Most crucially, the bureaucratic process is extremely complex, and few borrowers have enough documentary evidence of their illegal credit transactions to build a strong case. The fragmentation of the loan application mechanism, which requires police investigations and the involvement of multiple institutions, means that it takes an average of 18 months for funding requests to be considered (Commissario, 2019), and the vast majority are rejected. This is compounded by Italy's chronically slow judicial system, which forces many cases beyond the statute of limitations, resulting in few convictions. The lender's assets are then returned, including the victim's post-dated cheques, property deeds, and other documents that enable the lender to resume demands for repayment (Busà & La Rocca, 2006), potentially reactivating the debt-trapping relationship. Although the plaintiff's debts are frozen for a year, this protection is much briefer than the time it takes to receive the state loan, plunging the borrower back into a vortex of unmanageable repayment demands, many of them from state entities.

Moreover, the civil and penal courts are often out of synch, resulting in the usury victims' homes and businesses being sold off while they are still in the process of demonstrating that usury has occurred. They must thus also fight the stripping of their assets in the civil courts, paying legal fees that they are unlikely to afford. The state loan, if it does arrive, adds another layer of debt to be repaid in instalments, often making the business's recovery even more difficult (Commissario, 2019). Consequently, 80% of these loans are not repaid, incurring losses for the state and the danger of additional court cases for the borrower. Since the penal system's slowness results in few guilty verdicts, the borrower then risks encountering the lender in their daily life and suffering psychological and physical violence for having gone to the authorities. Indeed, NGOs argue that a major factor in refusal to press charges lies in the state's inability to guarantee the victim's safety throughout the legal process. Those who do embark on this journey typically regret it: "they soon realize that they have entered a long tunnel by the end of which they will be a different person. They all tell us they would not have done it had they known." The masters of ceremonies tasked with guiding the victim through the lengthy rite of passage into the security of the post-liminal phase are too numerous and too fragmented to support them through the emotional and psychological drama of each complex step.

Much of the formal sector's inadvertent obstructionism is temporal: the same structural slowness that spurs people to resort to speedy and flexible informal loans in the first place reappears at this stage in the disconnection between the state's inertia and the usury victim's need to respond swiftly to economic demands that risk sinking them into further debt. Various attempts have been made in the state bureaucracy to address some of these problems, although success has been minimal. Bankruptcy legislation has been reformed but it is still slow and onerous to close a business: around 22% of the estate's value is lost to bureaucratic expenses (OECD, 2017). The state entity that coordinates anti-usury measures has digitalized procedures and connected the agencies in real time but slowness persists (Commissario, 2019). Some new sources of credit to businesses have been opened (Decreto-Legge 21 giugno 2013, n. 69, Art. 2) and Italy's system of credit unions (Banche di Credito Cooperativo) and microcredit institutions has expanded, although only a tiny proportion of small businesses turn to them. While bureaucratic simplification is important, its effects have been piecemeal and have done little to alter perceptions that the system is unable to respond with the speed necessary to save businesses from collapse. Although Italy's anti-usury mechanisms have been widely praised for providing extensive protections on paper, observers concur that in practice the system has failed and requires deep reform (Busà, 2017; Confesercenti, 2017; Commissario, 2019).

Conclusion

A broad variety of unofficial sources of credit thus exists in Rome and Italy more generally, ranging from zero-cost loans from kin and community, through different types of fees and non-monetary obligations, to illegal but manageable interest rates, to rapacious debt-trapping. Actors move along this progressive scale according to their needs, the viability of their financial projects, their cultural, social, and economic capital. Informal and illegal borrowers do not necessarily end up in the dangerous zone of inescapable debt. However, the liminality of the entire sector – its invisibility and separation from institutional monitoring and protection – means that the potential for inadvertently falling prey to loan sharks is very real. While lenders with diverse strategies and interests populate the market, its vast size and potential for wealth accumulation makes it an ideal environment for organized crime groups to expand their social legitimacy and legal holdings. Informality thus intertwines with illegality more extensively here than in the other fields explored in this book. This is not a marginal niche, though. It potentially draws in actors from across Rome's disparate social and business environments where economic risks are a daily reality.

It has become normalized practice for agents to make cost-benefit analyses of whether their interests are better served by formal state and banking institutions or by informal and potentially criminal networks. Contrary to dominant narratives that borrowers' profligacy and incompetence pushes them into destructive debt, the discussion shows that demand reflects a combination of systemic factors: chronically high unemployment, rising economic precarity across social classes, a weak welfare system that provides inadequate financial safety nets, overly rigid banking restrictions, the absence of an affordable and efficient system for winding down unsuccessful businesses, the bureaucratic and fiscal burdens that make operating entirely in the legal economy difficult. Informal and illegal lending fills a void between the constraints of a formal environment that is often obstructive and the necessity to adopt economic practices that are likely to require recourse to unofficial credit. The economic crises following 2008 and then the coronavirus pandemic have merely aggravated problems that had already been afflicting Italy's small businesses and families for decades.

The sector is thus a direct product of Italy's political economy and the inadequacy of legal and institutional frameworks to address its weaknesses. In compensating for services that are difficult to access legally, the field produces opportunities for meso-level brokers who can bridge those needs: not only OCGs but the lawyers, bankers, and other professionals who also profit as mediators or lenders. The hierarchies that thereby emerge place many borrowers in positions of acute subordination, unable to resist their creditors' conditions and demands. The cost of buying temporal capital – in the form of financial flexibility and control over time – is not only material but includes the price of social opprobrium and possible physical vulnerability. Their cultural and legal stigmatization mean that acting collectively with other borrowers or forming alliances with better-positioned actors in the field is impracticable. Isolation and invisibility obstruct many informal borrowers from building the social and symbolic capital necessary to push against the established power relations or subvert the dominant assumptions and practices that structure the field.

Unlike the case studies in other chapters, these hierarchies are not the result of bureaucrats' discretionality or top-down rule-bending to promote institutional and elite interests. They are a consequence of legislation that, though well intentioned, has not had the expected results. A quarter century since its introduction, the rate-capping mechanism upon which Italy's anti-usury law is based has not only failed to curb demand for and supply of illegal loans, but has probably augmented them. At the time, Anderloni (1997) stressed that a purely financial instrument (interest rate caps) would be unlikely to resolve social problems: "a state that wants to protect its weakest citizens cannot expect to do so by limiting the price of credit; it is not through more or less expensive loans that one can solve problems of lack of income" (p. 159). While the years immediately following the promulgation of the 1996 usury law were marked by optimism that informal and illegal borrowers would emerge from the shadows, emboldened by the promise of state support and protection, the steady reduction in reports in the last two decades has dashed those hopes. Three strategies for reform are urgently needed to address these failures. First, a policy must be introduced that incentivizes access to microcredit and that expands the currently very limited types of mutual credit associations permitted.[17] In addition to meeting financial needs, this would make an important step towards destigmatizing borrowers. Second, a deep restructuring of the tax and bureaucratic burdens of small enterprises is essential. Third, the system for supporting debt-trapped individuals requires greater simplification, defragmentation, and acceleration than has so far been enacted. For many borrowers, state and civil society support comes too late, when a cycle of economic disintegration has become too entrenched to be easily resolved. State protection must be effective and continuous and its currently punitive and shaming approach must be replaced by adequate financial and social support.

Notes

1 Some paragraphs of this chapter were previously published in: Clough Marinaro, I. (2017). Loan-sharking in a time of crisis: Lessons from Rome's illegal credit market. *Trends in Organized Crime, 20*, 196–215.
2 It should be noted that mafias both contribute to and benefit from the fragility of small businesses, especially in the South. Bank interest rates are in fact higher in mafia-dense areas than elsewhere in the country, further feeding the demand for informal sources of credit (Bonaccorsi di Patti, 2009; CPI, 2012).
3 See, for example, the high refusal rates encountered by researchers in Naples when seeking interviewees on this subject (Di Gennaro et al., 2017). Herzfeld (2009) faced the same problems in Rome.
4 The Devoto and Oli (2007) dictionary states that by extension the term *usuraio* refers to "a person dominated by sordid avarice," underlining the moral condemnation that permeates the language.
5 79.5% of Italy's businesses are defined as microenterprises (*microimprese*) and have 3–9 employees (ISTAT, 2020a).
6 For example, a general reduction in bankruptcies and company closures in the 15 months running up to November 2019 (Cerved, 2019).
7 Productivity growth stayed sluggish, private consumption grew minimally, and per capita GDP remained at the same level as in 2000 (OECD, 2019).
8 Italy ranks very low internationally in terms of businesses' access to credit (119th out of 190 economies) and enforcement of contracts (122nd) (World Bank, 2019b).
9 See, for example, the "Rinascita Scott" investigation into 'Ndrangheta investments in commercial outlets throughout the capital (Di Corrado, 2020).
10 The Guarnera family in Acilia, Franco Gambacurta in Montespaccato, and Salvatore Nicitra in north and west Rome are among those to have been arrested in recent years for usury, among other crimes (Regione Lazio, 2019).
11 In 2020, the Supreme Court ruled that there were in fact two distinct organizations: one involved in corruption of civil servants and politicians, headed by Salvatore Buzzi and Massimo Carminati, the other dedicated to extortion. Consequently, it rejected the existence of a single organization employing mafia methods of intimidation and subjugation based on members' criminal reputations. Nevertheless, Massimo Carminati was brought to trial again in 2020, specifically on charges of usury. A verdict had not yet been reached at the time of writing.

12 That credit rationing by banks is not the only reason for borrowing illegally is confirmed at the European level: a study of EU businesspeople found that 32.8% of those who claimed to have used illegal credit sources did so because of a bank refusal, while almost 40% reported other reasons (Dugato, 2013).
13 The IMF instead estimates that it constituted 17.5% of official GDP (Medina & Schneider, 2018).
14 By December 2019, a record number of Italians – more than three million – were employed with short-term contracts (ISTAT, 2019b).
15 Further examples of non-payment by the state can be found in Pardo (2000) and Manco (2013).
16 Pardo (2000) noted similar allegations in Naples, suggesting that such relationships are historically established and systemic.
17 Until the late 1990s, Rome had an array of rotating savings and credit associations (ROSCAs) that partially met the need for small, quick, and flexible loans and operated on the basis of community trust (see Clough Marinaro, 2017; Herzfeld, 2009). The tightening of credit regulations pushed most ROSCAs from informality into illegality and many closed, although some politicians noted that this would increase the risk of people turning to loan-sharks instead (Senato della Republica, 1998). A system does exist for operating "self-financed communities" (*comunità auto-finanziate*: CAF) legally; however, the sums they lend are small (usually capped at 600 euro) and their capital must be above 250,000 euro (Abenante, 2018). Few associations have the large number of members necessary to put together that amount.

References

Abenante, P. (2018). Il rapporto fra migranti e finanza informale. Osservatorio Nazionale sull'Inclusione Finanziaria dei Migranti. www.migrantiefinanza.it/.

Anderloni, L. (1997). Sovrindebitamento delle famiglie e politiche di prevenzione: Alcune esperienze estere e prospettive per l'Italia. In D. Masciandaro & A. Porta (eds), *L'usura in Italia* (pp. 75–122). EGEA.

Becucci, S. (ed.). (2019). *Oltre gli stereotipi: La ricerca-azione di Renzo Rastrelli sull'immigrazione cinese in Italia*. Firenze University Press.

Benvenuti, M., Casolaro, L., & Ciani, E. (2017). Informal loans, liquidity constraints and local credit supply: Evidence from Italy. Bank of Italy Working Papers, no. 1099. www.bancaditalia.it/pubblicazioni/temi-discussione/2017/2017-1099/index.html?com.dotmarketing.htmlpage.language=1.

Bianconi, G. (2018). Prestipino: "Cresce l'omertà e i clan cercano il consenso sociale". *Corriere della Sera*, 18 July. https://roma.corriere.it/notizie/cronaca/18_luglio_17/casamonica-prestipino-cresce-l-omerta-clan-cercano-consenso-sociale-f79c0c48-89f3-11e8-8bbc-b107b233a106.shtml.

Bonaccorsi di Patti, E. (2009). Weak institutions and credit availability: The impact of crime on bank loans. Bank of Italy Occasional Papers, no. 52. www.bancaditalia.it/pubblicazioni/qef/2009-0052/QEF_52.pdf.

Boni, S. (2014). Legal hyper-invasiveness and anti-legal practices in contemporary Italy. *Journal of Modern Italian Studies*, 19(5), 514–527. https://doi.org/10.1080/1354571x.2014.962252.

Bosio, R. (2017). Per un uso responsabile del denaro. Manuale antiusura. http://images.vc.camcom.it/f/Varie/74/7463_CCIAAVC_232017.pdf.

Busà, L. (2017). La legge 108/1996. Venti anni dopo. *Sos Impresa*. www.sosimpresa.it/2581/la-legge-10896-venti-anni-dopo-.html.

Busà, L., & La Rocca, B. (2006). *L'usura. Le usure. Tempi, modi e luoghi di un fenomeno antico e moderno*. Edizioni Commercio.
Busà, L., & La Rocca, B. (2011). L'Italia incravattata: Diffusione territoriale ed evoluzione del fenomeno usuraio. *Sos Impresa*. www.sosimpresa.it/userFiles/File/Documenti5/italia_incravatta_busa-larocca.pdf.
Casolaro, L., Gambacorta, L., & Guiso, L. (2006). Regulation, formal and informal enforcement, and the development of the household loan market: Lessons from Italy. In G. Bertola, R. Disney, & C. Grant (eds), *The economics of consumer credit* (pp. 93–134). MIT Press. https://doi.org/10.7551/mitpress/2607.003.0005.
CENSIS (Centro Studi Investimenti Sociali). (2013). Italy today: Social picture and trends. Censis.
Cerved. (2019). Fallimenti, procedure e chiusure di imprese. https://know.cerved.com/wp-content/uploads/2020/03/Fallimenti-e-chiusure-d%E2%80%99impresa-3q-2019.pdf.
CGI Mestre. (2021). Per il lavoro nero il 2021 sara' un anno d'oro. www.cgiamestre.com/per-il-lavoro-nero-il-2021-sara-un-anno-doro/.
Cimmarusti, I. (2019). La Cassazione: Il clan Casamonica di Roma è una mafia. *Il Sole 24 Ore*, 30 April. www.ilsole24ore.com/art/la-cassazione-clan-casamonica-roma-e-mafia-ABPtcBtB.
Clough Marinaro, I. (2017). Loan-sharking in a time of crisis: Lessons from Rome's illegal credit market. *Trends in Organized Crime*, 20, 196–215. https://doi.org/10.1007/s12117-016-9279-y.
Clough Marinaro, I., & Borselli M. G. (2019). Camorra expansions into Rome. In F. Allum, I. Clough Marinaro, & R. Sciarrone (eds), *Italian mafias today: Territory, business and politics* (pp. 174–190). Edward Elgar.
CNEL (Consiglio Nazionale dell'Economia e del Lavoro). (2008). Usura: Diffusione territoriale, evoluzione e qualità criminale del fenomeno. http://usura.liberapiemonte.it/wp-content/uploads/sites/7/2011/09/Rapporto-usura-2008.pdf.
Commissario (Commissario per il coordinamento delle iniziative antiracket e antiusura e presidente del comitato di solidarietà). (2015). Relazione annuale attività dicembre 2015. www.interno.gov.it/sites/default/files/relazione_2015_0.pdf.
Commissario (Ufficio del Commissario straordinario del Governo per il coordinamento delle iniziative antiracket e antiusura). (2019). Relazione annuale attività 2019. www.interno.gov.it/sites/default/files/relazione_2019.pdf.
Commissario (Commissario per il coordinamento delle iniziative antiracket e antiusura e presidente del comitato di solidarietà). (2021). Relazione annuale attività (aggiornata al 31 dicembre 2020). www.interno.gov.it/sites/default/files/2021-03/relazione_annuale_2020.pdf.
Confcommercio. (2017). Le determinanti dell'evasione fiscale: Un'analisi regionale. www.confcommercio.it/documents/20126/480933/Le+determinanti+dell%27evasione+fiscale.pdf/b105562c-9e50-730d-83a7-205a697d7dbc?version=1.1&t=1505299123000.
Confcommercio. (2020a). Confcommercio: Nel 2020 oltre 300mila imprese in meno, l'80% a causa del Covid. www.confcommercio.it/-/comunicato-203-2020-300mila-imprese-in-meno-causa-covid.
Confcommercio. (2020b). Criminalità in aumento nel terziario, 40mila imprese a rischio usura. www.confcommercio.it/-/imprese-rischio-usura.
Confcommercio. (2020c). Sulle imprese lo "spettro" dell'usura. www.confcommercio.it/-/spettro-usura-sulle-imprese.

Confcommercio. (2021). Congiuntura Confcommercio, N. 1 (gennaio 2021). www.confcommercio.it/documents/20126/3212567/Congiuntura+Confcommercio+%28CC%29+1-2021.pdf/07e88554-dd1b-9183-1bf0-b08132b833f0?t=1610980188809.

Confesercenti. (2017). L'usura dopo la crisi, tra vecchi carnefici e nuovi mercati. Il Rapporto 2017 SOS Impresa. www.confesercenti.it/blog/lusura-dopo-la-crisi-tra-vecchi-carnefici-e-nuovi-mercati/.

CPI (Commissione parlamentare di inchiesta sul fenomeno della mafia e sulle alter associazioni criminali, anche straniere). (2012). Dimensione delle attività criminali, costi per l'economia, effetti della crisi economica. www.sosimpresa.it/userFiles/File/Documenti7/bankitaliantimafia2012citazionerapporto.pdf.

Crow, D. (2020). Virus renews fears over strength of Italy's banks. *Financial Times*, 26 March. www.ft.com/content/35a1ce1c-6d58-11ea-89df-41bea055720b.

Della Bella, C. (1997). Gestione finanziaria delle piccole e medie imprese e fenomeni di usura. In D. Masciandaro & A. Porta (eds), *L'usura in Italia* (pp. 39–59). EGEA.

Dell'Oste, C., & Parente, G. (2018). Italiani innamorati del contante. Tutti i rischi dei pagamenti cash. *Il Sole 24 Ore*, 25 June. www.ilsole24ore.com/art/italiani-innamorati-contante-tutti- rischi-pagamenti-cash-AERqsGAF.

Demos. (2019). Rapporto gli italiani e lo stato 2019. www.demos.it/rapporto.php.

Devoto, G., & Oli, G. C. (2007). *Il Devoto-Oli. Vocabolario della lingua italiana*. Le Monnier.

Di Corrado, V. (2020). Ecco i negozi nel salotto di Roma in cui la 'ndrangheta riciclava. *Il Tempo*, 10 January. www.iltempo.it/roma-capitale/2020/01/10/news/ndrangheta-roma-inchiesta-catanzaro-gratteri-negozi-punti-vendita-centro-riciclaggio-soldi-boss-cosche-vibo-valentia-castelromano-outlet-1264761/.

Di Gennaro, G., Donnarumma, G., & Gaudino, F. (2017) Risultati di un'indagine di vittimizzazione nel napoletano sull'usura: Fattori di rischio e propensioni alla domanda di credito illegale. In G. Di Gennaro & R. Marselli (eds), *Criminalità e sicurezza a Napoli. Secondo rapporto* (pp. 287–313). Federico II University Press.

Domani. (2021). L'Antimafia conferma le inchieste di Domani: Covid affare d'oro per i clan. *Domani*, 24 February. www.editorialedomani.it/politica/italia/le-mani-sul-recovery-le-mafie-puntano-green-e-sanita-lallarme-della-dia-c46ytnby.

Dugato, M. (2013). The crime against businesses in Europe. A pilot survey. *Transcrime*. www.transcrime.it/wp-content/uploads/2013/11/EU-BCS-Final-Report_GallupTranscrime.pdf.

EC (European Commission). (2019). Regional Innovation Monitor. Lazio. https://ec.europa.eu/growth/tools-databases/regional-innovation-monitor/base-profile/lazio.

Ellison A., Collard S., & Forster, R. (2006). Illegal lending in the UK. www.bristol.ac.uk/medialibrary/sites/geography/migrated/documents/pfrc0707.pdf.

Esselink, H., & Hernandez, L. (2017). The use of cash by households in the euro area. European Central Bank Occasional Paper Series, no. 201. www.ecb.europa.eu/pub/pdf/scpops/ecb.op201.en.pdf.

Eurispes. (2016). Usura: Quando il credito è "in nero". https://eurispes.eu/wp-content/uploads/2016/09/Eurispes_Rapporto_Usura_2016.pdf.

Eurispes. (2020). Rapporto Italia 2020. Fiducia nelle Istituzioni, il trend positivo si arresta. Governo e Parlamento giù di 10 punti. www.leurispes.it/rapporto-italia-2020-fiducia-nelle-istituzioni-il-trend-positivo-si-arresta-governo-e-parlamento-giu-di-10-punti/.

Favale, M., & Tonacci, F. (2012). Roma capitale dell'usura dal boss all'impiegato l'esercito dei nuovi strozzini. *La Repubblica*, 13 January. https://ricerca.repubblica.it/

repubblica/archivio/repubblica/2012/01/13/roma-capitale-dellusura-dal-boss-allimpiegato-esercito.html.
FAI (Federazione Antiracket Italiana). (2014). *Prevenzione e contrasto usura. Dieci anni di attività*. FAI.
Federlazio. (2020). Indagine congiunturale: Segnali ancora negativi per le PMI del lazio. www.federlazio.it/single-post/2020/02/12/Indagine-Congiunturale-Pmi-Lazio-ancora-in-forte-affanno.
Fiano, F. (2017). Usura, 17 arresti e 50 indagati: Emersi legami con il boss Michele Senese. *Corriere della Sera*, 16 June. http://roma.corriere.it/notizie/cronaca/17_giugno_16/usura-17-arresti-50-indagati-emersi-legami-il-boss-michele-senese-6823b0f0-5292-11e7-a6f1-62717796370c.shtml.
Fiasco, M. (2011). Credito illegale e indebitamento patologico a Roma tra imprese e famiglie produttrici. www.rm.camcom.it.
Fiasco, M. (2019). Effetti di dieci anni di crisi sull'esposizione all'indebitamento patologico e al rischio di usura nelle province italiane. www.chiesadimilano.it/wp-content/uploads/2019/06/Relazione-di-Maurizio-Fiasco.pdf.
Filotto, U. (1997). L'usura e il sistema finanziario italiano. In D. Masciandro & A. Porta (eds), *L'usura in Italia* (pp. 139–165). EGEA.
Giuffrida, S. (2019). Lazio, l'usura è un'emergenza sociale: In 40 mila a rischio. *La Repubblica*, 20 May. https://roma.repubblica.it/cronaca/2019/05/20/news/lazio_e_allarme_usura_in_40_mila_a_rischio-226732394/?ref=search.
Guano. E. (2010). Taxpayers, thieves, and the state: Fiscal citizenship in contemporary Italy. *Ethnos*, 75(4), 377–401. https://doi.org/10.1080/00141844.2010.522246.
Herzfeld, M. (2009). *Evicted from eternity. The restructuring of modern Rome*. Chicago University Press. https://doi.org/10.7208/chicago/9780226329079.001.0001.
Il Giornale delle PMI. (2019). Continua la contrazione del credito alle imprese. www.giornaledellepmi.it/continua-la-contrazione-del-credito-alle-imprese/.
Il Sole 24 Ore. (2021). Istat: Nel 2020 calo occupazione "senza precedent": 456mila con il Covid. *Il Sole 24 Ore*, 12 March. www.ilsole24ore.com/art/istat-2020-calo-occupazione-senza-precedenti-456mila-il-covid-ADrqKiPB?refresh_ce=1.
ISTAT. (2020a). Censimento permanente delle imprese 2019: I primi risultati. www.istat.it/it/files/2020/02/Report-primi-risultati-censimento-imprese.pdf.
ISTAT. (2020b). Delitti denunciati dalle forze di polizia all'autorità giudiziaria. http://dati.istat.it/Index.aspx?DataSetCode=DCCV_DELITTIPS#.
ISTAT. (2020c). L'economia non osservata nei conti nazionali. Anni 2015–20. www.istat.it/it/files/2020/10/Economia-non-osservata-nei-conti-nazionali.pdf.
Ito, S. (2003). Microfinance and social capital: Does social capital help create good practice? *Development in Practice*, 13(4), 322–332. https://doi.org/10.1080/0961452032000112383.
Lanzara, F. (2020). Coronavirus: Razzante (Crst), "rischio boom criminalità economica dopo emergenza". *AdnKronos*, 18 March. www.adnkronos.com/razzante-crst-rischio-boom-criminalita-economica-dopo-emergenza-coronavirus_6mhkBXQS8fhZRfQsW72Q1h.
Legorano, G. (2019). Italian banks, long a drag on Europe, are making good on bad loans. *Wall Street Journal*, August 9. www.wsj.com/articles/italys-banks-ditch-bad-loans-but-vulnerabilities-remain-11565357638.
Libera. (2015). Mafie nel Lazio. www.regione.lazio.it/binary/rl_main/tbl_documenti/OSL_RA_mafie_lazio_23_03_2015.pdf.
Manco, R. (2013). Italo. [Video.] www.youtube.com/watch?v=Ptyf2uYdILE.

Martone, V. (2017). *Le mafie di mezzo. Mercati e reti criminali a Roma e nel Lazio.* Donzelli.
Masciandaro, D. (2001). In offense of usury laws: Microfoundations of illegal credit contracts. *European Journal of Law and Economics*, 12(3), 193–215. https://doi.org/10.1023/A:1012813724643.
Mayer, R. (2012). Loan sharks, interest-rate caps, and deregulation. *Washington and Lee Law Review*, 69(2), 807–848.
Medina, L., & Schneider, F. (2018). Shadow economies around the world: What did we learn over the last 20 years? IMF Working Paper. www.imf.org/en/Publications/WP/Issues/2018/01/25/Shadow-Economies-Around-the-World-What-Did-We-Learn-Over-the-Last-20-Years-45583.
Monizzi, F. M. (2018). Usura tra ieri, oggi e domani. www.baccarato.org/2019/02/11/usura-tra-ieri-oggi-e-domani/.
Mugellini, G. (2012). Le imprese vittime di criminalità in Italia. *Transcrime.* www.transcrime.it/wp-content/uploads/2013/11/16_Le_imprese_vittime_di_criminalit%C3%A0_in_Italia1.pdf.
OECD. (2017). *OECD economic surveys: Italy 2017.* OECD Publishing. www.oecd.org/economy/surveys/italy-2017-OECD-economic-survey-overview.pdf.
OECD. (2019). *OECD economic surveys: Italy 2019.* OECD Publishing. www.oecd.org/economy/surveys/Italy-2019-OECD-economic-survey-overview.pdf.
Pardo, I. (2000). Credit, entrepreneurship and the repayment of debt: Mismatched conceptions of legitimacy in Italy. *Self, Agency and Society*, 2(2), 51–87.
Pignatone, G., & Prestipino, M. (2015). Le mafie su Roma, la mafia di Roma. In E. Ciconte, F. Forgione, & I. Sales (eds), *Atlante delle Mafie*, vol. 3. (pp. 95–130). Rubbettino.
Regione Lazio. (2018). Mafie nel Lazio. Le infiltrazioni della criminalità organizzata nell'economia legale del Lazio. www.regione.lazio.it/binary/rl_osservatorio_legalita_sicurezza/tbl_news/Osservatorio_legalit__sicurezza_le_infiltrazione_criminalita_2018_Stampa_1_ok.pdf.
Regione Lazio. (2019). Mafie nel Lazio. IV Rapporto. www.regione.lazio.it/binary/rl_main/tbl_news/Notizia_report_mafie_lazio.pdf.
Savatteri, G., & Grignetti, F. (2015) *Mafia Capitale. L'atto di accusa della Procura di Roma.* Melampo.
Saviano, R. (2020). I soldi marci che divorano l'Italia onesta. *La Repubblica*, 20 May. www.repubblica.it/cronaca/2020/05/20/news/i_soldi_marci_che_divorano_l_italia_onesta-257115956/.
Saviano, R. (2021). L'usura al tempo del Covid: Così le mafie stanno soffocando l'economia. *Corriere della Sera*, 16 January. www.corriere.it/video-articoli/2021/01/16/cosi-l-usura-mafie-soffoca-l-economia/3953c852-5769-11eb-8f51-2cbbf1c2346f.shtml.
Savona, E., & Riccardi, M. (2015). *From illegal markets to legitimate businesses: The portfolio of organised crime in Europe.* Transcrime. www.transcrime.it/wp-content/uploads/2015/12/ocp.pdf.
Scaglione, A. (2014). Estimating the size of the loan sharking market in Italy. *Global Crime*, 15(1/2),77–92. https://doi.org/10.1080/17440572.2014.886035.
Senato della Repubblica. (1998). Risposte scritte ad interrogazioni. www.senato.it/service/PDF/PDFServer/DF/17789.pdf.
Spina, R., & Stefanizzi, S. (2007). *L'usura: Un servizio illegale offerto dalla città legale.* Bruno Mondadori.

Trocchia, N. (2019). *Casamonica: Viaggio nel mondo parallelo del clan che ha conquistato Roma*. UTET.
Turner, V. (1967). *The forest of symbols: Aspects of Ndembu ritual*. Cornell University Press.
Unioncamere. (2014). Studio conoscitivo sul fenomeno dell'usura. www.unioncamere.gov.it/P42A2417C189S123/on-line-lo–studio-conoscitivo-sul-fenomeno-dell-usura-.htm.
UPI (Unione Province Lazio). (2018). Rapporto 2018 sullo stato delle province del Lazio. www.un-industria.it/canale/studi-ricerche/notizia/76841/upi-lazio-e-eures-novembre-2018-rapporto-2018/.
Williams, C. (2014). Out of the shadows: A classification of economies by the size and character of their informal sector. *Work, Employment and Society*, 28(5), 735–753. https://doi.org/10.1177/0950017013501951.
World Bank. (2019a). Doing business 2020. Ranking. www.doingbusiness.org/content/dam/doingBusiness/pdf/db2020/Doing-Business-2020_rankings.pdf.
World Bank. (2019b). Economy profile of Italy. Doing business 2020. www.doingbusiness.org/content/dam/doingBusiness/country/i/italy/ITA.pdf.

5 Garbage

Managing liminal matter through multi-layered informalities

Introduction

Waste is liminal matter *par excellence*: the inevitable by-product of our daily lives that we constantly strive to keep separate and at a distance, where we are safe from its power to pollute (Douglas 2002).[1] Both symbolically valueless and a valuable commodity, it acts as a contestable marker between inside and out, clean and contaminating, useful and useless. What we consider to be "waste" and how we treat it are the outcomes of ambivalent, historically mutable, and often conflict-laden processes (Hawkins & Muecke, 2003; Lindner & Meissner, 2015; Scanlan, 2005). Naturalized as merely a technical component of urban management systems, the politics of waste in fact reveal processes of governance and planning that are far from neutral. How waste is constructed as a problem and the strategies that are implemented to contain and hide it are wedded to economic and political valuations about urban space and the social groups living and working in it. It is especially when the boundaries between cleanliness and disorder begin to leak, when the infrastructure that is supposed to make waste vanish efficiently shows its flaws, that hierarchies are most prominently displayed. Informal waste-related practices become visible, along with the taken-for-granted assumptions that underlie them.

Rome's waste management system has attracted condemnation from all sides for over a decade. Its residents view it as a key factor in the city's low quality of life and services (ACOS, 2020; ASPL, 2019). The international media regularly disseminate images globally of its streets filled with garbage (Horowitz, 2018; Roberts, 2019). Reports by environmental watchdogs identify it as one of the most waste-polluted locations in the country and one of the most prone to environmental crime (Legambiente, 2019a). The EU has sanctioned the Lazio region for failing to implement waste management plans (EC, 2008), for not respecting regulations on waste treatment in its biggest landfill (EC, 2013), and for repeatedly failing to address illegal waste dumping on its territory (EC, 2019a; EP, 2013). The city is exposed to cyclical "waste emergencies" whenever its fragile and precarious system becomes overwhelmed; for example, when one of its treatment plants is damaged or an agreement to export the waste

DOI: 10.4324/9780429353321-6

elsewhere comes to an end. These repeated moments of emergency are the periodic materializations of a structural dysfunctionality that has built up and crystallized for over half a century.

Since the 1960s, the city's waste management arena has become more tightly entangled with the urban economy and with its political system than ever before. It has become populated by actors at all levels of the city's social hierarchy, all of whom are affected, in different ways, by its multiple layers of ever-shifting and erratically implemented regulations. Rome therefore provides a useful case study for tracing the interconnections between actors' relative positions of power and their use of informal practices to navigate regulatory gaps and obstacles in order to advance or defend their interests. It also permits analysis of whether there are concatenations in these practices: whether the informalities of actors in dominant positions directly influence those at subordinate levels or vice versa. The aim is to map how actors of different standing in the field – its economic and bureaucratic elites, meso-level figures, and small-scale waste reclaimers – use the resources available to them to navigate and challenge the stakes of this crucial sector of urban governance.

The first section briefly outlines the historical development of the waste management field in Rome, identifying the processes by which positions of domination have become established. It highlights how elite actors in the post-war decades used multiple informal practices to consolidate their positions, and then traces how these have been affected by the arrival of external challenges since the early 2000s. Environmental legislation at the EU and national levels, and the spreading of an ethos of sustainability within civil society, have in fact significantly altered the symbolic value of waste-related practices. However, these developments have only partially translated into a more transparent and ecologically sound approach to waste reduction and disposal in Rome. The third section maps how chronic dysfunctionalities in legal waste management directly resulting from ongoing informal practices "from above" have created the conditions for lucrative illegal waste economies to thrive. The two have become as interdependent as are informalities with official practices at the other end of the rule-bending spectrum. The final section then focuses on the role of informal waste collectors and resellers within this chain of relationships, arguing that their gleaning and repurposing activities are actually in line with the EU's principles of waste prevention and reuse. The absence of any infrastructural and regulatory support from municipal institutions means, however, that these activities remain suspended in a condition of protracted lack of authorization, constantly exposed to legal crackdowns. This does not only perpetuate positions of weakness and vulnerability at the lowest level of the field. In politically strategic moments, it is actively used by the authorities to deprive poor urbanites of their most basic access to an income. Roma gleaners, in particular, are subjected to the symbolic violence of ethnicizing discourses and policies that construct them and their work as an urban threat. In response, they cultivate social capital both to maintain their livelihoods and to redefine the symbolic value of waste-related activities by harnessing pollution and sustainability tropes to reframe themselves as a resource for the city's future.

Historicizing waste and its power relations in Rome

Rome has struggled to deal effectively with the accumulation of solid waste in its streets ever since it became the great metropolis of antiquity. The ancient city did set the basis for an advanced and complex system of drainage and sewage that exists to this day and that allowed part of the population's biological waste and superficial urban debris to be flushed away (Davies, 2012; Hopkins, 2012; Koloski-Ostrow, 2015). However, household and production-related refuse appears to have always posed greater challenges. Throughout Rome's history, the authorities issued countless ordinances to try to govern where and how residents jettisoned their garbage and to regulate its removal from the city centre. Yet, just like the many edicts that sought to manage street trading (see chapter 3), these were only sporadically successful at best. Accounts from the Renaissance onwards convey a strong impression of streets covered in refuse of all types (Isabella et al., 1997; Roscioni, 2005). Although the Counter Reformation popes tried to enforce more effective street sanitizing methods (Rinne, 2012), there was no attempt to publicly organize garbage collection until the 17th century. Despite gradual improvements over time, though, the reach and effectiveness of these services remained only partial until the country's unification.

The city's new role as capital from 1870, and the intense population growth that it sparked, required rapid change. Waste collection and disposal, which had previously been outsourced to a collection of small private firms, was now taken over by the municipality and extended greatly. With the start of the 20th century, some processes were also mechanized, but these developments in engineering came to a halt with the onset of World War I (Isabella et al., 1997). Rather than advance and rationalize the system further, the Fascist regime that followed reprivatized much of the service, reintroducing the problems of inefficiency and fragmentation that had plagued garbage collection under papal rule. World War II made the situation even more dysfunctional: the city's sanitation infrastructure was heavily damaged and, by the end of the conflict, the municipality owed vast debts to its private contractors. The financial situation was so critical that the city could not bring waste disposal facilities back under public management. Most of the system consequently remained in the hands of six private companies, although day-to-day street cleaning activities did get placed under local government control (Rigon, 2005). The intention was to eventually return the entire sector to the city authorities, but this goal was never achieved. The municipality's inability to manage its finances endured and private contracts were thus repeatedly extended until 1959. Sorting of waste was still being carried out mostly manually, in fields, with no safety and hygiene precautions, and the equipment used for collection was similarly outdated (Bettini Prosperi et al., 2003).

The economic boom years of the late 1950s and 1960s presented the critical moment in which the city should have planned a technologically advanced and integrated refuse management infrastructure and a clear regulatory framework to order it. Rome's population had by then reached over two million and its consumption patterns were radically changing with mass production of disposable goods. The vast amount of packaging that accompanied rising consumerism was generating waste on an unprecedented scale. However, the city administration did not come up with a suitable long-term response. It simply continued to add services and infrastructure in a piecemeal and disjointed fashion, coherent with the lack of long-term strategy with which it was responding to the unplanned and unauthorized development of entire neighbourhoods at the time (see chapter 2, this volume, and Rigon, 2005). In the immediate term, Rome also needed to face the logistical difficulties of hosting the 1960 Olympic games and the massive influx of visitors it would attract.

This convergence of institutional incapacity and the critical need for speedy solutions set the mould for how the field of waste management would be structured for the next half-century. The financial and political stakes were now at their highest as an industrial scale system for treatment and disposal became indispensable. In 1960, therefore, the municipality issued an invitation to tender for private companies equipped with their own treatment and incineration facilities to transport and eliminate the city's burgeoning waste. Three of the four companies selected were under the control of a single local entrepreneur, Manlio Cerroni (Bettini Prosperi et al., 2003). The fourth was a public consortium, SORAIN, which proved unable to develop the necessary infrastructure and lagged far behind its private competitors for the following two decades. This resulted, in essence, in the entire sector being dominated by one private actor. Subsequent attempts, in the mid-1980s, to expand the public sector's role failed dramatically and much of the remaining public infrastructure and personnel was placed under the umbrella of Cerroni's private firms (Rigon, 2005). Meanwhile, Cerroni had been establishing a landfill site in a disused quarry in Malagrotta that became authorized, in 1975, to take in by-products of the meat industry. In 1984 the city issued a contract for all unrecyclable refuse to be dumped there, consolidating Cerroni's private monopoly of waste disposal. Although garbage collection in the streets returned to municipal management in 1973, other companies within Cerroni's conglomerate subsequently participated in various public-private-partnerships, further cementing his centrality in the city's expanding refuse management system.[2]

On the international and national levels, awareness was beginning to spread about the need to recover reusable waste. Rising pressure from central government to implement selection and treatment methods was ignored in Rome, however, and most of the material dumped in Malagrotta continued to be raw and potentially hazardous waste. The primary reason for this inaction was financial: Cerroni was charging the municipality very modest fees for the service. Inevitably, with no pressure from the public sector to invest and innovate, this led to the machinery becoming outdated and ever less efficient. The private monopoly nevertheless continued to make a profit. The far more labour-intensive and less lucrative part of the waste system (street-cleaning, collection, and transportation of refuse) instead remained under the municipality. The public garbage company AMNU (now AMA) repeatedly argued that it should take over disposal to achieve economies of scale across a unified refuse management scheme, implementing waste-to-energy and reuse technologies that would offset the expense in the long term (Rigon, 2005). Instead, Rome's dependency on the private landfill continued uninterruptedly until the late 1990s, despite clear European Community legislation (Directive 1991/156/EEC) requiring environmentally safe disposal and extensive recycling. In fact, the Malagrotta site grew to become Europe's biggest landfill, eventually covering 240 hectares of land and taking in 4,500 to 5,000 tons of waste per day – at a cost of 44 million euro a year – until it was closed in 2013, having long since exceeded its capacity (CPI, 2011).[3]

Two developments in the late 1990s plunged this arrangement into crisis. In 1997, national legislation (Decreto Legislativo, 5 febbraio 1997, n. 22) was introduced to implement the European regulations. The regions were now delegated the task of formulating waste management in accordance with the new law. Their responsibility covered all levels of the waste hierarchy, from disincentivizing the production of refuse to decontaminating polluted sites to identifying locations and treatment methods for new sites. Constructing an integrated system of sorting and recovery, would – it was hoped – result in only minimal residues needing to be dumped in landfills or incinerators. This legislation instead laid bare the critical situation that had by then developed in the capital through the failure of successive administrations to produce any significant alternative to the Malagrotta landfill. Meanwhile, preparations were underway for the Catholic Jubilee of 2000 which would see the arrival of millions of pilgrims to Rome. The crisis was such that the Italian government declared a state of emergency for the city and its province in February 1999, intended to last for a year. Instead, the emergency measures were extended yearly until 2008 and, from 2002, were expanded to include the rest of the region. The president of Lazio was nominated extraordinary commissioner, tasked with designing an effective waste management strategy and identifying sites on which to build energy-producing plants to replace the outdated and inadequate infrastructure. Despite nine years of this emergency management, though, no plan was successfully developed to move beyond the reliance on landfills.

Given these chronic failures, in 2007 the European Court of Justice ruled that Lazio was operating in violation of EU law. In 2012, therefore, the region devised a new plan, setting itself the ambitious goal of bringing the proportion of Rome's recycled waste to 60%. Reality remained far behind formal declarations, though: by 2012 only 22.6% of waste was recycled (ISPRA, 2014) and to this day Rome produces well below those targets (an estimated 45% in 2020: ACOS, 2020). Although the number of sorting and selection plants for recyclable waste gradually increased, no waste-to-energy plants were built.[4] The unusable residues therefore continued to flow into the region's growing number of landfills. By 2011, EU and national legislation had banned any untreated waste from being deposited in such sites, but in Lazio the practice continued. This triggered another European Commission infringement procedure in 2011, confirmed by a European Court of Justice ruling in 2014 (C-323/13).[5] A new state of emergency was consequently declared, again with the hope of unblocking the system's persistent problems.

Malagrotta had reached full capacity by 2004 and was slated for closure in 2011 but repeated deferrals by the region allowed it to continue operating until October 2013. Its two mechanical biological treatment (MBT) plants are still in operation today, though, processing about half of the city's unsorted rubbish. The closure of the landfill, after forty years of existence, has made the dysfunctionality of Rome's waste system even more evident. Regional and municipal authorities cyclically air the possibility of creating new landfill sites or reopening decommissioned ones, but communities around Rome have so far vocally resisted them.[6] It is striking that the governing institutions continue to re-present the same stop-gap proposals. This illustrates their ongoing inability to devise a sustainable strategy for Rome's environmental future or to substantially reduce waste production in the present. In fact, an estimated million tons a year are still being incinerated or deposited in landfills (Legambiente Lazio, 2018). The city continues to lack adequate reuse and recycling centres and can only manage one third of its unsorted rubbish (Pelati, 2017). The rest is therefore treated in other parts of Lazio and Abruzzo and then exported to 62 sites around the country and abroad for final disposal. The cost of doing so comes close to 100 million euro per year.[7] Its existing plants are operating at maximum capacity. Consequently, any setback – such as a fire that destroyed the Salaria MBT plant in December 2018 – produces backlogs and garbage piling up on the streets (Figure 5.1). Ambitious new waste management plans were announced by the region in 2019 with higher goals for recycling, initiatives for circular economies, and requiring each sub-area of Lazio to become self-sufficient in its waste disposal (Regione Lazio, 2019). By mid-2021, however, there was no evidence that the situation had significantly improved. In fact, the closure of another landfill triggered yet another crisis and the build-up of waste on the streets, while the region and municipality accused each other of inaction (Scarlino, 2021).

The material impacts of this history on the lives of today's Romans are firstly financial. City residents pay some of the highest waste taxes in the country and the municipality is engaged in ongoing legal battles with Cerroni. So far, it has been ordered to reimburse him 92 million euro for past unpaid services (Salvaggiulo, 2017). The second, more worrying impact, concerns public health. The firm that ran the Malagrotta landfill was placed under investigation in 2019 for environmental disaster (*disastro ambientale*), accused of not treating the leachate and thereby contaminating the groundwater (Radio Radicale, 2019). Numerous medical studies over the years have recorded high rates of ill-health among residents living near the site (Alagia &

Figure 5.1 Uncollected garbage outside a health facility

Iervolino, 2011; CDCA, 2013). However, its full environmental impact has yet to be clearly measured and made public. In fact, the region never imposed a cohesive regime of environmental authorizations and checks on Malagrotta (CPI, 2017). This negligence was part of a wider pattern of regulatory gaps through which informal practices were able to flourish, as the next section demonstrates further.

Political economies of waste informality

The legal history of waste management in Rome is extremely complex and the brief overview provided above barely hints at the myriad court cases and technical and judicial investigations that have been initiated since the 1980s. Nevertheless, it shows that public institutions enabled and perpetuated the domination of the field by a single private actor. This was achieved through multiple and systemic informal practices, some of which blurred into full illegality. From the 1970s onwards, for example, none of the disposal contracts were allocated via competitive public calls for tender (CPI, 2017). In the early years of the field's development, the lack of expansive rules concerning safe waste management allowed the private sector to establish its power with few state-imposed restrictions. Its informal practices at this stage were "complementary" (Altrock, 2016), providing necessary services while the local authorities postponed any long-term planning and regulation. However, as EU and national waste laws were passed, they were enforced in Rome with years of delay. When they were eventually implemented, local bureaucrats applied them only partially, occasionally using "bizarre" and "at times distorted" interpretations of the law (CPI, 2017, pp. 13, 19). This was not a benign form of "supplementary" informality, making up for the state's inability to implement its own regulations (Altrock, 2016). It was a "calculated" informality, where the authorities' systematic by-passing of higher-level regulations was purposive. This was non-planning as "a planning regime" (Roy, 2009, p. 80): informality used as an instrument to allocate and accumulate resources benefitting only a select group of highly positioned individuals.

A few examples of the stratagems through which actors, private and public, manoeuvred around the rules suggest that elite-level informal practices became a common, taken-for-granted way of operating. Not the exception, but the rule. There is evidence, for instance, of Cerroni having repeatedly carried out works in his plants without the necessary authorizations, in the expectation of post hoc formalization (Bonaccorsi et al., 2012: CDCA, 2013; Iervolino & Tozzi, 2013). Most notably, his company dug a new landfill site intended to replace Malagrotta after its closure; in doing so, the geological barrier protecting the water table from contamination was destroyed. No geological study had been carried out before the works were initiated, despite the requirements of EU law (CPI, 2017). Although the venture was ultimately blocked, the fact that Cerroni was confident enough to make such expensive infrastructural investments without authorization indicates that the non-application of rules by the authorities was systemic and predictable. In fact, the authorities failed to carry out various mandatory technical studies at Malagrotta and, in cases when they were done, several technicians had clear conflicts of interest due to prior relations with Cerroni's firms (Iervolino & Tozzi, 2013; CPI, 2017). This casual approach to monitoring hydrogeological safety was not limited to Malagrotta. Various other potential landfill sites were approved without the necessary *in situ* tests having been performed, in one case risking major contamination of a river, an aqueduct, and local agriculture (Bonaccorsi et al., 2012; Iervolino & Tozzi, 2013).

Another case is emblematic of the subordination of the public good to private interests. In 2010, the region ordered that waste shredders be installed in Malagrotta and in an AMA-owned plant. The purpose was to exploit a legal loophole allowing a new code to be applied to shredded waste, permitting this untreated refuse to be exported out of the region, contrary to EU regulations (CPI, 2017). A parliamentary investigation subsequently noted that neither project was assigned by open tender. Moreover, AMA "did nothing to deliver on its [own] project" (CPI, 2017, p. 89). In fact, it agreed to transport a guaranteed minimum daily quantity of garbage to Cerroni's site at above-market rates,[8] thereby ensuring a constant flow of money to the private firm while having no incentive to use its own recycling infrastructure (CPI, 2017). This example displays how all parties involved violated regulations: the region's own rule breaking enabled Cerroni's firm and AMA to ignore its orders and simultaneously bypass legal processes for public procurement. All this to the benefit of Cerroni's enterprises and the disadvantage of taxpayers and public health.

Much blurring of boundaries between legality and illegality was facilitated by the emergency administration that ran the waste system for ten years. Under this type of regime, ordinary decision-making processes, which follow clear legal protocols, are suspended. The purpose is to permit the authorities to implement urgent solutions when faced with calamities such as earthquakes. In Lazio, though, it effectively created a state of exception allowing the institutions to operate outside formally established regulations. The special administration was not used to restructure a dysfunctional waste system, but to create a condition of protracted legal liminality within which to expand institutional freedom of action. This informality from above prolonged the dominance of apex actors, entrenching power hierarchies of the field, despite intense external pressures to destabilize this structure.[9]

Clearly, Cerroni benefitted financially from his position: he was allegedly making about 80 million euro a year before Malagrotta was closed (Iervolino & Tozzi, 2013). It is less evident what advantages this presented for the public officials involved. Legal charges brought against Cerroni in 2014 claimed that he had created a criminal association, together with several regional bureaucrats, to maintain his monopoly. The group was also accused of waste trafficking and fraud. However, the 2018 verdict found all the defendants not guilty of criminal association and no evidence of bribery was identified (Tribunale Penale di Roma, 2019).[10] It appears, therefore, that the informal practices that bolstered Cerroni's dominance were not aimed at functionaries' personal enrichment but had political goals. Since any initiative to develop new waste treatment plants inevitably generates public outcry and its harnessing by political opponents, the prolonged institutional inaction can be understood as a tactic to maintain political capital in the short term. Voter hostility was thereby averted and the electoral costs of the system's accumulating inadequacies were displaced onto future politicians. The priority was to channel the city's scarce financial capital away from electorally unrewarding investments in waste infrastructure, towards sectors where public demand was more pressing and vocal (Iervolino & Tozzi, 2013). It should be remembered that Rome has always struggled under immense municipal debts accumulated through the post-war decades, resulting in a system of public services rarely in line with the needs and expectations of its residents. Calculations over the highest possible convertibility of economic capital into political capital became critical in these circumstances.

The trajectory of Cerroni's monopoly further exemplifies how informalities may become vectors of different types of capital and the means of their conversion. The initial economic capital developed by his enterprises in the 1960s and 1970s made his infrastructure indispensable as the city's needs grew, expanding the ties between his companies and public bodies. The municipality's failed attempt to run waste disposal publicly in the 1980s further raised the value of the private sector as the only functional alternative. Cerroni's economic capital translated over the years into vast social capital underpinning his personal and often close dealings with officials at all levels (Cerroni, 2014; CPI, 2017; Tribunale Ordinario di Roma, 2008; Tribunale Penale di Roma, 2019). This, in turn, converted into symbolic capital: he consistently presented himself as the only person able to resolve the city's waste-related problems, even writing to the president of the Republic in 2018 to offer his intervention in the latest garbage crisis (Scarlino, 2018). This view that he was indispensable to the city was widely shared. For example, when he was acquitted in 2018 of the charges of criminal organization, the judges declared that the authorities had turned to him not for reasons of corruption but because of his organizational abilities and the size of his enterprises. They added that his decades-long experience in the field had made him the only player able to avert an escalating environmental crisis in the late 1990s and early 2000s (Tribunale Penale di Roma, 2019). Temporal capital was thereby explicitly acknowledged as a significant element in his domination of the field, producing symbolic capital that circularly fuelled his wealth.

Legacies of informality in a restructured field

The system was finally destabilized in 2013 through a combination of legal action by EU bodies and the election of two mould-breaking politicians as mayor (Ignazio Marino) and regional president (Nicola Zingaretti). Looming EU fines now threatened unprecedented financial damage to the region and the municipality. This dramatically altered the valuations of the field, destroying the symbolic capital of actors who had previously controlled it through informal negotiations. Political legitimacy was now with those willing to apply the law. With Malagrotta closed, and the city's dependency on it interrupted, major legal investigations were finally undertaken. New far-reaching national legislation to curb environmental crimes (Legge 22 maggio 2015, n. 68) added further pressure. Cerroni has now been indicted for running the Rocca Cencia shredding plant without authorization and generating undue profits of up to a million euro a week over a three-year period (Affari Italiani, 2019; Izzo, 2018). He is also accused of having dumped untreated waste in Malagrotta from 2006 to 2013. The charges are of waste trafficking, fraud, and abuse of office. Co-defendants include managers of his plants but also a former director of the municipal waste company, AMA, and the head of Rome province's Environmental Department. The case is ongoing. In 2017, his main holding company, E. Giovi Srl, was placed under judicial administration – a measure that is usually used in anti-mafia investigations – until the case is concluded.

The field of waste politics has expanded to include numerous civil society organizations and NGOs that campaign vocally against waste-related informalities and illegalities, using social media to amplify their presence. Their public legitimacy is such that several have actively participated in recent legal enquiries.[11] This does not mean, however, that the field's positions of power have been entirely overturned, given that Cerroni's treatment plants are still essential to the current disposal system. Nevertheless, his symbolic and social capital are notably weakened. For example, in 2016 a municipal councillor for the environment and former consultant to AMA, Paola Muraro, was forced to resign following allegations – and media outcries – that she had promoted his interests.[12] Although the city's waste system continues to be very precarious, with AMA remaining financially fragile and stop-gap tactics still predominating over long-term solutions, recourse to calculated informalities of the scale witnessed in the 1990s and early 2000s appears to be waning as political and judicial attention remains focused on it.

Nevertheless, informalities have endured at the meso-level, especially channelled through opaque operations within AMA. For example, investigations in 2010 found that many high-powered positions in the company had been allocated to close associates of the mayor, Gianni Alemanno, through nepotistic hiring practices that bypassed transparent recruitment regulations (Peronaci, 2010). The scandals echoed similar ones in the public transport company, ATAC, indicating that such informalities were operating across different public agencies. In 2012, eight top managers of AMA, including its CEO, were indicted for having hired 841 employees who lacked the required qualifications.[13] Forty-one others were issued post-dated contracts to circumvent new hiring rules (La Repubblica, 2012). Hundreds of other individuals were employed through temping agencies, allegedly to similarly avoid competitive procedures (Capponi & Menicucci, 2010). Such a large-scale recruitment drive was widely interpreted as a means to build a reservoir of votes for the incumbent candidates at the next election (Peronaci, 2010). Subsequent investigations revealed that at least one labour union (CISL) was also involved in a well-structured system of bribes for hiring and promotion within the company (Peronaci, 2012, 2017a). This was, in short, a transversal system that included citizens, private firms, unionists, and public employees across different levels of the field. The levels of corruption, however, went much further. The former CEO of AMA, Franco Panzironi, has been found guilty of not only nepotistic hiring practices but also external involvement with the criminal group commonly dubbed *Mafia Capitale*. He was found guilty of corruption and of helping the organization obtain lucrative public works projects through illicit means. Although such extreme cases of rule-breaking have been uprooted from the company and structural reorganization is underway, from a financial point of view its chronic mismanagement has cost the city and its residents dearly: investigations by the Court of Auditors (*Corte dei Conti*) indicate that AMA managers failed to transfer 240 million euro of taxes to the municipality (Solani, 2020). Rather than force repayment of the funds, the city government has agreed to give the firm a further 150 million euro to help it avoid bankruptcy (de Ghantuz Cubbe, 2021). These judicial investigations have been fundamental in highlighting some of the ways in which systemic rule-bending and breaking within a public company became a channel for advancing the interests of a variety of actors. Decades of strategic blind-eye-turning by the institutions that should have monitored its activities have resulted in a company close to collapse and propped up by public money.

From informalities to waste crimes

Both the parliamentary commission on waste illegalities (CPI, 2017) and the environmental watchdog Legambiente (2019b) have declared that the long-term mismanagement of waste in Lazio has fostered major vulnerability to crimes. So far, there is no evidence that organized criminal groups have infiltrated the official waste management system in Rome, unlike in traditional mafia territories (Martone, 2019). Nevertheless, Lazio follows immediately behind the four Southern regions in terms of frequency of environmental crimes of all types (7.7% of the total). Strikingly, it ranks first, nationally, for those committed through bribing public officials (Legambiente, 2019b). Waste crimes are the most common typology of environmental illegalities in Italy and among the most lucrative, worth approximately 2.8 billion euro annually. Lazio comes sixth in regional rankings of waste crimes, with Rome third of all the provinces in the country. Investigations into such crimes have risen dramatically throughout the country since the late 1990s, partly due to intensified law enforcement attention but also because the phenomenon is growing thanks to the immense profits it can generate (Legambiente, 2019b).

In Lazio, persistent informalities from above have directly opened opportunities for illegal activities at the levels below. In particular, the need to transport most garbage out the region, combined with a weak system for monitoring the firms and identifying the content of their cargo, has produced multiple avenues for circumventing the law.[14] The lack of effective territorial surveillance adds a further problem, exposing the region to widespread illegal dumping and burning of refuse. Much of this occurs on a systematic scale: private waste disposal and recycling companies are alleged to produce fraudulent documentation that mis-certifies the special waste as ordinary refuse (Legambiente, 2019b). Alternatively, they dump it in disposal plants while declaring that it has been recycled. The main purpose is to undercut the fees charged by firms that treat the material in accordance with environmental legislation (Legambiente, 2019b). Much of this mechanism is invisible to the public eye. Nevertheless, there is also a parallel system of unauthorized open-air dumps around the countryside and in peri-urban areas. These are mostly accumulations of construction debris (including asbestos), electronics, tyres, and bulky domestic waste. Approximately 1,000 such sites existed around Rome in 2021, according to a map produced by Legambiente (Roma Today, 2021). Numerous less conspicuous dumps are also under investigation by environmental police forces, such as underground caves filled with discarded engine oil or with abandoned plastic sheeting used in the cultivation of mushrooms.[15] In 2014, excavations by ARPA (the regional environmental protection body) in a field in eastern Rome where crops were being cultivated, revealed a 1.5m-thick layer of pharmaceutical, medical, and cosmetic waste. Its depth indicated that the dumping had occurred systematically over many years (Belli et al., 2015).

One of the most pressing concerns is that of electrical and electronic waste, some of which appears to be methodically "re-routed towards a parallel illegal disposal chain" through systematic use of fraudulent accounting (CPI, 2017, p. 10). These are corporate crimes (Legambiente, 2019b), driven by the financial interests of legal firms positioned at the meso-levels of Rome's political economy of waste. Law enforcement agents believe that much of the problem originates with major retail chains for electrical and household appliances that are obliged to take back customers' used equipment. In return for subsidies, they must have the appliances disposed of according to Italy's e-waste legislation. Instead, it appears that some of the disposal companies hired by these outlets carry out illegal dumping to bypass the high costs of safe demolition.[16] That this occurs on a substantial scale is evidenced by the periodic detection of large sites such as a 60-hectare area in the Aniene valley containing hundreds of dismantled refrigerators (Bisbiglia & Gennaro, 2018).

By law, such sites must be decontaminated by the authorities when they are on public land or on private property if the owners are unable to do so. However, the historic build-up of institutional incapacity and lack of resources has resulted in many such dumps being left untouched "even for decades" (CPI 2017, p. 204). In some cases, AMA has received funds to sanitize them but has failed to do so, often without being sanctioned (see for example De Cicco & Mozzetti, 2019). The macro-history of dysfunctional application of the law and short-sighted financial (non)planning discussed in previous sections have thus produced a terrain in which multiple other forms of rule-breaking thrive with limited counteraction. This interconnection between institutional informalities and environmental crimes is structural and protracted. Just as informalities develop out of the cracks and contradictions of formality, so criminal activity flourishes best where institutions' capacity to regulate and enforce has become eroded over time. Indeed, Lazio and Rome's high positions in the rankings of environmental crime are not a recent or passing phenomenon; they have been among the most critical areas in the country since at least 2010.[17] The consequences of protracted waste informalities thus persist long term.

Ethnicization and the social hierarchies of waste

A further layer in the social hierarchies of waste has emerged from this intertwining of waste crimes with institutional neglect of environmental hazards. Many of Rome's illegal dumps are in immediate proximity to publicly built Roma camps. As chapter 2 outlined, these are ethnically concentrated and socially excluded reservations, often positioned close to industrial plants and far from public services. Residents face a variety of grave environmental problems that compound precarious health conditions linked to high poverty levels. Among these is the systematic dumping of construction debris and e-waste outside the fences by firms that often pay a self-proclaimed camp "boss" for permission (Belli et al., 2015). Some of the residents then dismantle the appliances, burning through the plastic and insulation materials to retrieve metals which they sell on to scrapyards. Although burning is only carried out by a small number of camp residents, it exposes the entire community and nearby neighbourhoods to toxic smoke. Since 2017 the frequency of such fires has provoked intense campaigns by media and residents' committees, resulting in heightened law enforcement attention. The fines and confiscations have reduced the fires but have not resolved their two underlying causes. Economic discrimination against Roma persists, leaving them with few alternatives to selling recovered goods (see chapter 3), including metals. Moreover, no large-scale inquiries into systematic dumping by firms have been carried out, so the practice continues.

Nevertheless, a 2019 investigation into the destination of some metals unveiled the existence of a criminal network composed of residents of three camps, the non-Roma owners of a scrapyard that fraudulently documented the metals and resold them at a profit of 400,000 euro, and the driver of the lorries that collected the materials from the camps and delivered them to the demolition yard (Fiano & Frignani, 2019). In public discourse, such illegal metal trading networks are routinely described in ethnicized terms, for instance: "over the years a fully-fledged supply chain has developed, run by these subjects of Romani ethnicity who make sizeable incomes from it" (CPI, 2017, p. 10).[18] As the 2019 case showed, such chains are in fact made up of diverse actors operating at various levels of the local economy, many of them non-Roma benefitting financially from Roma's poverty and their relegation to isolated locations where dumping and dismantling can easily be carried out. Moreover, many camp residents are aware of the health hazards that these practices expose them to and, in some cases, protest vocally against them. The community discussed in the next section, for example, filmed trucks illegally dumping waste by their homes and successfully convinced the borough to temporarily install surveillance cameras, achieving an important step in their right to environmental safeguarding. Here, residents' long-established relationships with local officials were effective in focusing attention on a problem which inhabitants of other camps complain is persistently ignored by the authorities. It is therefore clear that social capital is equally essential to Roma's participation in waste economies as it is to obtaining rare institutional protections. Despite repeated promises by Rome's municipality over the last twenty years to provide Roma with avenues for legal and safe employment, these have never materialized. Many therefore continue working in this dangerous and illegal sector despite the risks.

While Roma are widely constructed as the source of environmental problems in the city, there is little parallel recognition that they are frequently exposed to environmental dangers of a more structural nature. For example, the Via di Salone camp was built by the municipality on a disused quarry where waste had been dumped illegally for years, and next to a former GPL storage site contaminated with heavy metals and hydrocarbons (Belli et al., 2015). A few hundred metres away was an incinerator of toxic and hazardous waste owned by the multinational firm BASF (Associazione 21 luglio, 2014). By the time it was shut down in 2016, the population of the nearby camp had reached 1,200 inhabitants. The closure of the incinerator was triggered by the company's repeated failure to implement mandatory environmental monitoring, and evidence that the area's groundwater had been poisoned (Belli et al., 2015). Epidemiological studies found that neighbourhood residents had higher than average cancer rates, diseases of the central nervous system, and heart malformations at birth (Dipartimento di Epidemiologia del Servizio Sanitario Regionale, 2015). Similarly, the Barbuta camp was rebuilt in 2012 to house around five hundred Roma. Located under the landing path of Ciampino airport, it was next to another historic hazardous waste dump which was only superficially cleansed before construction began (Belli et al., 2015). A third case of institutional complicity in exposing Roma to environmental hazards emerged in a judicial investigation of 2016. This revealed that a building contractor who had received public funds to clean three other municipally owned camps instead buried asbestos and toxic waste there (Pitoni, 2016), doubly profiting by saving on legal waste disposal fees. The inquiry also pointed to entrenched corrupt relations between the contractor and some municipal officials. These cases are emblematic of informalities as a system of communicating vessels: at the top level, thirty years of informal or illegal management of Roma camps (chapter 2) have fused with even longer-term institutional failure to coherently implement waste legislation. This has produced a vast grey space in which law-breaking by private firms has thrived. Although these investigations are evidence of some institutional attempts to address the phenomenon, many other hazardous situations in and around camps have been ignored unless the health risks have concerned other, non-Roma, city residents.

Waste-reclaiming and prospects for a circular economy

Roma's spatial relegation to valueless and often contaminated wasteland and their widespread poverty are both cause and consequence of the entrenched symbolic violence through which they continue to be constructed as pollutants, dehumanized as a biological and moral threat to the urban social body.[19] Elsewhere I have shown how discriminatory public policies have repeatedly been accompanied by rhetorics portraying hazardous conditions in camps as evidence of an essentialized Roma culture or biology (Clough Marinaro, 2014, 2018). A circular logic follows: Roma live in dirty, disease-ridden places because they themselves are dirty and polluting and must therefore be kept at a safe distance from clean society, in the dirty non-spaces of the city. They are frequently referred to through faecal imagery, but also as rats and other vermin (Clough Marinaro, 2014). A common trope in political and media discourse defines camps as "discariche a cielo aperto" (open-air rubbish dumps) and their removal as "bonifica" (reclamation or decontamination).[20] Such images do not distinguish between the human residents of the camps and the garbage they allegedly surround themselves with. They also extend beyond housing, to Roma's livelihoods. In fact, the eviction of Roma traders from the Porta Portese flea market discussed in chapter 3 hinged on repeated accusations that they were selling "literally garbage recovered from dumpsters" (Martelli, 2007).

It is often suggested that the centuries-old stigmatization and ongoing discrimination against Roma communities in Italy has isolated them from mainstream economies. Their historic positioning at the lowest levels of the social hierarchy certainly burdens them with massive constraints to social mobility. This does not mean, however, that they are disconnected from local and global economic flows and the social networks through which those trades are organized. On the contrary, as chapter 3 underlined, they exert agency, adapting to and engaging with economic and political developments and opportunities in the city, activating and expanding their social and cultural capital to maintain financial autonomy. Moreover, they use material waste and its mobile discursive meanings as a resource through which they attempt to subvert the social order and its value systems. The next section presents an ethnographic discussion of the informal/illegal waste salvaging of some Roma traders, unpacking the close connections that exist between this apparently marginal activity and the broader political economies of waste. The analysis does not consider these to be ethnic-specific forms of income generation. Rather, it draws from scholarship that demonstrates how socially marginalized groups around the world identify and capitalize on niches that emerge within value chains and markets (Agamuthu, 2010; Gidwani & Reddy, 2011; Guillard & Roux, 2014; Rutkowski & Rutkowski, 2015; Storey et al., 2015). In some contexts, such workers are also successful in demanding rights and recognition of their labour (Machado-Borges, 2015; Schurman et al., 2017).

That waste picking is not an "ethnic" practice is confirmed by its marked rise in many Italian cities, including Rome, since the economic crisis of 2008. Impoverished Italians and migrants of all backgrounds are resorting to gleaning what they can from garbage containers for personal use or resale: food, metals, reusable electronics, and household goods (Scarpa, 2011; Masia, 2016). The spread of this practice is an indicator of Italy's ongoing difficulties in addressing the economic needs of its long-term poor population (ISTAT, 2020). In 2017, Rome's municipality responded to the situation by transforming what was previously an informal activity, subject to unclear regulations and generally tolerated, into an illegal one. It introduced fines for pickers, provoking criticism from civil society associations for further aggravating the economic precarity of these actors.[21] Since these provisions do not alleviate the poverty that underpins the phenomenon, they appear to have had little effect. Indeed, as the discussion below shows, some Roma who have worked in this sector for decades are diversifying their sources of income in response to rising competition. At the same time, little has been done by Rome's public authorities to foster a legal regeneration and reuse economy, in contrast with cities such as Milan, Brescia, and Turin, where municipalities have worked with NGOs to create spaces for donation and exchange of reusable goods to benefit poor residents.[22] This negligence is doubly striking given that waste reduction and reuse are positioned high on the EU's hierarchy for sustainable waste management, and recovery of metals and electronic components is of particular importance in the EU's Waste Framework Directive (EC, 2019b, EC, n.d.). The more recent European Green Deal has placed even greater emphasis on developing a circular economy that "work[s] for people, regions and cities" (EC, 2020).

Artisanal-level waste gleaning has been demonstrated, in countries as varied as Brazil and Spain, to be a sustainable, environmentally low-impact means of advancing a circular economy while producing demarginalizing work for low-income groups (Cattaneo, 2017; Rutkowski & Rutkowski, 2015). In Italy, it is estimated that 500,000 tons of materials currently destroyed as waste could be retrieved and reused if a functional system were in place (CdD, 2018). This would significantly reduce the costs and ecological damage that regions such as Lazio continue to generate by exporting large quantities of garbage. For recovery methods to be effective, gleaners would need to be allocated basic work and storage facilities and minimal infrastructure for sorting and cleaning the goods. The extensive social networks that Roma and other salvagers have built up over the years could, if supported institutionally, become an important asset. However, Rome and Lazio have not provided any facilities or incentives, despite strong pressure from environmental groups. Instead, the EU's regulations on hazardous materials have been applied in ways that severely restrict possibilities for lawful recovery and resale by small-scale collectors.

The challenges are particularly complex for those who collect scrap metals, as many Roma have done for decades. Since 2015, metal traders have been required to implement expensive and complex quality management procedures to monitor and certify that the materials they resell comply with EU criteria and document this conformity in all transactions.[23] They must also record where and from whom they obtained each item. Thus, a salvager who collects some old lamps from a dumpster and disused construction materials from a building site must document the contents of the dumpster, provide a legal receipt to the construction firm, and certify the purity of metals and other components. In addition, all salvagers must open a legal garbage collection firm, register with the chamber of commerce, and file for a financially burdensome tax status whose bureaucratic complexity is such that hiring expensive tax consultants often becomes unavoidable. These requirements are unrealistic for most gleaners. They are consequently forced to operate illegally and at constant risk of arrest and the confiscation of their vehicles and materials. The obstacles also enhance tensions and inequalities among groups, reinforcing hierarchies by effectively only allowing rich traders to regularize their status. While Italy's cumbersome implementation of EU waste recovery rules has affected independent salvagers nationally (Palumbo, 2016), in Rome its application appears to have directly targeted Roma, with police periodically instructed to monitor the roads near camps in what may be considered a form of ethnic profiling (Associazione 21 luglio, 2016). For metal collectors, the situation has been aggravated by a parallel set of crackdowns on scrap yards, making it very difficult for unregistered traders to sell there (Roma Capitale, 2014). This reduction in sales outlets, coupled with the rise in competition among metal traders, has caused the resale value of scrap iron to halve from around 13 cents/kg to 7 cents/kg over the last decade.

Strategies of sustainable waste recovery between illegality and informality

To explore more closely how these macro-level forces have affected small-scale gleaners, I draw on my fieldwork since the mid-1990s to focus on three extended families living in an unauthorized camp. During this quarter-century, I have visited those families at least once every six months, although often much more intensively. The account that follows is based on our many conversations about their changing financial and employment circumstances, together with my observations of their gleaning work. Over that time, these reclaimers have diversified their trades from metals to second-hand commodities of all types in response to the shifting legal barriers and market forces. To do so, they have exploited and expanded their well-established social networks and logistical and spatial techniques for sourcing goods. Most of the families living in the camp refuse to burn plastics due to the health risks involved and a reluctance to attract the kind of neighbourhood protests and police incursions seen elsewhere. Maintaining the, albeit fragile, political and social capital that they have built up in their neighbourhood takes priority over immediate economic gains. Alternative techniques of metal recovery involve physically exhausting labour and possible injuries that no longer appear financially justified. The gradual transition to trading reusable consumer goods permits them to work with reduced risk. Since household goods are often less bulky than metal they can be transported by car, attracting less police attention. Moreover, they fall into a regulatory grey zone, making them less easily classifiable as special waste and thus subject to fewer risks of fines and confiscation. Their informal, rather than illegal, status makes the investment of time and petrol to collect them a much safer economic strategy. While traders still try to resell metals if they find them, hoping that the long-term relations they have built with the scrapyard managers will induce the latter to buy small amounts from them covertly, this commodity flow is becoming ever more marginal. These Roma are therefore making a deliberate choice to move as much as possible along the spectrum from illegality towards informal activities. The process takes time and involves ongoing strategic investments in social capital as a vector through which they hope to achieve the long-term goal of moving out of the protracted liminality that is inherent to their unauthorized work and the vulnerability that accompanies it.

While much salvaging in the city is carried out with shopping trolleys, especially in central and residential areas, this group of reclaimers rely on a shared van to scour the sprawling industrial peri-urban areas where the largest quantities of goods can be sourced. Their historical rootedness in the city is key to how they organize their work, enabling them to constantly update mental maps of their commercial and social networks. Three or four times a week they drive along well-established routes, visiting illegal dumpsites as well as warehouses and bulk stores where they have built friendly relations with managers who donate unsold items that would otherwise be destroyed. Similarly, foremen at construction sites allow them to take unwanted materials. Salvagers also dedicate time and effort to cultivating contacts in their neighbourhood, and among NGOs and small business owners throughout the city. Relationships are often so consolidated that clients call with requests to empty cellars or remove unwanted materials. Managing work on the phone ensures efficiency and further reduces exposure to police controls. Indeed, an essential form of spatial and social knowledge is the ability to predict the location and timing of police checks and the communicative skills to convince officers to turn a blind eye if one is caught transporting materials illegally. Many individuals have worked hard to build friendly relations with police, aware that establishing oneself as a *brava persona* (an honest person) can often avert asset confiscation.

On returning to the camp, the salvaged goods are sorted and cleaned in the open spaces around homes, with all members of the family participating according to their individual strength and skill, and then stored in sheds or under plastic sheeting until they can be resold. What passers-by view as piles of useless debris are in fact logically ordered valuable materials. Old windows and wooden planks are saved for expanding or repairing homes, an old sofa provides a safe place for small children to play, furniture awaits repair, old supermarket trolleys hold items too heavy to carry (Figure 5.2). Most goods first flow through the domestic sphere; every item is evaluated for its immediate or longer-term utility to the household and for its market value. Some are used temporarily and then sold when a better replacement is found. Long-term stockpiling is impossible, though, as residents fear their goods may be stolen or damaged or that authorities will evict and demolish the camp and their wares. Consequently, they try to sell them as quickly as possible, on the informal street markets discussed in chapter 3 or directly to their web of private clients. Indeed, their sales networks are as extensive and diverse as their suppliers. These include collectors and merchants of antiquities and vintage goods, second-hand furniture dealers, and migrant traders who regularly visit to source specific categories of goods for export primarily to Africa. This last group focus particularly on good-quality second-hand sports shoes, construction tools and machinery, replacement parts for household appliances, and electronic components for computers and cell phones. The reuse economy within which Roma traders operate is not merely a local

Figure 5.2 Objects for repurposing and resale stored outside a camp

phenomenon, therefore, but is integrated within global consumption chains. Dealers consciously participate in the transformation of symbolic and financial value of the objects along these globalized chains, as one interviewee made clear: "I make money, the next guy makes money, and the next one, that's how this shit turns into valuable stuff."

Defining their goods as "shit" can be understood as a strategy to distance themselves from symbolic contamination by the waste they work with, presenting themselves as detached intermediaries between those who discard goods and those who buy them. Simultaneously, though, these traders establish a moral superiority by affirming themselves as environmental innovators and cleansers of a city destroyed by its "real pollutants": corruption and lack of civic responsibility. To quote another gleaner:

> People throw away stuff that ends up in dumps and gets burned. Instead, we make it live again. It doesn't get wasted. It allows us to eat and the people who buy the things are happy. We clean the city. We take the washing machines that people dump illegally because they don't want to pay to have their waste taken away. We give them a service free of charge – not like their corrupt politicians – and instead of thanking us they fine us and confiscate our vans.

This harnessing of sustainability discourses and the emphasis on returning life to objects seeks to overturn the associations with death, pollution, and disorder that waste-related work often arouses (Lyons & Snoxell, 2005). By asserting their role as generators of life, gleaners construct the centrality of their presence to the long-term functioning of the city. They thus seek to convert their temporal and social capital into symbolic capital, attempting to alter the established positions, power relations, values, and unspoken assumptions that pervade the field of waste politics in Rome. Unfortunately, these discourses have not translated yet into political or entrepreneurial organization or achieved a concrete improvement in conditions. Roma lack the collective symbolic capital necessary to shift prevailing attitudes about their work from stigmatization to legitimization. Until such dominant perspectives are reshaped, they will remain stuck in this liminality of perpetual informality.

In fact, some Roma traders have made sporadic requests to formalize their salvaging work and various administrations in Rome have, over the years, promised to create special licenses for a few individuals, so far without any follow-through. In 2019, for example, the municipality declared its intention of regularizing 36 Roma metal collectors and integrating them into the AMA recycling system (De Cicco, 2019). Such projects are problematic because their very limited scale does nothing to resolve the wider issue of lack of infrastructure for an effective economy of regeneration and reuse. It is also symbolically harmful because it perpetuates the historic ethnicization that connects Roma to waste, while ignoring the diversity of actors that are involved. More promisingly, some NGOs are working to recast widely shared negative connotations about trading second-hand goods, rebranding them as a "chic" new production and consumption model (Occhio del Ricilone, n.d.). They are thus capitalizing on growing interest among Italian consumers towards recycled commodities now marketed as "vintage" or "pre-loved," especially through the internet (Doxa, 2021; Fury, 2020). Other NGOs are attempting to expand good practices developed in northern Italy for training Roma in legal recovery methods and integrating them into wider consortia of independent traders (Consorzio Equo, n. d.). Such projects are important in providing solutions to the complex bureaucratic obstacles that hamper formal participation in the sector. However, without appropriate infrastructure provided by the authorities, their impacts are limited. In 2019 a citizens' initiative bill was submitted to Rome city government that, if passed, would decentralize waste collection to the boroughs and create a system for recovery or reusable materials. It has yet to be debated by the city council.[24] A bill was also submitted to the national parliament in 2018 aiming to provide the legal framework for simplifying procedures, tax statuses, and licences for reclaimers and traders (CdD, 2018). This would bring Italy more closely in line with the countries that support small-scale waste collectors as an asset in developing a sustainable, circular economy. It would also provide crucial symbolic legitimation to counter the stigmatization of this sector.[25] However, the bill is still waiting to be discussed. Meanwhile, salvagers in Rome continue to operate in a situation of protracted liminality.

Conclusion

The political economies of managing waste in Italy's largest metropolis have produced a hierarchical structuring of positions in this field whose material, political, and social consequences are still very much in evidence. A long series of informal practices at the municipal and regional levels were originally enacted as short-term expedients to overcome institutional incapacities. Yet, these accumulated over time, generating ever more entrenched and complex manoeuvrings to avoid making the onerous legal and financial adjustments necessary to build a functional and sustainable waste management system. Informal practices thus took on long-term structural properties. The dynamics discussed in this chapter are a clear example of how informalities may be generated by state institutions through calculated avoidance or manipulation of regulations, motivated by macroscopic political and economic rationales. The result was to open spaces for accumulation and power at the top of the field by a single private actor able to accommodate the institutions' financial constraints and take advantage of the emergent opportunities for negotiation and rule-bending. A symbiotic relationship was thus woven between these complementary sets of interests through strategic use of regulatory malleability and discretionality. Together, institutional and non-state actors co-produced a system that permitted, normalized, and legitimized informal practices as the main governance approach within the field. The state is, however, a fragmented and multi-scalar space within which political interests do not always cohere. While the national state long permitted these informal local-level dynamics, its obligations to the European Union ultimately forced it to develop and impose a strong legislative framework on its lower levels. Although both municipal and regional institutions have gradually implemented the basic legal requirements, their representatives' claims to prioritizing the protection of public health and the environment for the future have not translated into the radical overhaul necessary to begin managing waste sustainably.

Rome's history of informality-rife waste governance has created a chain of opportunities linking different hierarchical layers. Among the many legacies that decades of institutional mismanagement have left is the lack of adequate surveillance and enforcement systems able to deter the increasingly sophisticated waste-related crimes that the region has become exposed to. These failures have fostered multiple intertwinings of waste informalities and illegalities that are organized and lived in very different ways according to the social levels at which they occur. For waste salvagers in the lowest positions of the field, they have engendered opportunities but also constraints. The symbolic weakness of these actors has meant that their concrete contribution to waste reuse and regeneration continues to be delegitimized. Indeed, they are forced to act informally and sometimes illegally due to the complexity of legislation and the lack of institutional support to comply with regulatory requirements. They are thus deeply "disadvantaged by their inability to be 'formal'" (Banks et al., 2019, p. 2). In turn, they respond tactically and dynamically to the shifting legal constraints and market opportunities, adapting as much as their restricted economic capital allows. The crucial value of social capital is most evident here: it is the networks that gleaners weave with other economic actors that enable them to reduce their vulnerability by operating at the more legal end of the spectrum of informal waste practices. Their growing links with NGOs in the field are also gradually valorizing their environmental work and will hopefully facilitate their future integration into legal recycling systems. The process of counteracting deeply rooted symbolic violence and the pollution taboos connected to waste-related work is a slow one against which social resistance is strong. Nevertheless, changing values concerning acceptable and appropriate consumption and reuse practices may offer possibilities for incremental shifts in the field's social structures. Roma reclaimers are certainly using the movable meanings of waste to influence value systems where they can. As governance priorities begin to similarly recognize the social and economic value of refuse, this is the time for public policies to actively commit to undoing decades of discriminatory treatment of those who work with it.

Notes

1 Some paragraphs of this chapter were previously published in the following two articles: Clough, Marinaro, I. (2017). The informal faces of the (neo-)ghetto: State confinement, formalization and multidimensional informalities in Italy's Roma camps. *International Sociology, 32*(4), 545–562.

Clough Marinaro, I. (2018). Salvaging Rome: Roma waste traders and the city's "garbage crisis". *Etnografia e ricerca qualitativa, Rivista quadrimestrale* 1/2018, 11–31, doi:10.3240/89692.

2 See CPI (2017, p. 428) for a detailed organigram of the firms that made up Cerroni's business empire.

3 In 1989 the Lazio Region approved the dumping of waste from the rest of the region, in addition to that of the capital, in the Malagrotta landfill. Since then, various other landfills in the region have also been expanded (Bonaccorsi et al., 2012).

4 Lazio has one incinerator, located in San Vittore, about 80 km from Rome, which opened in 2002.

5 Over 200 landfills across Italy were addressed in the ruling.

6 For example, in 2019 the region resurrected suggestions, initially made in 2012, to build two new landfills; one in Corcolle (near the UNESCO heritage site of Hadrian's Villa) and one in Riano, in the Tiber valley. In 2021, Mayor Raggi requested that a site be opened in Colleferro, south of the city.

7 In 2018 Rome budgeted 188 million euro to ship this waste out of the region for the following two years (Ulivieri, 2018).

8 AMA paid 45 euro per ton to Cerroni. Similar plants in Campania were charging 34.85 euro per ton (CPI, 2017).

9 It is emblematic of the tightness of relations between the dominant political and entrepreneurial powers that a former President of the Lazio region, Bruno Landi, was subsequently employed as a lawyer for Cerroni's firms (Tribunale Ordinario di Roma, 2008). Similarly, a former employee of a Cerroni enterprise was hired as the head of ARPA, the region's environmental protection agency (CPI, 2017).

10 Various other charges had instead expired under the statute of limitations.

11 For example, environmental associations like the WWF, as well as residents' committees, were co-plaintiffs in the 2014–2018 case on criminal association, and various have been consulted by the Parliamentary Commission on waste-related crimes (CPI, 2017).

12 The case was subsequently dismissed.

13 Three were ultimately found guilty (ANSA, 2018).

14 This problem is not exclusive to Lazio. Legambiente (2019b) points out that outsourcing recycling and waste processing to the private sector, and the inability of the authorities to systematically monitor what happens to that waste, makes the system vulnerable nationally, with areas of greater and lesser criticality.

15 Confidential interviews between 2016 and 2020 with a member of the Social and Environmental Emergency section of Rome's municipal police.

16 Confidential interviews, see previous note.

17 See Legambiente Lazio for yearly reports on the region and capital's positions in the rankings: www.legambientelazio.it/. Since 2011, Lazio has remained stable as the country's main hub of environmental crimes after the four mafia-intense Southern regions (it had risen to second place nationally in 2010). Rome oscillated between second and fourth worse-affected province throughout the decade.

18 A similar example of ethnicizing portrayals was provided in this newspaper headline: "The Roma 'environmental mafia': This is how they disposed of hazardous waste" (Benignetti, 2020). The article goes on to state that the organization was in fact run by non-Roma owners of a construction company. Some residents of two camps were then paid to dispose of the waste.

19 Roma are thus the most recent category of people who have been marginalized and secluded because of their construction as dirty/polluting during Rome's long history. See Bradley and Stow (2016) for discussion of similar treatment of Jews, prostitutes, and vagabonds.

20 I have been tracking such discourses since 2010. It is interesting to note that critique of this language is now beginning to appear in some media outlets. See, for example, Merli (2020).

21 A poster distributed around town and reproduced in a flyer to inform citizens of new municipal police rules provides no reflection of the poverty that drives such activities, while implying that gleaners spread rubbish outside the dumpsters. See: https://m.facebook.com/virginia.raggi.m5sroma/photos/a.470151043167350/1412816915567420/?type=3&source=54.

Rome's waste management company does collaborate with six NGOs that collect books, bicycle parts, aids for disabled people, and functioning mobile phones and tablets to donate to disadvantaged people. However, it does not provide information about whether or when the NGOs are present at the reusable waste collection sites. Residents must thus contact the NGOs directly, adding a significant logistical deterrent to making donations. See: www.amaroma.it/raccolta-differenziata/disposizioni-generali/4953-raccolte-di-beni-usati-per-il-terzo-settore.html.

22 See, for example: www.cauto.it/progetto/isola-del-riuso/ and https://inlinea.cittametropolitana.mi.it/newsletter/doc/Indicazioni_costituzione_centri_del_riuso.pdf.

23 At the national level, Legge 28 dicembre 2015, n. 221 updated existing environmental legislation (Decreto legislativo 3 aprile 2006, n. 152) and introduced narrow guidelines stipulating the kind of businesses that can legally recover and store metals, as well as banning itinerant metal trading. This law, like many others concerning waste and second-hand goods collection, includes various contradictions which directly affect small-scale waste collectors' access to licenses to operate legally (see, for example, Paone, 2013; Palumbo, 2016).

24 The full text of the bill can be viewed at www.comune.roma.it/web-resources/cms/documents/RC.2019.22894.pdf.

25 https://documenti.camera.it/leg18/pdl/pdf/leg.18.pdl.camera.1065.18PDL0026380.pdf.

References

ACOS (Agenzia per il controllo e la qualità dei servizi pubblici locali di Roma Capitale). (2020). Relazione annuale 2020. www.agenzia.roma.it/it-schede-850-relazione_annuale_2020.

Affari Italiani. (2019). Rifiuti e Cerroni, si organizza un nuovo maxi processo sui Tmb di Roma. *Affari Italiani*, 14 March. www.affaritaliani.it/roma/rifiuti-cerroni-si-organizza-un-nuovo-maxi-processo-sui-tmb-di-roma-593603.html.

Agamuthu, P. (2010). The role of the informal sector for sustainable waste management. *Waste Management Research*, 28, 671–672. https://doi.org/10.1177/0734242x10377834.

Alagia, P., & Iervolino, M. (2011). *Con le mani nella monnezza. I disastri della partitocrazia: Il caso Malagrotta*. Reality Book Editions.

Altrock, U. (2016). Conceptualising informality: Some thoughts on the way towards generalization. In C. McFarlane & M. Waibel (eds), *Urban informalities: Reflections on the formal and informal* (pp. 171–193). Routledge. https://doi.org/10.4324/9781315548814.

ANSA. (2018). Parentopoli Ama, condannato Panzironi. *ANSA*, 5 April. www.ansa.it/lazio/notizie/2018/04/05/parentopoli-ama-condannato-panzironi_5ac1cc65-2219-420c-b2a5-d80cd3d4f331.html.

ASPL (Agenzia per il controllo e la qualità dei servizi di Roma Capitale). (2019). XII Indagine sulla qualità della vita e dei servizi pubblici locali a Roma. www.affaritaliani.it/static/upl2019/xii_/xii_indagineqdv2019_agenziaservizipubblicirmcapitale.pdf.

Associazione 21 luglio. (2014). Quell'inceneritore vicino al "campo rom". www.21luglio.org/quellinceneritore-vicino-campo-rom/.

Associazione 21 luglio. (2016). Posti di blocco nei "campi rom": I controlli che violano la libera circolazione. www.21luglio.org/posti-di-blocco-nei-campi-rom-i-controlli-che-violano-la-libera-circolazione/.

Banks, N., Mitlin, D., & Lombard, M. (2019). Urban informality as a site of critical analysis. *Journal of Development Studies*, 56(2), 223–238. https://doi.org/10.1080/00220388.2019.1577384.

Belli, E., Granata, R., Risi, E., & Vivona, V. (2015). *A ferro e fuoco: Fumi tossici nella "città eterna"*. Kogoi.

Benignetti, A. (2020). La "mafia ambientale" dei rom: così smaltivano i rifiuti pericolosi. *Il Giornale*, 21 May. www.ilgiornale.it/news/roma/mafia-ambientale-dei-rom-cos-smaltivano-i-rifiuti-pericolosi-1864570.html.

Bettini Prosperi, M., Bonincontro, I., & Lisi, C. (2003). Archivio del servizio della nettezza urbana del Comune di Roma inventario. Istituto Poligrafico e Zecca dello Stato.

Bisbiglia, V., & Gennaro, A. (2018). Roma, la "frigo-valley" in riva all'Aniene. "È opera delle aziende di smaltimento delle grandi catene di elettrodomestici". *Il Fatto Quotidiano*. www.ilfattoquotidiano.it/2018/04/03/roma-la-frigo-valley-in-riva-allaniene-e-opera-delle-aziende-di-smaltimento-delle-grandi-catene-di-elettrodomestici/4234264/.

Bonaccorsi, M., Trocchia, N., & Sina, Y. (2012). *Roma come Napoli: Il malaffare di politica e signori della monnezza che mette in ginocchio il Lazio e la capitale*. Castelvecchi.

Bradley, M., & Stow, K. R. (2016). *Rome, pollution and propriety: Dirt, disease and hygiene in the Eternal City from antiquity to modernity*. Cambridge University Press.

Capponi, A., & Menicucci, E. (2010). Parentopoli, Ama sotto inchiesta: Uso disinvolto delle agenzie interinali. *Corriere della Sera*, 24 December. https://roma.corriere.it/notizie/cronaca/10_dicembre_24/nuovo-ama-parentopoli-vigilia-natale-181140660873.shtml.

Cattaneo, C. (2017). Natural resource scarcity, degrowth scenarios and national borders: The role of migrant squats. In P. Mudu & S. Chattopadhyay (eds), *Migration, squatting and radical autonomy* (pp. 257–271). Routledge. https://doi.org/10.4324/9781315673301-21.

CDCA (Centro di documentazione sui conflitti ambientali). (2013). Monnezza blues. La gestione dei rifiuti nel Lazio: Emergenzialità, conflitti sociali e nuovi modelli. http://asud.net/wp-content/uploads/2013/06/MonnezzaBlues.pdf.

CdD (Camera dei Deputati). (2018). Proposta di legge. No. 1065. Disposizioni per la disciplina dell'economia dei beni usati e la promozione del settore del riutilizzo, nonché istituzione del Tavolo di lavoro permanente sul riutilizzo. http://documenti.camera.it/leg18/pdl/pdf/leg.18.pdl.camera.1065.18PDL0026380.pdf.

Cerroni, M. (2014). Storia e cronaca a volo d'angelo sulla monnezza di Roma e del Lazio. https://it.scribd.com/doc/225083141/Storia-e-Cronaca-a-Volo-d-Angelo-Sulla-Monnezza-Di-Roma-e-Del-Lazio-dal-1944-Al-9-Gennaio-2014-e-Non-Solo.

Clough Marinaro, I. (2014). "Sporco zingaro". I rom e l'integrità del corpo della nazione. In C. Lombardi Diop & C. Romeo (eds), *L'Italia postcoloniale* (pp. 93–108). Le Monnier-Mondadori Accademia.

Clough Marinaro, I. (2017). The informal faces of the (neo-)ghetto: State confinement, formalization and multidimensional informalities in Italy's Roma camps. *International Sociology*, 4(32), 545–562. https://doi.org/10.1177/0268580917706629.

Clough Marinaro, I. (2018). Salvaging Rome: Roma waste traders and the city's "garbage crisis". *Etnografia e ricerca qualitativa*, 9(1), 11–31.

Consorzio Equo (n.d.). http://consorzioequo.org/.

CPI (Commissione parlamentare d'inchiesta sulle attività illecite connesse al ciclo dei rifiuti). (2011). Relazione territoriale sulle attività illecite connesse al ciclo dei rifiuti nella Regione Lazio. hwww.senato.it/service/PDF/PDFServer/BGT/526516.pdf.

CPI (Commissione parlamentare d'inchiesta sulle attività illecite connesse al ciclo dei rifiuti e su illeciti ambientali ad esse correlati). (2017). Relazione sul ciclo dei rifiuti di Roma Capitale e fenomeni illeciti nel territorio del Lazio. www.senato.it/service/PDF/PDFServer/BGT/1063695.pdf.

Davies, P. (2012). Pollution, propriety and urbanism in Republican Rome. In M. Bradley with K. Stow (eds), *Rome, pollution and propriety: Dirt, disease and hygiene in the Eternal City from antiquity to modernity* (pp. 67–80). Cambridge University Press. https://doi.org/10.1017/cbo9781139028479.007.

De Cicco, L. (2019). Roma, i "rovistatori" dei cassonetti diventano operatori del riciclo. *Il Messaggero*, 6 March. www.ilmessaggero.it/roma/news/roma_rovistatori_cassonetti_diventano_operatori_ama_riciclo-4251501.html.

De Cicco, L., & Mozzetti, C. (2019). Roma, incendio al Collatino: "Vendetta dei rom". Ama sotto inchiesta: bonifiche mai fatte. *Il Messaggero*, 27 April. www.ilmessaggero.it/roma/news/collatina_incendio_roma-4454072.html.

de Ghantuz Cubbe, M. (2021). Roma, ok al bilancio Ama: dal Campidoglio 250 milioni di euro per salvare la società. Ma il fallimento è ancora possible. *La Repubblica*, 8 March. https://roma.repubblica.it/cronaca/2021/03/08/news/roma_approvato_il_bilancio_ama-290997403/.

Dipartimento di Epidemiologia del Servizio Sanitario Regionale. (2015). Valutazione epidemiologica dello stato di salute della popolazione residente in prossimità dello stabilimento BASF Italia Srl. www.deplazio.net/it/archivio-news/188-valutazione-epidemiologica-dello-stato-di-salute-della-popolazione-residente-in-prossimita-dello-stabilimento-basf-italia-srl.

Douglas, M. (2002). *Purity and danger: An analysis of concepts of pollution and taboo.* Routledge. https://doi.org/10.4324/9780203361832.

Doxa. (2021). Osservatorio second hand economy: Sono 23 milioni gli Italiani che nel 2020 hanno comprato o venduto oggetti usati. www.bva-doxa.com/osservatorio-second-hand-economy-sono-23-milioni-gli-italiani-che-nel-2020-hanno-comprato-o-venduto-oggetti-usati/.

EC (European Commission). (2008). Italy: Commission pursues legal action over waste management in the Campania and Lazio regions. 6 May. https://ec.europa.eu/commission/presscorner/detail/en/IP_08_705.

EC (European Commission). (2013). Environment: Commission takes Italy to Court over inadequate treatment of waste landfilled in Lazio. https://ec.europa.eu/commission/presscorner/detail/en/IP_13_250.

EC (European Commission). (2019a). List of landfills covered by the judgment of 2/12/2014-situation of the expiry of the ninth semester following the judgment (3/12/2018–2/6/2019). https://ec.europa.eu/environment/legal/law/press_en.htm.

EC (European Commission). (2019b). The environmental implementation review 2019. Country report Italy. https://ec.europa.eu/environment/eir/pdf/report_it_en.pdf.

EC (European Commission). (2020). Circular economy action plan. https://ec.europa.eu/environment/strategy/circular-economy-action-plan_en.

EC (European Commission). (n.d.). Waste framework directive. https://ec.europa.eu/environment/topics/waste-and-recycling/waste-framework-directive_en.

EP (European Parliament). (2013). Working document on Fact Finding Mission to Italy, from 29 to 31 October 2012, concerning waste management in Lazio and Campania. www.europarl.europa.eu/meetdocs/2014_2019/documents/peti/dt/942/942408/942408en.pdf.

Fiano, F., & Frignani, R. (2019). Il business dei rifiuti dietro i roghi tossici nei campi rom: 15 arresti e 57 indagati. *Corriere della Sera*, 16 January. https://roma.corriere.it/notizie/cronaca/19_gennaio_16/business-rifiuti-dietro-roghi-tossici-campi-rom-15-arresti-57-indagati-b5a37936-1957-11e9-8af3-37b4f370f434.shtml.

Fury, A. (2020). Il boom del mercato vintage: Gli acquisti corrono online. *Il Sole 24 Ore*, 23 November. www.ilsole24ore.com/art/il-boom-mercato-vintage-acquisti-corrono-online-ADW3ng3.

Gidwani, V., & Reddy, R. N. (2011). The afterlives of 'waste': Notes from India for a minor history of capitalist surplus. *Antipode*, 43(5), 1625–1658. https://doi.org/10.1111/j.1467-8330.2011.00902.x.

Guillard, V., & Roux, D. (2014). Macromarketing issues on the sidewalk: How "gleaners" and "disposers" (re)create a sustainable economy. *Journal of Macromarketing*, 34(3), 291–312. https://doi.org/10.1177/0276146713518562.

Hawkins, G., & Muecke, S. (2003). *Culture and waste: The creation and destruction of value.* Rowman & Littlefield.

Hopkins, J. (2012). The "sacred sewer": Tradition and religion in the Cloaca Maxima. In M. Bradley with K. Stow (eds), *Rome, pollution and propriety: Dirt, disease and hygiene in the Eternal City from antiquity to modernity* (pp. 81–102). Cambridge University Press. https://doi.org/10.1017/cbo9781139028479.008.

Horowitz, J. (2018). Rome in ruins. *New York Times*, 24 December. www.nytimes.com/2018/12/24/travel/rome-pollution-trash.html.

Iervolino, M., & Tozzi, M. (2013). *Roma, la guerra dei rifiuti.* Infinito.

Isabella, C., Rubrichi G., & Sensi F. (1997). *Per una storia della nettezza urbana a Roma dal 1870 al 1960.* Vol. 1, *Dal canestraro al netturbino.* Editrice Cel.

ISPRA (Istituto superiore per la protezione e la ricerca ambientale). (2014). Rapporto rifiuti urbani. www.isprambiente.gov.it/files/pubblicazioni/rapporti/RapportoRifiutiUrbani2014_web.pdf.
ISTAT. (2020). Le statistiche dell'ISTAT sulla povertà. Anno 2019. www.istat.it/it/files//2020/06/REPORT_POVERTA_2019.pdf.
Izzo, E. (2018). Dramma rifiuti nella Capitale, chiesto nuovo processo per Cerroni e altri 6. *La Stampa*, 16 June. www.lastampa.it/roma/2018/12/18/news/dramma-rifiuti-nella-capitale-chiesto-nuovo-processo-per-cerroni-e-altri-6-1.34067848.
Koloski-Ostrow, A. (2015). *The archaeology of sanitation in Roman Italy: Toilets, sewers, and water systems.* University of North Carolina Press. https://doi.org/10.5149/northcarolina/9781469621289.001.0001.
La Repubblica. (2012). Ama, Panzironi a processo per 841 assunzioni irregolari. *La Repubblica*, 7 December. https://roma.repubblica.it/cronaca/2012/12/07/news/ama_-48265139/.
Legambiente Lazio. (2018). Dossier rifiuti a Roma, Legambiente su reazioni da parte del Campidoglio ai dati presentati. www.legambientelazio.it/dossier-rifiuti-a-roma-legambiente-su-reazioni-da-parte-del-campidoglio-ai-dati-presentati/.
Legambiente. (2019a). Ecosistema urbano 2019. www.legambiente.it/comunicati-stampa/ecosistema-urbano-2019/.
Legambiente. (2019b). *Ecomafia 2019*. Edizioni Ambiente.
Lindner, C., & Meissner, M. (2015). *Global garbage.* Routledge. https://doi.org/10.4324/9781315732251.
Lyons, M., & Snoxell, S. (2005). Sustainable urban livelihoods and marketplace social capital: Crisis and strategy in petty trade. *Urban Studies*, 42(8), 1301–1320. https://doi.org/10.1080/00420980500150631.
Machado-Borges, T. (2015). "Have you ever seen a thief wearing a uniform?!" Struggling for dignity in urban southeastern Brazil. *Ethnography*, 16(2), 207–222. https://doi.org/10.1177/1466138114547623.
Martelli, G. (2007). Maxi retata a Porta Portese. *Il Tempo*, 24 September, p. 1.
Martone, V. (2019). Mafie, ecomafie e (dis)economie ambientali: Attori e contesti di operatività. In D. Scarabelli (ed.), *Mafie tossiche* (pp. 68–81). Crim.Int. Edizioni.
Masia, V. (2016). Dal cassonetto al mercatino, viaggio tra chi di rifiuti ci vive. *ADN Kronos*, 17 October. www.adnkronos.com/2016/10/17/dal-cassonetto-mercatino-viaggio-tra-chi-rifiuti-vive-video_UDJzOTAnzDNLYOfUHeAmbL.html.
Merli, G. (2020). A Roma si "bonificano" i rom. *Il Manifesto*. https://ilmanifesto.it/a-roma-si-bonificano-i-rom/.
Occhio del Ricilone. (n.d.). Guida al riuso nella Provincia di Roma. www.spazioriuso.it/wp-content/uploads/Guida-Riuso.pdf.
Palumbo, L. (2016). Legge "Green Economy": Che pasticcio sui rottami ferrosi. www.riciclanews.it/normative/collegato-ambientale-rottami-ferrosi_4250.html.
Paone, V. (2013). La raccolta e il trasporto dei rifiuti in forma ambulante. *Ambiente e Sviluppo*, 2, 111–115.
Pelati, M. (2017). Rifiuti di Roma trasferiti in Puglia: l'ok della Regione dopo lo scontro Raggi-Zingaretti. *Corriere della Sera*, 5 April. https://roma.corriere.it/notizie/cronaca/18_giugno_08/rifiuti-roma-trasferiti-puglia-l-ok-regione-lo-scontro-raggi-zingaretti-08808e1e-6b25-11e8-9458-812edbd9a164.shtml.
Peronaci, F. (2010). Parentopoli, dopo l'Atac scoppia il caso Ama. *Corriere della Sera*, 8 December. https://roma.corriere.it/notizie/cronaca/10_dicembre_8/parentopoli-si-allarga-ama-18134334805.shtml.

Peronaci, F. (2012). Ama, la promozione "costa" 500 euro. *Corriere della Sera*, 24 October. https://roma.corriere.it/roma/notizie/cronaca/12_ottobre_24/ama-promozione-pagamento-2112392249790.shtml.

Peronaci, F. (2017a). Tangenti e assunzioni facili all'Ama dialoghi-choc all'esame della Procura. *Corriere della Sera*, 3 January. https://roma.corriere.it/notizie/cronaca/17_gennaio_03/tangenti-assunzioni-facili-all-ama-dialoghi-choc-all-esame-procura-5e41fef2-d1f0-11e6-a55b-632cc5cf8e9f.shtml.

Peronaci, F. (2017b). Assunzioni facili all'ama, ecco tutti i trucchi: I nomi passati dai sindacati alle agenzie interinali. *Corriere della Sera*, 8 January. https://roma.corriere.it/notizie/cronaca/17_gennaio_07/assunzioni-facili-all-ama-ecco-tutti-trucchi-nomi-passati-sindacati-agenzie-interinali-28e795ba-d505-11e6-a429-dbd66ce5e88f.shtml.

Pitoni, A. (2016). Altre tangenti in Campidoglio, sei arresti per i campi rom. *La Stampa*, 29 June. www.lastampa.it/politica/2016/06/29/news/altre-tangenti-in-campidoglio-sei-arresti-per-i-campi-rom-1.34991107.

Radio Radicale. (2019). Processo a Manlio Cerroni e a Francesco Rando per disastro ambientale (discarica di Malagrotta). *Radio Radicale*, 15 May. www.radioradicale.it/scheda/573990/processo-a-manlio-cerroni-e-a-francesco-rando-per-disastro-ambientale-discarica-di.

Regione Lazio. (2019). Piano regionale di gestione dei rifiuti della Regione Lazio 2019–2025. www.regione.lazio.it/rl_rifiuti/?vw=newsDettaglio&id=63.

Rigon, L. (ed.) (2005). *I venti anni dell'Ama di Roma 1985–2005. Da azienda municipale per la nettezza urbana a impresa per la tutela dell'ambiente.* FrancoAngeli.

Rinne, K. (2012). Urban ablutions: Cleansing Counter-Reformation Rome. In M. Bradley with K. Stow (eds), *Rome, pollution and propriety: Dirt, disease and hygiene in the Eternal City from antiquity to modernity* (pp. 182–201). Cambridge University Press. https://doi.org/10.1017/cbo9781139028479.015.

Roberts, H. (2019). Romans fume and sweat surrounded by mountains of rubbish. *The Financial Times*, 9 July. www.ft.com/content/5d650548-a19f-11e9-a282-2df48f366f7d.

Roma Capitale. (2014). Deliberazione n. 181. Linee di indirizzo programmatiche in materia di interventi per la delocalizzazione e/o stabilizzazione dei Centri di autodemolizione e rottamazione nel territorio di Roma Capitale. www.comune.roma.it/resources/cms/documents/DelibGCn181del25giugno2014prorogaAttivitaAutodemolitori.pdf.

Roma Today. (2021). Mille discariche abusive in città, Legambiente presenta la mappa: "Gestione dei rifiuti è un fallimento". *Roma Today*, 1 April. www.romatoday.it/politica/mille-discariche-roma-mappa-legambiente.html.

Roscioni, L. (2005). Sanità e decoro. La nettezza urbana a Roma tra antico regime e unità. In L. Rigon (ed.), *I venti anni dell'Ama di Roma 1985–2005. Da azienda municipale per la nettezza urbana a impresa per la tutela dell'ambiente* (pp. 15–29). FrancoAngeli.

Roy, A. (2009). Why India cannot plan its cities: Informality, insurgence and the idiom of urbanization. *Planning Theory*, 8(1), 76–87. https://doi.org/10.1177/1473095208099299.

Rutkowski, J. E., & Rutkowski, E.W. (2015). Expanding worldwide urban solid waste recycling: The Brazilian social technology in waste pickers inclusion. *Waste Management & Research*, 33(12), pp. 1084–1093. https://doi.org/10.1177/0734242x15607424.

Salvaggiulo, G. (2017). Arbitrati da 175 milioni. Trasporti e rifiuti, in Campidoglio gli atti esecutivi. *La Stampa*, 3 September. www.lastampa.it/cronaca/2017/09/03/news/arbitrati-da-175-milioni-1.34441152.

Scanlan, J. (2005). *On garbage.* Reaktion Books.

Scarlino, M. (2018). Rifiuti, Cerroni scrive a Mattarella: "Roma discarica a cielo aperto, ma gli impianti ci sono". *Roma Today*, 6 January. www.romatoday.it/politica/rifiuti-roma-cosa-sta-succedendo-gennaio-2018.html.
Scarlino, M. (2021). Perché a Roma c'è una nuova emergenza rifiuti e cosa serve (con urgenza) per uscirne. *Roma Today*, 4 June. www.romatoday.it/politica/emergenza-rifiuti-roma-perche.html.
Scarpa, G. (2011). A caccia di cibo nei cassonetti della spazzatura. Effetto crisi, la spesa di disoccupati e pensionati. *La Repubblica*, 4 November. https://roma.repubblica.it/cronaca/2011/11/04/news/a_caccia_di_cibo_nei_cassonetti_della_spazzatura_effetto_crisi_la_spesa_di_disoccupati_e_pensionati-24459887/.
Schurman, S. J. et al. (2017). *Informal workers and collective action: A global perspective*. ILR Press. https://doi.org/10.7591/9781501707964.
Solani, M. (2020). Il pasticcio dei bilanci Ama, c'è una nuova inchiesta. *Il Foglio*, 12 May. www.ilfoglio.it/cronache/2020/05/12/news/il-pasticcio-dei-bilanci-ama-ce-una-nuova-inchiesta-317781/.
Storey, D., Santucci, L., Fraser, R., Aleluia, J., & Chomchuen, L. (2015). Designing effective partnerships for waste-to-resource initiatives: Lessons learned from developing countries. *Waste Management and Research*, 33(12), 1066–1075. https://doi.org/10.1177/0734242x15602964.
Tauber, E. (2017). "When a breach arises." Good bureaucratic action and informal scrap metal collection in Northern Italy. *ANUAC*, 6(2), 155–173.
Tribunale Ordinario di Roma. (2008). Ordinanza applicativa di misure cautelari personali e decreto di sequestro preventivo. N. 7449/2008 R.G.N.R; N. 13928/2008 R.G.GIP. www.manliocerroni.it/files/accusa.pdf.
Tribunale Penale di Roma. (2019). Sentenza. N. 14783/18 Sent.
Ulivieri, V. (2018). Rifiuti, 40 milioni di tonnellate in giro per l'Italia. E i costi di smaltimento (e trasferimento) li pagano i cittadini. *Il Fatto Quotidiano*, 23 June. www.ilfattoquotidiano.it/2018/06/23/rifiuti-40-milioni-di-tonnellate-in-giro-per-litalia-e-i-costi-di-smaltimento-e-trasferimento-li-pagano-i-cittadini/4445125/.

6 When in Rome

Mapping Romans' attitudes and understandings of informal practices

Paola Castelli and Isabella Clough Marinaro

Introduction

The previous chapters have shown how informal practices occur at all social levels within the four specific sectors of Rome's economic life and urban governance examined. In analyzing these practices, the empirical case studies have confirmed some core theoretical propositions outlined in chapter 1. On the one hand, they have shown that informalities are co-produced by institutional representatives, professionals, and private actors, who all make use of regulatory gaps and contradictions to serve their interests. On the other hand, they have demonstrated that such practices are primarily driven by methods of governance within public offices: rules are often purposefully left open to interpretation and negotiation, their enforcement is selective rather than arbitrary, and their temporalities alternate between slowness and sudden, often unpredictable, accelerations. Non-institutional actors in turn navigate these obstacles and opportunities by drawing on their cultural, social, and symbolic capital, seeking to influence those processes as best they can.

This chapter examines whether these phenomena are perceived to exist beyond the delimited spheres of the case studies; whether they are understood to be widespread features in the public's engagements with formal institutions and their regulations. It is notable that studies of informality across the globe rarely directly ask ordinary citizens how they make sense of and evaluate those informal practices. Their normative views are either ignored or are inferred from the behaviours and discourses of the particular "informal actors" on which the studies centre, without exploring whether the latter's understandings of regulatory malleability are widely shared within the broader population. This becomes problematic when extrapolations are made concerning the existence of coherent local norms – or, conversely, that the norms are limited to distinct domains and contexts –, without these assertions being tested. This last chapter presents the outcomes of a preliminary attempt at tackling this gap. Specifically, we report on the results of an online survey carried out in 2020 aimed at exploring Romans' views of informal practices and the bureaucratic and legal procedures that may promote and perpetuate them.

DOI: 10.4324/9780429353321-7

The present study

Our investigation had three overarching aims. First, we wished to explore whether public bureaucracies, regulations, and services are considered to be clear, efficient and equitable. Chapter 1 argued that informalities generally emerge when the wording of rules is unclear or is contradicted by other regulations, when procedures do not follow the letter of the rule, or when laws are absent, inappropriate, or unhelpful. It also highlighted the critical theoretical proposition that legal frameworks are generally formulated to reflect the ideological views and practical interests of social elites. Where informal practices are a direct consequence of institutional inefficiency and disparity of application, we should expect legal inadequacy to also be the prevalent perception among the city's general population.

Second, we considered the theoretical notion that informality is symbiotically intertwined with formal regulations and their implementation; that people move between formal and informal activities, often engaging in both at once or acting "in light of the rules" without rigidly adhering to them (Chiodelli & Moroni, 2014). In other words, we investigated whether informal practices are seen as a regular facet of people's engagements with official rules and procedures, used endemically by those who live and work in the city, rather than just being the habitus of specific groups. We also explored what factors may influence people's tolerance for informal behaviours. To the extent that people consider them to be a common feature of urban governance dynamics and directly driven by bureaucratic processes and timeframes, we should expect respondents to be more likely to accept informal practices as a viable solution to the shortcomings of institutional behaviours.

Third, we examined whether people's normative acceptance of informal practices is in any way associated to the type of violation being considered, the categories of actors believed to predominantly engage in them, and their presumed motivations. As chapter 1 outlined, theoretical debates present informalities both as the forced survival tactics of disempowered actors structurally excluded by the law, and as voluntary strategies enacted by financially and politically powerful ones to maintain and reinforce their positions of dominance. If respondents understand informalities to be conditioned by power differentials, we should expect them to be more tolerant of violations stemming from necessity as opposed to those used for personal financial benefit or to obtain bureaucratic shortcuts and favours. In examining each of these three macroscopic hypotheses, we also investigated whether similar attitudes cross demographic groups, or whether reliable differences in perceptions emerge according to demographic characteristics.

Method

Participants

Two hundred and nineteen (219) Italian-speaking people volunteered to participate in our study. Forty-four (44) were later excluded from analyses as they reported not having ever lived in Rome or residing there in the present. Three additional participants were excluded as they only completed the demographic questionnaire. Our final sample thus comprised 172 participants (60% females) whose average age was 44 years (SD = 14; range = 19 years – 79 years). Most of the participants held at least an undergraduate university degree and reported a yearly income of between 15,000 and 55,000 euro. About a quarter of our sample reported dealing frequently with bureaucratic procedures, whether for professional or for personal reasons. Detailed demographic characteristics of our final sample are reported in Table 6.1.

Materials

- *Demographic questionnaire*. This questionnaire gathered basic information about our participants, such as age, gender identity, education, and income level.
- *Perception of Informality questionnaire* (PIQ). This set of 43 questions tapped into individuals' perceptions of formal and informal rules and practices, as well as their opinions on who may engage in informal behaviours. For each item, participants were asked to rate their level of agreement on a seven-point scale (1= strongly disagree to 7= strongly agree).
- *Attitudes towards Rule-violating Behaviours questionnaire (ARVB)*. This 14-item questionnaire listed a series of rule-violating behaviours (e.g., borrowing from an *usuraio*: an unauthorized moneylender) and asked respondents to rate their level of approval of each behaviour on a 7-point scale (1= strongly disapprove to 7= strongly approve).
- *Attitudes towards Punishment of Rule-violating Behaviours questionnaire (PRVB)*. This questionnaire listed the same 14 rule-violating behaviours covered in the previous one (ARVB). For each behaviour, respondents rated whether they approved of it being legally sanctioned on a seven-point scale (1= strongly disapprove to 7= strongly approve).

Procedure

Through social media (i.e., Facebook), through distribution of a flyer containing a QR code in shops and bars around the city, and via word of mouth, we invited participants to take part in an anonymous survey concerning attitudes towards the rule of law, informality, and bureaucracy. Participants independently accessed the link to the survey via mobile phone or computer. They were offered a chance to win a 50-euro Amazon gift card in return for their participation. Clicking on the shared link directed potential participants to the study consent form. Those who consented to participate were directed first to the demographic questionnaire. After completing this section, respondents accessed the questionnaire on perceptions of informality, followed by the one on attitudes towards rule-violating behaviour. Lastly, they were presented with the questionnaire on attitudes towards punishment of rule-violating behaviours. After finishing this last set of questions, participants were thanked for their participation and redirected to a separate Google form where they could enter the lottery to win the Amazon gift certificate.

Results

Preliminary analyses

To analyze participants' perceptions of informality, mean composite scores were computed from items in the PIQ (see Table 6.2 for a translated list of items included in each composite and for reliability values). Three composites represent respondents' perceptions of potential determinants of informal behaviour: (1) *Clarity of Legal Norms* (e.g., "Following one rule often implies violating others"), (2) *Inefficiency of Bureaucracy* (e.g., "It is impossible to benefit in a timely manner from institutional services if one follows official procedures"), (3) *Legal Alienation* (e.g., "Legal and regulatory frameworks generally reflect the interests of those in a position of power, and rarely those of common citizens"). Two additional composites represent people's perception of informal behaviour: *Informality as Endemic* (e.g., "Rule bending is the norm in many instances of everyday life") and *Tolerance of Informality* (e.g., "When rules are absent, it is normal for individuals to resort to informal practices").

To examine respondents' attitudes towards different types of rule-violating behaviour,[1] composite scores were also created for the items in each of the ARVB and the PRVB questionnaires. These composites represented approval towards rule-violating behaviours potentially driven by (1) Lengthy bureaucracy (e.g., "Renovating one's home without requesting proper authorizations"), (2) Necessity (e.g., "Doing undeclared work"), (3) Financial gain ("Paying workers under the table"), as well as approval of legally sanctioning these actions (see Table 6.3 for a list of items included in each composite and for reliability values).

Mean composite scores were used in all subsequent analyses. Preliminary analyses indicated no significant difference in attitudes depending on level of education, thus this variable will not be considered further. Only significant results are reported next.

Perception of formal rules and regulations

To explore whether public bureaucracies, regulations, and services are deemed to be clear, efficient, and equitable, we examined participants' patterns of response to items related to the three potential determinants of informal behaviours: *Clarity of Legal Norms, Inefficiency of Bureaucracy*, and *Legal Alienation*.

As can be gleaned from the means in Table 6.4, when considering *Clarity of Legal Norms*, participants tended to view laws and official regulations as complex and often contradictory. Analysis of individual items indicated, for example, that many agreed that our laws are often too convoluted to be understood by laypersons (agree: 72%; disagree: 13%),[2] that they are often in conflict with one another (agree: 45%; disagree: 24), that following one rule often implies violating others (agree: 44%; disagree: 24%), and that the sheer number of existing laws as well as their contradictions undermine their actual efficacy (agree: 62%; disagree: 16%). A regression analysis was conducted to explore whether demographic variables (i.e., age, gender, income level) would predict people's perceptions of norms as coherent. No predictors emerged, suggesting that people's view of legal norms as confusing and often incoherent was not related to their demographic characteristics.

Looking at the mean value for the *Inefficiency of Bureaucracy* composite, it is apparent that participants perceived bureaucracy to be slow, ineffective, and rarely transparent. For example, most respondents agreed that it is practically impossible to receive a service from a public institution in a timely manner if one follows the official bureaucratic procedure (agree: 51%; disagree: 34%), and that respecting such procedures when requesting services or authorizations is not always compatible with citizens' own time frames (agree: 83%; disagree: 10%). Only a small group agreed that most public institutions have transparent rules and procedures (agree: 22%; disagree: 58%), and even fewer conceded that these are easy for common citizens to understand and follow (agree: 15%; disagree: 73%). Regression analysis where *Inefficiency of Bureaucracy* was entered as a dependent variable revealed no effect of demographic variables. Thus, people's generally negative perception of bureaucratic processes was not linked to their age, gender, or income level.

In relation to the dimension of *Legal Alienation*, mean ratings suggest that respondents were inclined to see the law as not being exclusively in the public interest. Indeed, many agreed to the statement that legal norms generally reflect the interests of those in a position of power, and rarely those of common citizens (agree: 47%; disagree: 29%), that laws are not enforced equally for all citizens (agree: 81%; disagree: 9%), and that disadvantaged people are often forced to operate on the margins of the law (agree: 54%; disagree: 32%).

Hierarchical regression analysis examined whether perceptions of legal norms and bureaucratic procedures were linked to ratings of *Legal Alienation* (see Table 6.5). In Model 1, $F\ (3, 159) = 3.50$, $p < .05$, we controlled for demographic characteristics. Age was a significant predictor, such that older people had greater ratings of legal alienation. Entering perceptions about clarity of norms and inefficiency of bureaucracy in Model 2 significantly improved the model, explaining an additional 46% of variation in legal alienation. Gender emerged as a significant predictor, such that men were more likely than women to feel alienated from the law. Additionally, to the extent that people saw legal norms as confusing, and bureaucracy as inefficient, they were more likely to perceive laws as not serving citizens. Taken together, variables in Model 2 explained a significant proportion of variance in participants' ratings of legal alienation, $R^2_{\text{adjusted}} = .51$, $F\ (5, 159) = 34.29$, $p < .001$, with perceptions of bureaucratic inefficiency uniquely explaining 16% of the variance.

Perception of informal behaviours

To explore whether informal practices are seen as intrinsic to how citizens and institutions operate, as well as identify potential predictors of tolerance for such practices, we examined responses to items addressing informal behaviours, specifically those concerning the extent to which informal practices are seen as embedded in the city's culture, and the extent to which they are tolerated as solutions to governance failures. As seen in Table 6.4, mean ratings on perceptions of *Informality as Endemic* indicate that participants were likely to see informal behaviour as a normal facet of everyday life. Most stated that bypassing the rules is typical of Italian culture (agree: 75%; disagree: 14%), and that some economic sectors can only function through informal practices (agree: 57%; disagree: 25%). Likewise, many reported that most of their acquaintances have benefitted from "exceptions to the rule" at least once (agree: 67%; disagree: 16%).

We conducted hierarchical regression analyses to investigate whether attitudes towards formal rules (i.e., clarity of legal norms, inefficiency of bureaucracy, and legal alienation) predicted people's perception of informality as endemic. Model 1 controlled for demographic characteristics. The contribution of attitudes towards legal norms was examined in Model 2 (see Table 6.5). Model 1 was not significant. Including clarity of norms, inefficiency of bureaucracy, and legal alienation in Model 2, F (6, 158) = 17.54, p <.001, significantly improved the model, explaining an additional 39% of variation in perceptions of informality as an endemic phenomenon. Legal alienation was the only reliable predictor, suggesting that greater feelings of legal alienation were associated with higher likelihood of seeing informality as endemic. Variables in Model 2 explained 39% of the variation in respondents' opinion on this dimension of informality.

Mean ratings on *Tolerance of Informality* highlight how opinions on this matter were instead more divergent. On the one hand, most respondents agreed that where clear rules are absent, it is normal that informal practices will emerge (agree: 54%; disagree: 32%). They also mostly agreed that individuals will bypass the rules when institutional control is lacking (agree: 48%; disagree: 35%). On the other hand, many disagreed that rule-bending is the only way to force institutions to change inadequate laws (agree: 25%; disagree: 60%), or that violating a rule is justified when one does not agree with it (agree: 7%; disagree: 87%). Most affirmed, in fact, that official rules should always be followed, even when they seem unfair (agree: 78%; disagree: 12%).

Hierarchical regressions explored whether attitudes towards formal rules, and perception of informality as endemic, informed people's tolerance of informality (see Table 6.6). In Model 1 we controlled for the effect of demographic variables. Attitudes towards formal rules were entered in Model 2. Model 3 tested for the contribution of perceptions of informality as endemic.

Model 1 was not significant. The inclusion of variables measuring attitudes towards formal rules in Model 2, F (6, 155) = 10.52, p <.001, explained an additional 27% of variation in tolerance for informality. Legal alienation was the only reliable predictor, such that the more people perceived the law as not serving citizens, the more tolerant they were of informal behaviours. Entering informality as endemic in Model 3, significantly improved the model. Legal alienation and perception of informality as endemic were the only significant predictors, indicating that respondent expressed greater tolerance of informality when they perceived informal practices as embedded in the culture. Taken together, variables in Model 3 explained 32% of the variation in tolerance ratings, R^2_{adjusted} =.32, F (7, 155) = 11.43, p <.001.

Acceptance of informal behaviours: the role of violators and violation type

Perceptions of rule-violators

To further explore whether participants' tolerance of informal practices was related to their perceptions about those who engage in them, additional items for the PIQ were analyzed. These items directly addressed perceptions of who breaks the rules and are presented individually, as they did not converge on a reliable scale. First, almost every participant reported seeing themselves as rule-abiding (agree: 98%; disagree: 1%). Similarly, respondents generally believed that most people follow the rules, even if not blindly (agree: 67%; disagree: 13ì%), and that those who do not do so are fundamentally dishonest people (agree: 60%; disagree: 22%). Reflecting specifically on rule-bending, most did not view this behaviour as characteristic of people with low socio-economic status (agree: 9%; disagree: 81%). On the contrary, many saw it as typical of people in a position of power (agree: 66%; disagree: 19%).

A series of multiple regression analyses were conducted on each of the above variables to explore demographic predictors as well as to examine whether perception of informality as endemic would predict the category of people that respondents perceived as engaging in informal practices. Several predictors emerged from these analyses (see Table 6.7). First, when considering people's view of themselves as rule-abiding, results indicated that older people and women more strongly viewed themselves as respecting the rules. Of interest, viewing informality as endemic was also a significant predictor, suggesting that the more likely people were to share that view, the less likely they were to declare themselves as rule-abiding. Variables in the regression explained 13% of the variance in participants' response to this item. Second, age and perceptions of informality as endemic also predicted people's view of rule-violators as dishonest. Specifically, older participants and those less likely to see informality as an endemic phenomenon were more likely to view those who bend the rules as fundamentally dishonest. A significant proportion of variance in participants' responses to this item was explained by variables in the regression. Third, when considering people's view of rule-bending as typical of those in power, results indicated that the more people agreed that informality is an endemic phenomenon, the more likely they were to perceive informal behaviours as typical of those in a position of power. Variables in the regression accounted for 20% of the variance in people's rating on this dimension. No significant predictor emerged for the two remaining items discussed above.

Lastly, we examined whether perceptions of who violates rules could contribute to explaining differences in expressed tolerance for informality. A hierarchical regression was thus conducted with *Tolerance of Informality* entered as a dependent variable. Model 1 controlled for the influence of *Legal Alienation* and perceptions of *Informality as Endemic*, which were previously found to be predictors of tolerance. Model 2 tested for the unique contribution of perceptions about rule-breakers (i.e., rule-breaking is typical of low-income people, rule-breaking is typical of those in a position of power, rule-breakers are fundamentally dishonest). Model 1 mimicked the results of previous regression analysis on tolerance, F (2, 160) = 40.9, p <.001. Even though perception of rule-breaking as typical of those in power emerged as an additional predictor (β = -.17, p <.05), entering perceptions about rule-breakers in Model 2 only explained an additional 2% of the variance in people's tolerance for informality, which did not represent a significant improvement from Model 1.

Perceptions of violation type

To address whether acceptance of informal practices was linked to the type of violation considered, we looked at participants' responses to the ARVB and PRVB surveys. As can be seen from the means in Table 6.4, most of our respondents disapproved of the behaviours presented regardless of their potential underlying motivation, albeit to different degrees. A repeated measure ANOVA explored the influence of violation type (i.e., motivated by lengthy bureaucracy vs. necessity vs. financial gain) on approval ratings, revealing a significant effect of violation type, F (2, 166) = 18.6, p <.001.

Post hoc comparisons clarified that violations motivated by bureaucracy were the most disapproved of, followed by violations motivated by financial gain. Rule violations driven by necessity were the least disapproved of. Indeed, when we looked at patterns of responses to individual items in the composites, "doing undeclared work" as well as "selling on the street without proper authorization" (behaviours often driven by necessity) were the least disapproved violations (approve: 11% for both; disapprove: 66% and 69% respectively). On the other hand, "leaving rubbish on the street" was unequivocally disapproved of by 100% of the respondents.

We examined potential predictors of approval in a series of hierarchical regressions (see Table 6.8). In Model 1 we controlled for the effect of demographic characteristics. Model 2 explored the contribution of attitudes towards informality (i.e., legal alienation, informality as endemic, and tolerance of informality). Model 3 explored any additional contribution of perceptions about rule-breakers (i.e., rule-breaking is typical of low-income people, rule-breaking is typical of those in a position of power, rule-breakers are fundamentally dishonest).

When approval of *Bureaucracy Motivated Behaviours* was entered as a dependent variable, all models were significant, *Fs* (9, 158) ≥ 3.79, *ps* ≥.05. In Model 1, age was the only significant predictor (see Table 6.8), such that older people were more likely than younger ones to disapprove of rule violations motivated by lengthy bureaucracy. Including attitudes towards informality in Model 2 explained an additional 8% of variation. Informality as endemic and tolerance of informality emerged as additional predictors, such that those more likely to see informality as an endemic phenomenon and those more tolerant of informality were less likely to disapprove of rule violations motivated by bureaucracy. Adding perceptions of rule-breakers further improved the model. Besides age, which remained a reliable predictor, legal alienation, rule-breaking as typical of those in power, and seeing rule-breakers as fundamentally dishonest, were the only other predictors. This indicates that the more people agreed that the law is unfair, and that rule-breakers are fundamentally dishonest, the more likely they were to disapprove of rule-breaking motivated by bureaucracy. On the other hand, they were more tolerant of such behaviours when they perceived rule-breaking as typical of those in power. Taken together, variables in Model 3 explained 15% of variation in people's approval of rule-breaking behaviours motivated by lengthy bureaucracy.

When approval of *Necessity Motivated Behaviours* was entered as a dependent variable, Model 1 was not significant (see Table 6.9). Including attitudes towards informality, *F* (6, 155) = 3.54, *p* <.01, explained an additional 8% of variation. Age and tolerance of informality were significant predictors, suggesting that older people and those less likely to tolerate informal behaviours were less likely to approve rule-breaking behaviours motivated by necessity. Adding perceptions of rule-breakers further improved the model, *F* (9, 155) = 5.13, *p* <.001. Perception of rule-breakers as fundamentally dishonest emerged as an additional predictor, indicating that the more people viewed rule-breakers as dishonest, the less likely they were to approve of rule-breaking behaviours driven by necessity. Income level also approached significance (*p* =.07) suggesting that there was a tendency for people with higher income to be more approving of violations motivated by necessity. Taken together, variables in Model 3 explained 19% of variation in people's approval of rule-breaking behaviours motivated by bureaucracy.

When approval of *Financially Motivated Behaviours* was entered as a dependent variable, all models were significant, *Fs* (9, 158) ≥ 2.92, *ps* ≥.05. In Model 1, age emerged as a reliable predictor (see Table 6.10), suggesting that older people were more likely than younger ones to disapprove of violations motivated by financial gain. In Model 2, tolerance of informality emerged as an additional predictor indicating that the more tolerant people were of informal behaviours, the more likely they were to approve of financially motivated violations. Model 3 further improved the model. Besides age and tolerance of informality, perception of rule-breakers as fundamentally dishonest emerged as a significant predictor. Similar to previous results, to the extent that people viewed rule-violators as fundamentally dishonest, they were more likely to disapprove of violations driven by financial gain. Taken together, variables in Model 3 explained 17% of variation in people's approval ratings of this type of violations.

Looking at attitudes towards punishment, analyses of responses on the PRVB survey indicated that most respondents believed that the violations presented should be punished by law (see Table 6.4). A repeated measure ANOVA exploring the influence of violation type (i.e., motivated by lengthy bureaucracy vs. necessity vs. financial gain) on punishment ratings, revealed a significant effect of violation type, F (2, 165) = 6.23, p <.01. Post hoc comparisons indicated that participants were less likely to approve of punishing violations motivated by necessity compared to the other two. No significant difference emerged between attitudes towards punishment of bureaucratically and financially motivated violations. Indeed, patterns of responses to individual items showed that only about half of our respondents approved of punishing behaviours such as "borrowing from an unauthorized moneylender" or "selling on the street without proper authorization" (approve: 50% and 54% respectively; disapprove: 38% and 33% respectively). On the other hand, most people believed that "lending money at high interest" and "illegal dumping" should be punished by law (approve: 69% and 72% respectively; disapprove: 28% and 27% respectively).

In a series of hierarchical regressions, we next explored potential predictors of punishment attitudes. Specifically, we tested whether approval of specific types of violation, as well as other potentially relevant attitudes, would predict whether people supported their being legally sanctioned. For punishment of violations motivated by lengthy bureaucracy, in Model 1 of the regression we controlled for variables that previously emerged as predictors of approval for such violations (i.e., age, tolerance of informality, rule-breakers as dishonest, rule-breaking as typical of those in power). In Model 2 we explored the added contribution of approval for bureaucracy driven violations and of people's general perceptions of bureaucracy. Model 1 was not significant. Variables in Model 2 significantly improved the model, explaining an additional 6% of the variance. Approval of bureaucracy motivated violations and perceptions of bureaucracy emerged as reliable predictors (ß = -.20, p <.05 and ß = -.22, p <.05, respectively), such that the more likely people were to approve bureaucracy motivated violations and to view bureaucratic procedures as slow and inefficient, the less likely they were to approve of punishing such behaviours. Taken together, variables in Model 2 explained 4% of variation in punishment ratings, $R^2_{adjusted}$ =.04, F (6, 154) = 2.14, p =.05.

Looking at predictors of punishment for violations motivated by necessity, in Model 1 we entered predictors of approval for such behaviours (i.e., age, tolerance of informality, rule-breakers as dishonest), and tested the unique contribution of approval for such behaviours in Model 2. Model 1 was not significant. Model 2 indicated approval of necessity-motivated violations as the only predictor for attitudes towards punishing this type of violations (ß = -.60, p <.001), such that the more people approved of these violations, the less supportive they were of them being punished. Taken together, variables in

Model 2 explained 6% of variation in punishment ratings, $R^2_{adjusted}$ =.06, F (4, 150) = 3.43, p =.01.

When considering punishment for violations motivated by financial gain, we entered predictors of approval for such behaviours in Model 1 (i.e., age, tolerance of informality, rule-breakers as dishonest). In Model 2 we tested for the added contribution of approval of this type of behaviours, as well as examined whether seeing informality as endemic and seeing rule-breaking as typical of those in power would predict people's attitudes towards punishing financially motivated violations. Both models failed to reach conventional levels of statistical significance.

Discussion

The goal of our study was to explore people's perceptions of formal rules and informal behaviours to understand whether the perspectives often attributed to informal actors are widely shared among "regular" citizens. Specifically, one of our aims was to examine people's perceptions of the efficacy and clarity of the law since lack of clear regulations and institutional control are often identified as creating fertile ground for informal activities. Two results are worthy of consideration in this regard. First, we documented how most Romans shared a negative view of legal norms and of the bureaucratic procedures that stem from them. People viewed laws and regulations as often too complex to be understood by regular citizens, and contradictory to the point of being ineffective. They perceived them as mostly representing the needs of the elites, often forcing the least fortunate to operate at the edge of legality. Similarly, respondents viewed bureaucratic procedures as not easily accessible nor helpful. Rather, they shared a view that institutional processes are time-consuming, inefficient, and disturbingly slow even in rectifying their own mistakes or omissions. It is important to note that these views were expressed by most respondents, irrespective of their age, gender, education, or income.

These results indicate that shortcomings in regulations and their enforcement are not confined to specific areas of governance or social groups. They are instead pervasive and experienced in the everyday dealings of "regular" citizens. Indeed, our findings chime with the results of a recent Eurobarometer study (EC, 2019) exploring people's attitudes towards the rule of law. These show that 58% of the Italians surveyed "definitely" believed that improvement was needed to ensure that "[t]he laws applying to your everyday life, work, or business are clear, stable and predictable. You understand the consequences of your actions." The relevance of negative opinions concerning bureaucracy is further underlined by a second interesting result of our study: that individuals' perceptions about the clarity of laws and, most importantly, about the effectiveness of bureaucratic procedures, were directly linked to their feelings about the actual legitimacy of the laws (i.e., what we identified as legal alienation). This suggests that people may distance themselves from laws and public institutions when they perceive them to be inaccessible or incompatible with citizens' temporal and other needs, an attitude that may contribute to rendering informal behaviours more acceptable, as we discuss later. It is worth noting that feelings of legal alienation were more common among men than women. Nevertheless, the widely spread negative views concerning the equity, coherence, and efficacy of legal norms and procedures offers support to the notion that it is regulatory inadequacy – and especially the perception that rules are not legitimate – that underpins practices of interpreting, bending, or ignoring rules.

A second aim of our study was to examine whether rule-bending is so intertwined with formal regulations as to be considered an endemic feature of the relationship between citizens and institutions, and as such likely tolerated, if not accepted, by most. Indeed, most respondents saw informal practices as characteristic of everyday relations, often tolerated by the very institutional agents mandated to oppose them, and frequently perceived as the only way to "get things done." Thus, borrowing from Gouldner's (1954) framework for classifying types of bureaucracy, it could be argued that Romans perceive the system to be a *mock bureaucracy*, where the ambiguity of rules combines with low emphasis on strict adherence, such that people think that enforcement is largely for show or ineffective. Notably, to the extent that people shared those views, they were also more likely to accept informal practices.

A few further results are also worth considering. First, contrary to what one may have expected, people's negative views about laws and procedures were not directly linked to their perceptions about the pervasiveness of rule-bending behaviours. Rather, the influence of these variables was mediated by feelings of legal alienation. Second, legal alienation was also the most important predictor of tolerance of informality, above and beyond the effect of people's view on the endemic nature of informal behaviours. Third, these views were not influenced by demographic characteristics or by perceptions of who breaks the rules.

Taken together, these results suggest that even when citizens see rule-bending behaviours as a common and often necessary means of navigating relations with institutions, they do not blindly approve of them. They only approve of them to the extent that they perceive the law as inadequate and not in the public interest, and rule-bending as a way to compensate for normative gaps. This points to a fundamental conclusion: informality is not the deeply embedded habitus of specific sub-cultural groups. It is widely understood as a pragmatic direct response to institutional inadequacies. In short, it is driven by the state and followed by citizens, who observe its patterns and learn to bend and adapt their behaviours accordingly.

One last goal was to explore people's perceptions of particular types of rule violations and of those who engage in them. Specifically, we were interested in examining whether Romans shared the common assumption that rule-breaking is the domain of the disadvantaged and whether their opinions on such behaviors reflected the potentially different motivations and actors behind them. A few notable results emerged. Contrary to much of the literature that portrays informalities as the practices of the poor and marginalized, our results suggested that Romans viewed them predominantly as the domain of the rich and powerful. They also considered rule-breakers to be fundamentally dishonest. These opinions were more strongly held when informal practices were seen as an endemic feature of urban life. This may suggest that people are sensitive to the idea that maintaining informality requires the cooperation and tolerance of those in power. In other words, they seem to share the view that institutions maintain a "façade of legal-rationality" (Chiodelli & Tzfadia, 2016, p. 7) for the purposes of political legitimacy while de facto participating in informalities. The data indicates that there is a generalized awareness of power differentials in these forms of "grey governance," in terms of both why they exist and how those who carry them out are treated. One could interpret this as a recognition that weak groups often need to bend rules or invest in personalized negotiations with public officials to access necessary resources, while the latter have the power to decide how far they are willing to allow those rules to be bent.

Second, Romans generally disapproved of all rule violations (a feeling that increased with age), but they also discriminated among different types of violating behaviours. As expected, people were less disapproving of rule violations that were possibly driven by necessity compared to those stemming from other reasons. However, given the generally negative view expressed in relation to bureaucratic efficacy, one might have also expected people to be somewhat more tolerant towards violations aimed at bypassing burdensome red tape, and somewhat less indulgent towards those committed for personal financial gain. Instead, the opposite was found. Indeed, we uncovered very strong negative opinions towards rule-breaking aimed at taking shortcuts around bureaucratically stipulated processes. Notably, for example, every single individual in our sample disapproved of people who do not respect waste disposal guidelines. In interpreting this finding, it may be useful to remember that most of our respondents see themselves as rule-abiding and may thus feel less tolerant towards those who do not follow regulations without an apparent justification (whether monetary, or for reasons of survival) other than "speeding things up." It is also worth noting that people were less approving of such behaviours when their ratings of legal alienation were high.

One possible interpretation is that people judge more harshly the behaviours that may have an immediate impact on their own access to services than violations that have longer-term impacts on institutional functioning, such as evading taxes and social security contributions.

In other words, they may see those who bypass or violate the law for bureaucratic reasons as contributing to the very institutional inefficiency and shortcomings that "law abiding" citizens confront on a daily basis (arguably because these types of violations are also under less intense scrutiny by those charged to enforce the rules) and that feed their sense of alienation from the law.

Third, people also deemed violations driven by necessity to be less worthy of punishment compared to other kinds of violations, confirming a general awareness of the disadvantages possibly faced by poorer social groups in dealings with Italian regulations. It is worth remembering that the majority of our respondents agreed that underprivileged citizens are often "forced" to act at the margins of the law, thus perhaps explaining their greater reluctance in punishing the resulting violations. We note that demographic variables had no impact on punishment attitudes, which were explained mostly by how approving people were of the specific types of behaviour considered. However, we should be cautious of drawing any conclusion in this regard, as it is possible that the restricted range of punishment ratings might have made it difficult for this effect to be detected. Future studies should address this more closely.

Conclusions

Despite the vast amount of research on informalities globally, little has been done to investigate how ordinary citizens judge such practices and whether they perceive them to be pervasive and open to a wide range of actors. This study is a first attempt at mapping Romans' attitudes regarding these issues and offers some useful insights while at the same time delineating interesting avenues for future research. One important conclusion to be drawn is that Romans do not think that the inadequacy of regulations and bureaucratic procedures justifies violating or bending the rules. Only to the extent that institutional inadequacy influences how alienated people feel from the law are such violations tolerated, regardless of who may engage in such practices. This suggests that, despite the stereotypes, rule bending is not normatively sanctioned, at least by our sample of Romans. We are not dealing here with a set of uncodified norms and practices that are more legitimate and widely shared than those created by formal institutions. Although the malleability of rules is clearly viewed as an institutional mechanism of grey governance, people do not generally approve of exploiting this malleability. The practical implications of this are significant. It suggests that there is not a deep-seated cultural resistance to formal rules; nevertheless, there is a strong sense that regulations are unfair and inefficient. Consequently, one can assume that institutional reform aimed at clarifying rules, speeding up bureaucratic processes, and explicitly enacting them in equitable and transparent ways would solve the needs that Romans feel fuel informalities. The tendency of public institutional actors to blame rule-breaking on residents' lack of education or civic sense – as is conveyed in the municipal fliers discussed in chapters 3 and 5, for example – is not borne out in our data.

Improving bureaucratic functioning is not only important in its own right, it is also fundamental to fostering the legitimacy of the rule of law. We have seen that people who think that laws are not efficient or only benefit elites are more likely to tolerate informal activities. The more widespread such views become, the more difficult it is for institutions to implement the rules systematically. This makes them more likely to develop additional regulatory layers, contributing to further legal alienation in what can easily degenerate into a vicious cycle.

A second important conclusion is that not all violations are tolerated to the same extent. While people are more understanding of navigating around the rules for necessity, they have especially negative opinions of those who bypass bureaucratic procedures. Although this confirms the theoretical assumption that informalities are power-inflected, it also suggests that there is a third possible interpretation that goes beyond the current dualistic view that informalities either constitute resistance against oppressive state power or the self-serving practices of the powerful. It indicates that people disapprove of the informalities of others on the basis of whether those activities may bring them noticeable disadvantages in the short term, such as delaying their own access to bureaucratic services. Instead, violations that do not have easily identifiable immediate victims, such as those aiming to cut costs, are less condemned. One practical significance of this finding is that people do not appear to be aware of how systemic informalities erode the quality and availability of public services for all social groups in the long term. There appears to be little perception that tax evasion, for example, has consequences on the hiring of personnel in public offices, or that squatting of housing undermines the fair distribution of public accommodation. It is clear that a two-pronged approach is needed by the institutions: bypassing of bureaucratic processes needs to be monitored and sanctioned as much as other types of informality are, in order to increase people's feeling that the law really does apply equally to all. This needs to be buttressed with intensive awareness-raising campaigns both among bureaucrats and the public concerning the long-term collective damage that discretionality and favouritism fosters.

The obvious third conclusion is that informalities are not restricted to marginalized groups. They are seen by Romans as endemic and actively supported by those in power. They are not, therefore, "departures from bureaucratic routine but, instead, constitute the essence of bureaucratic routine" (Martin et al., 2013, p. 551).

Limitations and future directions

In drawing these conclusions, several limitations need to be addressed. First, the data were collected during the COVID-19 pandemic, which made it difficult to reach an extensive and fully representative sample of Rome's population and redirected us towards a convenience sample. This resulted in some important groups (e.g., those with low educational qualifications and some professional categories, such as shop owners) being under-represented. Second, despite ensured anonymity in data collection, it is possible that fears of exposure, as well as the taboos associated with some of the practices covered, may have influenced participants' patterns of responses. Moreover, it is likely that issues of self-presentation resulted in respondents over-emphasizing their own normative adherence to formal rules. Third, the questionnaire on legal attitudes was positioned before the questions on rule-violating behaviors. It is thus possible that the order of presentation may have primed participants to think about the legitimacy of regulatory and legal frameworks, potentially explaining the low variability in approval observed in the last sets of questions.

The study was exploratory in nature and several potential avenues of investigation emerged as we analyzed our results. Our results, for example, indicate the possibility that citizens may be more alert to (and consequently more disapproving of) violations with visible short-term impacts compared to those that may more slowly erode institutional mechanisms and procedures. An in-depth examination of people's awareness and understanding of the impact of informal practices on the quality and availability of public services is thus warranted.

The current research purposefully did not ask respondents about their own rule-violating behaviours, given the methodological difficulties of building trust and overcoming the pressures of positive self-representation in a closed-question survey. Future research will use in-depth narrative and reflexive interview methods to try to trace the connections between the perspectives explored here and their roles in participants' own decision-making processes and actions in relation to rules. Our preliminary findings indicate that there are scales in people's normative understandings of which rules are more or less acceptable to break. One of the next tasks will be to more clearly map how those views intersect with and are used to legitimize rule-bending. Although this study is only the start of what hopes to be more systematic and detailed research, it provides an important step towards investigating the nuances and possible contradictions underlying the widespread view that informalities are an endemic feature of Italian public life.

Table 6.1 Summary of demographic characteristics of study sample

Gender *(N = 172)*	
Female	60.00%
Male	40.00%
Other	0.00%
Age groups (N = 172)	
Less than 25-yrs-old	16.30%
25–44-yrs-old	29.00%
45–64-yrs-old	50.00%
65-yrs and older	4.70%
Education level (N = 172)	
High school diploma or less	29.70%
University degree	39.50%
Post-graduate degree	30.80%
Income level (N = 168)	
Less than 15K	20.20%
15–28K	30.40%
28–55K	36.30%
More than 55K	13.00%

Table 6.2 Specific items in the mean composite scores for PIQ

Clarity of legal norms composite (*Cronbach* α =.72)
Local and national laws are rarely in contradiction with each other (R)
Our laws are often too convoluted to be understood by laypersons
Laws are often in conflict with one another
The sheer number of existing laws as well as their contradictions undermine their actual efficacy
Following one rule often implies violating others
It is not difficult for an honest person to understand and abide by the different rules that exist (R)
Inefficiency of bureaucracy composite (*Cronbach* α =.72)
It is impossible for common citizens to be up to date about all the institutional services they could benefit from
Bureaucratic procedures are easy for common citizens to understand and follow (R)
Respecting bureaucratic procedures when requesting services or authorizations is not always compatible with citizens' own time frames
It is practically impossible to benefit in a timely manner from institutional services if one follows official procedures
When institutions make mistakes, it takes a long time to rectify them
Bureaucracy is too slow to be of any real help to citizens
Most public institutions have transparent rules and procedures (R)
Even if often slow, official procedures serve to protect citizens and avoid possible abuses (R)
Legal alienation composite (*Cronbach* α =.72)
Laws are often too strict and rarely meet the actual needs of citizens
To act according to the rules, one often needs to enlist the help of an expert, which not everyone can afford
Police forces do not always enforce laws equally for all citizens
Laws are generally meant to simplify citizens' lives and protect their interests (R)
Disadvantaged people are often forced to operate on the margins of the law
Legal and regulatory frameworks generally reflect the interests of those in a position of power, and rarely those of common citizens
Bypassing the rules is a luxury not everyone can afford
Bypassing the rules is only easy for those who know the "right people"
Informality as endemic composite (*Cronbach* α =.68)
People who bypass the rules are rarely caught
Rule bending is the norm in many instances of everyday life
Some economic sectors can only function through informal practices
Bypassing the laws is typical of Italian culture
Most of my acquaintances have benefitted from "exceptions to the rule" at least once
When in need of institutional services (e.g., to obtain permits or other types of certificates), it is normal for people to seek informal shortcuts, rather than follow the official procedures
Institutions are often tolerant of rule bending behaviours
Law enforcement agencies often look the other way when someone doesn't follow the rules

Tolerance of informality composite (*Cronbach* α =.70)

In the absence of clear rules, it is normal for informal practices to emerge
Rule-bending is the only way to force institutions to change their regulatory frameworks
It is ok to violate a rule you do not agree with, as long as you don't get caught
When rules are absent or unclear, it is normal for citizens to take matters into their own hands
Bypassing the law is often the only way to benefit from a public service in a timely manner
Individuals will bypass the rules when institutional control is lacking
Rules should always be followed, even when they seem unfair (R)
Laws can often be interpreted to one's own advantage

Note: R= reverse scored.

Table 6.3 Specific items in the mean composite scores for ARVB and PRVB surveys

Bureaucracy motivated behaviours (*Cronbach* α =.69)
Relying on personal connections to obtain favours (e.g., skipping the queue, fast-tracking paperwork, finding a job, etc.)
Not disposing of waste according to official guidelines
Jumping ahead of the waiting list for public housing
Leaving rubbish on the streets
Renovating one's home without requesting proper authorizations
Necessity motivated behaviours (*Cronbach* α =.74)
Borrowing from an *usuraio* (i.e., an unauthorized moneylender)
Squatting in public housing
Selling on the street without proper authorization
Doing undeclared work
Financially motivated behaviours (*Cronbach* α =.78)
Lending money at high interest
Paying workers under the table
Paying a professional (e.g., a doctor, plumber, lawyer) at a discounted fee by forfeiting a tax receipt
Buying counterfeit goods
Providing professional services at a discounted price, without providing a tax receipt
Punishment of bureaucracy motivated behaviours (*Cronbach* α =.94)
Relying on personal connections to obtain favours (e.g., skipping the queue, fast-tracking paperwork, finding a job, etc.)
Not disposing of waste according to official guidelines
Jumping ahead of the waiting list for public housing
Leaving rubbish on the streets
Renovating one's home without requesting proper authorizations
Punishment of necessity motivated behaviours (*Cronbach* α =.91)
Borrowing from an *usuraio* (i.e., an unauthorized moneylender)
Squatting in public housing
Selling on the street without proper authorization
Doing undeclared work
Punishment of financially motivated behaviours (*Cronbach* α =.93)
Lending money at high interest
Paying workers under the table
Paying a professional (e.g., a doctor, plumber, lawyer) at a discounted fee by forfeiting a tax receipt.
Buying counterfeit goods
Providing professional services at a discounted price, without providing a tax receipt

Table 6.4 Mean ratings for all surveys composites (N = 167)

Clarity of legal norms composite	4.48	(.95)
Inefficiency of bureaucracy composite	5.02	(.84)
Legal alienation composite	4.5	(.96)
Informality as endemic composite	4.36	(.91)
Tolerance of informality composite	3.99	(.82)
Approval of bureaucracy motivated behaviours	1.84	(.80)
Approval of necessity motivated behaviours	2.21	(1.03)
Approval of financially motivated behaviours	2.07	(.95)
Punishment of bureaucracy motivated behaviours	4.77	(2.08)
Punishment of necessity motivated behaviours	4.54	(1.97)
Punishment of financially motivated behaviours	4.73	(1.93)

Note: Variables were scored 1 = Strongly Disagree/Disapprove to 7 = Strongly Agree/Approve. Standard deviation in parentheses.

Table 6.5 Summary of hierarchical regression analysis for variables predicting Legal Alienation and Informality as Endemic

	Model 1		*Model 2*	
Variables	*B(SE)*	β	*B(SE)*	β
Legal alienation (N = 159)				
Intercept	4.03 (.27)		.27 (.37)	
Age	.02 (.01)	.24**	.01 (.00)	.09
Gender	.18 (.15)	.19	.22 (.11)	.23*
Income	-.12 (.08)	-.13	-.06 (.06)	-.06
Clarity of norms			.29 (.07)	.29***
Inefficiency of bureaucracy			.55 (.07)	.49***
R^2	.06		.53	
F for Δ R^2			75.40***	
Informality as endemic (N = 158)				
Intercept	3.98 (.26)		1.16 (.39)	
Age	.01 (.01)	.14	-.00 (.00)	-.01
Gender	.01 (.15)	.02	-.07 (.12)	-.08
Income	-.02 (.08)	-.02	.05 (.06)	.06
Clarity of norms			.10 (.07)	.11
Inefficiency of bureaucracy			.11 (.09)	.10
Legal alienation			.47 (.09)	.50***
R^2	.02		.41	
F for Δ R^2			33.40***	

Note: *p ≤.05, **p ≤.01, ***p≤.001.

Table 6.6 Summary of hierarchical regression analysis for variables predicting Tolerance of Informality (N = 155)

	Model 1		Model 2		Model 3	
Variables	*B(SE)*	β	*B(SE)*	β	*B(SE)*	β
Tolerance of informality						
Intercept	3.78 (.23)		1.78 (.38)		1.47 (.38)	
Age	.00 (.00)	.05	-.00 (.00)	-.07	-.00 (.00)	-.07
Gender	.23 (.13)	.30	.15 (.11)	.19	.17 (.11)	.21
Income	-.01 (.07)	-.01	.05 (.06)	.06	.03 (.06)	.04
Coherence of norms			.08 (.07)	.10	.06 (.07)	.07
Inefficiency of bureaucracy			.02 (.09)	.02	-.01 (.09)	-.01
Legal alienation			.39 (.08)	.46***	.26 (.09)	.31**
Informality as endemic					.27 (.08)	.30***
R^2	.02		.30		.35	
F for ΔR^2			19.30***		12.20***	

Note: *p ≤.05, **p ≤.01, ***p≤.001.

Table 6.7 Summary of regression analysis for variables predicting perceptions of who breaks the law

Variables	*B(SE)*	β	R^2	*F*
I see myself as generally abiding with the rules (N = 163)			.15	6.96***
Intercept	6.62 (.34)			
Age	.02 (.00)	.26***		
Gender	-.38 (.12)	-.46**		
Income	-.05 (.07)	-.05		
Informality as endemic	-.20 (.07)	-.23**		
Those who bend the rules are fundamentally dishonest (N = 164)			.07	2.88*
Intercept	5.54 (.76)			
Age	.03 (.01)	.23**		
Gender	-.19 (.27)	-.11		
Income	-.15 (.15)	-.08		
Informality as endemic	-.31 (.15)	-.16*		
Bending the rules is typical of those in power (N = 164)			.22	11.50***
Intercept	1.28 (.64)			
Age	.01 (.01)	.07		
Gender	.21 (.23)	.13		
Income	-.14 (.12)	-.08		
Informality as endemic	.80 (.12)	.45***		

Note: *p ≤.05, **p ≤.01, ***p≤.001.

Table 6.8 Summary of hierarchical regression analysis for variables predicting Bureaucracy Motivated Behaviours (N = 155)

	Model 1		Model 2		Model 3	
Variables	*B(SE)*	β	*B(SE)*	β	*B(SE)*	β
Bureaucracy motivated behaviours						
Intercept	2.30 (.22)		1.44 (.37)		1.94 (.42)	
Age	-.00 (.00)	-.27***	-.01 (.00)	-.27***	-.01 (.00)	-.24**
Gender	.09 (.12)	.12	.07 (.12)	.09	.06 (.12)	.07
Income	.05 (.07)	.06	.03 (.06)	.04	.03 (.06)	.03
Legal alienation			-.15 (.08)	-.19	-.20 (.08)	-.25*
Informality as endemic			.17 (.08)	.20*	.11 (.08)	.13
Tolerance of informality			.22 (.09)	.23*	.17 (.09)	.17
Informality typical of poor					.00 (.04)	.01
Informality typical of power					.10 (.04)	.21*
Informals are dishonest					-.08 (.03)	-.19*
R^2	.07		.15		.20	
F for ΔR^2			4.67**		3.24*	

Note: *p ≤.05, **p ≤.01, ***p≤.001.

Table 6.9 *Summary of hierarchical regression analysis for variables predicting Necessity Motivated Behaviours (N = 155)*

	Model 1		*Model 2*		*Model 3*	
Variables	*B(SE)*	β	*B(SE)*	β	*B(SE)*	β
Necessity motivated behaviours						
Intercept	2.48 (.30)		.99 (.52)		2.25 (.56)	
Age	-.01 (.01)	-.20**	-.02 (.01)	-.23**	-.01 (.01)	-.17*
Gender	.05 (.16)	.05	-.07 (.16)	-.07	-.14 (.15)	-.13
Income	.17 (.09)	.14	.17 (.09)	.17	.15 (.08)	.14
Legal alienation			.10 (.11)	.09	.08 (.11)	.08
Informality as endemic			-.04 (.11)	-.04	-.09 (.11)	-.09
Tolerance of informality			.33 (.12)	.25**	.30 (.12)	.23*
Informality typical of poor					-.08 (.05)	-.12
Informality typical of power					.03 (.06)	.06
Informals are dishonest					-.19 (.04)	-.32***
R^2	.04		.12		.24	
F for ΔR^2			4.71**		7.40***	

Note: *p ≤.05, **p ≤.01, ***p≤.001.

Table 6.10 Summary of hierarchical regression analysis for variables predicting Financially Motivated Behaviours (N = 158)

	Model 1		*Model 2*		*Model 3*	
Variables	*B(SE)*	β	*B(SE)*	β	*B(SE)*	β
Financially motivated behaviours						
Intercept	2.63 (.28)		1.12 (.45)		1.95 (.51)	
Age	-.01 (.01)	-.22**	-.02 (.01)	-.24**	-.01 (.01)	-.19*
Gender	.15 (.15)	.17	.09 (.15)	.10	.08 (.14)	.08
Income	.00 (.08)	.00	-.01 (.08)	-.01	-.03 (.08)	-.03
Legal alienation			-.06 (.10)	-.06	-.09 (.10)	-.09
Informality as endemic			.17 (.10)	.16	.12 (.10)	.12
Tolerance of informality			.29 (.11)	.25**	.25 (.11)	.21*
Informality typical of poor					.00 (.05)	.01
Informality typical of power					.05 (.05)	.09
Informals are dishonest					-.14 (.04)	-.26***
R^2	.05		.16		.22	
F for ΔR^2			6.28***		3.72**	

Note: *p ≤.05, **p ≤.01, ***p≤.001.

Notes

1 Since informalities are a spectrum of behaviours that include breaking some rules and violating official processes, as well as bending or navigating around them, we asked questions covering these various gradations.

2 Note that for purposes of readability we do not report the "do not agree or disagree" responses.

References

Chiodelli, F., & Moroni, S. (2014). The complex nexus between informality and the law: Reconsidering unauthorised settlements in light of the concept of nomotropism. *Geoforum*, 51, 161–169. https://doi.org/10.1016/j.geoforum.2013.11.004.

Chiodelli, F., & Tzfadia, E. (2016). The multifaceted relation between formal institutions and the production of informal urban spaces: An editorial introduction. *Geography Research Forum*, 36, 1–14.

EC (European Commission). (2019). Rule of Law. Eurobarometer 91.3. https://europa.eu/eurobarometer/surveys/detail/2235.

Gouldner, A. W. (1954). *Patterns of industrial bureaucracy.* Free Press.

Martin, A. W., Lopez, S. H., Roscigno, V. J., & Hodson, R. (2013). Against the rules: Synthesizing types and processes of bureaucratic rule-breaking. *Academy of Management Review*, 38, 550–574. https://doi.org/10.5465/amr.2011.0223.

Conclusion

Rome is a city that defies categorization. It is not a global city or a megacity. It shares little, morphologically and in terms of governance, with cities labelled as part of the "Global South" or with many of those thrown together under the umbrella of "Global North." It is "ordinary" (Robinson, 2005) and unique. Any endeavour to define it, to subsume its sedimented layers of practices and its messy, often contradictory, urban politics into a single diagnosis, a grand theory, is unlikely to be successful. To make any such attempt would also run counter to all the findings of this book. Each of the four fields of urban life explored in the case studies has developed in its own singular way, shaped at once by specific external pressures and by the many actors that have populated it. An examination of other sectors not covered here, such as healthcare, urban planning, bureaucratic management of migrants, would likely reveal equally distinct logics. The empirical particularism of this book, in fact, is one of its core theoretical contributions. It demonstrates that we need to move beyond ontological theorizations of how cities and their governance systems work and what roles informality plays in them. The chapters together demonstrate that none of the many theories of informality are, alone, fully applicable to Rome. Informality does not emerge here specifically as a habitus of the poor, or as a means of gradually forcing political change from below. It is not exclusively a tactic of subaltern resistance, nor is it the privileged territory of the powerful. Rome's informalities rarely produce alternative sovereignties distinct from the state and they are not restricted to any particular economic sector or spatial domain. They are not just a result of capitalist structuring, nor are they simply a function of neoliberalism. Equally, the book's case studies indicate that no over-arching pattern can be extracted from Rome to readily explain the workings of other places in the world (or even in Italy) whose social histories and contemporary configurations are very different.

Paradoxically, it is precisely the demonstrated specificities of the Roman context that should be of use to scholars working in other urban contexts and governance spheres. By breaking with the sectoral perspectives usually taken (informality as economic strategy, as mode of urban planning, as welfare provision, etc.), the book demonstrates that informality is best understood as a *method* of study. It offers a way to look at how rules are made and used

DOI: 10.4324/9780429353321-8

and, through them, how power is negotiated in and across governance systems of all types. It can thus be applied to any institution, including private businesses, places of study, religious organizations, and numerous others. It can equally be used to understand power within informally constituted communities where rules may not be codified but are widely shared and adhered to. While the state should not be assumed to always be a player in such dynamics, it often does influence them, directly or obliquely.

This book has focused on how official regulations produced by various state agencies are moulded and interpreted in Rome, and to what ends. The approach makes visible how state power is always contextual, never absolute. It never loses sight, though, of the state's privileged capacity to define and categorise, to enforce and punish. The goal has thus been to paint a picture of Rome's social life that is on the one hand microscopic, descriptive of the everyday practices and decisions of some of the people whose activities tangle with official regulations, concurrently escaping them and conditioned by them. On the other hand, the analysis has connected those threads to the macroscopic patterns that have been woven over time in how official regulations have been conceived and implemented, contradicted and ignored. It is only by examining the threads and the political-economic fabric together that we can understand where the rule is used to distribute rights and resources equitably and where, instead, iniquitous effects emerge that need to be undone.

Each of the book's case-study chapters can be read independently, as a genealogical mapping of how a single field of urban governance has evolved and how actors within it have produced its hierarchies and logics. As the historical discussion of each one has shown, the emergence of its specific formal rules has mirrored its changing political and economic stakes. Informal practices have unfolded in symbiosis with those regulatory frameworks, within the latticework of constraints and opportunities that regulations and their (non) enforcement have fostered. An array of agents have moved within those spaces: not only the bureaucrats who have been shown to bend and interpret rules for multiple reasons, or just the actors who have difficulties dwelling and working in conformity with the letter of the rule. Other figures have also been found to inhabit those spheres of liminality. Some, like NGOs and community leaders, bridge the exigencies of those who operate informally with those who are tasked with implementing the rule. Others exploit the gaps between the rule and its application to their own advantage: high-interest moneylenders, illegal housing entrepreneurs, trickster political actors, and many others. Each set of actors thus mobilizes the skills, knowledge, and material resources available to them to stretch the rules or work around them. In doing so, they adapt to and simultaneously shape the ideologies that permeate the field: what practices are normalized and licit, whose interests and priorities carry most weight, and how far these can be contested and modified. Beyond the inherent empirical value of unpacking the dynamics and impacts of power in any sector of governance, these chapters offer a useful model for excavating archaeologies of how formal power builds on informal negotiations, how the visible and the invisible interlace, and how the socially powerful and the weak become interdependent. It is a heuristic strategy that can be implemented at any scale and in all political contexts.

Informalities as an institutionalized mode of rule

Looked at together, however, the case studies – combined with the survey data – reveal some overarching patterns in how informalities are used in Rome across different domains. First, in every one of the sectors discussed, informal practices have been shown to be the direct consequence of regulatory frameworks and processes that are opaque and often contradictory. These practices are not manifestations of specific subcultures or deep-rooted mechanisms of sociality and reciprocity. They do not occur in a dimension separate from the state, but *because of* the state. For centuries, unauthorized housing production, waste dumping and gleaning, borrowing money, selling on the streets, existed in Rome in the absence of adequate institutional infrastructure and management systems. At their origins, these informal practices were complementary to the state (Altrock, 2016), filling the gaps where institutions and official services were minimal or non-existent. However, as the stakes of each field rose, as the country and its capital were forced to respond to rapid post-war urban and economic growth, expansive regulatory mechanisms became unavoidable. Although these frameworks developed in different time periods, some incrementally – as in the case of street vending – and some more integrally – like the credit sector – they have all been implemented partially and selectively. Whether this has been caused by institutions' failure to enforce the rules, such as in the public housing sector, or because the law's formulation does not address the core needs of its targets, like anti-usury legislation, informalities have now become supplementary to regulatory systems that, though existent, are ineffective.

Second, Rome's particular informalities are not indicative that a process of regulatory rollback is underway. On the contrary, each of the governance sectors examined seems burdened by hyper-regulation. Rules are often convoluted and ambiguous in their formulation, layered on top of earlier ones or in contrast with ones emitted by other state agencies. We have also seen that the multiple forms of documentation often required, the frequent need to hire professionals to navigate labyrinthine bureaucracies, and the financial costs involved, mean that full conformity to official rules is difficult for many. The rigidities are such that workarounds must often be found for the processes to match the realities of the people they target. Yet, the ability to navigate the obstacles successfully is conditional on actors' personal resources, especially their knowledge of regulatory loopholes or unofficial patterns of enforcement. The frameworks in place thus do not make access to institutional services a right, transparently applied and equal for all. Indeed, even when the letter of the rule is univocal, its application frequently is not. A result is the exacerbated social exclusion of disadvantaged actors who lack the documents and social networks, cultural and economic capital necessary to work and reside fully within the law.

Third, in every sector studied, the bending of rules and violation of formal institutional goals is not merely the result of occasional actions by individual functionaries. The patterns have become macroscopic and systemic. For decades, public housing authorities have allowed a parallel private market to undermine their ability to provide homes to those most in need. Similarly longstanding rule-breaking by waste management authorities has incapacitated them from developing infrastructures to fully protect health and the environment in the present. The municipality continues to foster unauthorized street trading by not issuing enough licences to create new job opportunities. Loan-sharking victims requiring state support are repeatedly deprived of protection. While this does not suggest that all public services in the city are equally flawed – indeed, there are certainly sectors that operate efficiently and transparently – the specific failures mapped here indicate that in the capital of one of the world's most advanced economies, the state does not fully deliver basic rights to shelter, fair enterprise, or safety. In each case, there is a lack of accountability to the public that the institutions serve and an absence of consistent sanctions when they do not meet their mandates.

Chronic institutional slowness often directly results from this complexity of rules and procedures, forcing people into long periods of waiting that can have grave consequences on their access to other services and their ability to manage and plan their lives. Such governing through uncertainty is by no means specific to Rome (Tucker & Devlin, 2019). However, the results of our survey point clearly to the existence of widely shared views in the capital that lack of regulatory clarity merges with bureaucratic inefficiencies in driving informal practices as an alternative, often more efficacious, means of meeting one's needs. Of particular concern is the fact that many people view public institutions as slow in rectifying their own mistakes or omissions. This seems to connect with the findings of chapter 4 that some economic actors avoid dealing with public institutions where possible, perceiving them as a source of problems rather than service.

At the same time, the case studies show that the temporalities of the state go far beyond simple inertia and inefficiency. In each of the fields examined, the relevant institutions have engaged in periods of prolonged disappearance, during which they have not implemented official regulations and procedures at all or have done so minimally. This has often served to avoid conflicts with economically and politically important groups, tacitly fostering unofficial alternatives. These phases have alternated, though, with sporadic and sometimes dramatic reappearances at politically critical junctures, such as impending elections, EU deadlines, a build-up of tragic events or of material signs of institutional neglect. These temporalized pressures have then dictated *how* the relevant official bodies have made themselves felt. Roman authorities have calculated the relative political advantages or costs of their possible responses. In some situations, they have had an interest in negotiating, using selective formalizations to address the accumulated informalities that state absence has fuelled. In others, repression or the threat of violence have been chosen as the most effective tool to convey the state's potency and legitimacy.

Fourth, it is in these temporalized manoeuvres that the institutional production and management of informalities emerges most evidently as a mode of rule. At times for immediate tactical purposes, at times as part of a longer-term strategy, public institutions have been shown to repeatedly use regulatory *shifts* as a technology of power. Formal rules do not act; they must be enacted. By cancelling, replacing, layering rules, by ignoring them and then selectively enforcing them, Rome's authorities have moved informal practices into or out of regulatory clarity to achieve specific disciplinary goals. It is through this mutable labelling that state institutions have created the conditions for asserting coercive power, often placing in a state of illegality the survival activities of weak groups. Concurrently, they have repeatedly served to turn surveillance away from the actions of more powerfully positioned actors. The symbolic force of labels has been central to these mechanisms, with politicians and functionaries entwining regulatory manoeuvres with ideological ones, channelling and reinforcing the stigmatization of specific categories of people as informal/illegal while legitimizing rule-bending of institutional actors and of groups – such as Italian street vendors – who carry discursive weight through media and political campaigning.

An equally important disciplinary effect has been to constrain people to organize their informal practices in direct relation to the state's shifting definitions and temporalities. The case studies have highlighted how agents draw on their knowledge of past patterns of state behaviour to inform their actions in the present and the future. They act not just "in light of the rules" (Chiodelli & Moroni, 2014), but also in light of *how the rules have been applied*. Informality works not only as a means of grey governance, therefore, but of governmentality, fostering the subjectivities and savoirs through which people manage themselves and negotiate power, as the next sections discuss further.

Navigating regulatory opacity: informalities as vectors of capital

It is often implied that informal practices reflect and enact the habitus of specific social groups, especially subaltern ones for whom formal rules and processes can be deeply oppressive. The findings of this book show that the social reality in Rome is far more nuanced. Our survey provides preliminary data indicating that Romans perceive rule-bending in the city to be endemic and barely affected by social class or status, although they do attribute it more frequently to people with wealth than to disadvantaged groups. Even more significantly, they do not generally consider these practices to be the manifestation of unconscious attitudes into which people are socialized and which they absorb and imitate from others in their same social spheres. Rather, respondents appear to view these practices as rational, calculated navigations around institutional obstacles. While they may claim not to participate themselves, and often normatively disapprove of such actions, they understand them to be logical and often unavoidable ways of operating. Thus, if informality is a habitus – a coming together of attitudes, personal experiences, world views, skills and knowledge – it is a generalized one, enacted and reproduced across classes and contexts.

While informalities in Rome are not group- or environment-specific, the case studies demonstrate that there is great variance in how effective or, indeed, how dangerous, such practices may be. We have seen that the possibility of navigating the labyrinthine, movable pieces of the state and its demands is dependent on the resources that actors have available to them. All the forms of capital identified by Bourdieu are essential in seeking to avoid repression but also in stimulating helpful adaptations in the formulation and application of rules. In the context of this book, cultural capital is, in essence, the knowledge of *how to* successfully play with the rule. This is usually an accumulated, temporally based knowledge: it requires sustained observation and direct experience of how elastic a given set of rules may be; how much latitude there is to bend them. It also necessitates knowledge of institutional temporalities, so that future actions of official bodies can be predicted and acted on in an anticipatory way. Clearly, newcomers to a field generally lack such expertise. Intermediaries – official and informal service providers, NGOs, community representatives and go-betweens, but also criminal actors – thus acquire significant power when they have such knowledge. However, cultural capital also simply involves having the right educational background and formal qualifications to be able to engage dialectically with those tasked with interpreting and enforcing the rules. Strong command of the Italian language and the ability to harness the complexity of legal terminology are often crucial resources in negotiating institutional responses to informalities. Since cultural capital takes time to build up and is often predicated on economic capital, the ability of recent migrants and financially disadvantaged groups to accumulate and wield it to advance their interests and perspectives tends to be very limited.

For this reason, social capital has emerged in all the case-study chapters as a fundamental asset for operating and thriving in the spaces between moveable regulatory boundaries. This has manifested in people's ability to construct networks with other residents, with local shopkeepers and street vendors, or to find informal money lenders who can be trusted not to act rapaciously. When actors have established friendly relations with police officers and other street-level bureaucrats, they have accessed useful information, have managed to alter institutional deadlines and modalities of enforcement, or have successfully convinced them to turn blind eyes. In much of the fieldwork, the forbearance of individual officials was clearly founded on an ethics of solidarity, on a desire to find workable solutions when the rule was unhelpful. Nevertheless, the scope for discretionary decisions about what paperwork, what behaviour or situations fitted *closely enough* to the rule proved to be limited. While such institutional agents have the power to interpret, they do not have the power to overhaul. None of their actions have been able to fundamentally change the underlying institutional logics that foster the informalities in the first place. Their mitigating role is, at best, temporary and contingent.

At the other end of the spectrum connecting formality-informality-illegality, social capital has also caused informal practices to become entangled with illegal ones. Allegations of environmental crimes committed by corporate actors and allied public officials, collaborations between some gleaners and illegal waste traders, the dependency of some squatters on illegal housing entrepreneurs, the accusations of illegal advancement of cronies within municipal offices, all point to the fact that where there are spaces for informal practices, these may be exploited for criminal gain. There is no automatic connection between informalities and illegalities, however. Many informalities do not involve clear breaches of any legislation. When they do, their motivations and manifestations are varied. Nevertheless, we can conclude from the empirical cases that they do share a common tendency to flourish when the state protractedly neglects one, or both, of its core functions to protect social welfare and equitably apply the rule of law. Where these provisions are lacking or unbalanced, the unmet needs of parts of the public create opportunities for profit and power exploitable by those who can fill those gaps through illegal services. Repression may eventually occur but when it does, it rarely addresses the needs upon which those exchanges are founded. It thus leaves open the likelihood that new illegal entrepreneurs will step in.

While social networks are critically important for negotiating and operating informally, their mere extension is not enough to ensure the ability to do so safely and acquire legitimacy. Social capital is mediated through symbolic capital – through widespread recognition of agents' prestige, their official status, or their assumed indispensability to social functioning. Groups who have little symbolic power – because they have been systematically labelled as informal or illegal, territorially or racially stigmatized, discredited due to poverty, or pathologized because they are indebted – must all work to temper their symbolic disadvantage. The case studies have traced, for example, how Roma push against their racialization by harnessing discourses of environmental sustainability and ethical trading and consumption models. Differently, but to the same end, many overindebted actors submit to humiliation and their reframing as victims in order to neutralize their stigma. It is in such symbolic struggles that temporal capital acquires its particular significance. It is a means of claiming prestige when other, more conventional avenues are limited. By asserting inherent rights to tenancy, to public space, to visibility, dignity and voice, based on long-term activities or presence in the field, actors have sought to compensate for their deficit of other forms of capital. Temporal capital is thus a currency employed in the hope of achieving safety and stability in contexts where such security is always erasable. However, since there is fierce competition over the limited resources and recognitions for which weak actors bid, the construction of temporal capital has in many cases created new social cleavages and greater denigration of out-groups. This is evident in Corviale, for example, where people label other residents as more illegal, less deserving than themselves. The same mechanism emerges in the invention of a cultural and historic purity among Porta Portese vendors to demand rights for themselves by denying those of more recent arrivals. Consequently, the informal practices and associated discursive moves observed in this book have failed to generate any kind of commoning or alternative form of power-sharing and redistribution. On the contrary, in various cases, actors have employed their own exclusionary tactics to construct or reinforce divisions, thereby exacerbating inequalities.

Indeed, in none of the cases examined here have informal practices been able to significantly alter pre-existing social hierarchies. While the many disappearances of the state have permitted informalities of survival as well as for profit and self-advancement, the state's periods of reappearance have not then integrated the needs-based articulations of informality into formal rules and systems. Two apparent exceptions to this are the formalization of long-term squatters on the fourth floor of Corviale, and the inclusion of protracted street vending as an official criterion in allocating future licences. In both these cases, though, the institutional adaptations have been partial and isolated. They have addressed the practices of selected actors, while leaving others vulnerable to future repression. Crucially, they have done nothing to solve the structural lack of adequate affordable housing in Rome, or the shortage of equitable avenues to trading legally. In short, they have tackled the expressions of informality but not their causes. The power structures of each field have consequently remained largely intact; none of the informal practices examined have been able to subvert them. Thus, while informalities have operated as vectors of capital, enabling actors to mobilize resources to modify their positions, they have not significantly restructured how capital is distributed across each field. The informal practices observed have often been resistant, but they have never become insurgent.

Inhabiting liminal spaces

As we have seen, the dangers of engaging in informal practices are highly relative. People who can choose when and how to bend or ignore the rules are able to tactically modulate their behaviours, returning to formal practices when they anticipate institutional reappearances and crackdowns. Others, though, are stuck in informality, unable to avoid living between the rules. It is here, in these spaces of extreme and often inescapable liminality, that people must activate all the resources they can to control their circumstances and order their lives. It is these protracted survival informalities that tend to be the most visible in public space and thus are those most exposed to the symbolic violence of stigmatization and blame. Consequently, they are those most vulnerable to punitive state action. People inhabiting such situations do not only overtly harness the opportunities for discretionality and negotiation to influence institutional behaviours. They also often seek to encroach on formality, on what is officially permitted, as much as possible in the hope that acquiring some trappings of legality can alleviate the insecurity of their status. Even in these liminal states, though, there are great differences in the potential for action. We have seen how symbolically and politically weak groups, like Roma gleaners and traders, use their knowledge of regulatory flexibilities to adapt their work practices, moving towards goods and sales venues that provide them with greater security by being "less illegal" than other options. Theirs is a quiet encroachment that seeks to avoid dangerously antagonizing the state (Bayat, 2004). On the other hand, Italian street vendors and many people inhabiting public housing informally have enacted bold encroachment (Gillespie, 2017) in the form of very visible resistance, using their numbers and their political weight to force the state to continue its long-term inaction.

All the inhabitants of liminal spaces have been clearly shown to have a sharp knowledge of the rules and of how their own social status affects their potential to exploit regulatory malleability. Their knowledge of past institutional action is never a guarantee that patterns will repeat in the future, however. All liminal actors must consequently remain continuously vigilant, quick to adapt to unpredictable shifts in institutional behaviour. Their strategic timings, the careful actions through which they make themselves partially visible to the state while simultaneously organizing their activities to escape its surveillance, are a manifestation of this caution. It is in this juggling of visibility and invisibility that all the actors examined exert agency over their circumstances, resisting control while enacting practices of citizenship. Although the case studies show that for many "informals" it is difficult to achieve political solidarity and transformation writ large, the ethnographies also highlight the micro-politics of asserting rights and participating in shared activities that work towards improving well-being and a sense of belonging. This emerges in the day-to-day actions of mutual aid and protection among neighbours, vendors, employees, and NGOs in all the fields discussed. In multiple ways, the actors that populate this book stake a claim to the city and emphasize their centrality to urban life: its economy, its services, its social and cultural richness. They thereby engage explicitly with its dominant normative frameworks, contrasting their negative labelling and espousing alternative moral logics that foreground their physical and psychological labour of survival, their self-reliance and financial autonomy, the injustice of institutional rules that deprive them of the protections to which others have a right.

Their practices come together to create form and predictability to counterbalance the inherent stress of being in a liminal condition. Because liminality is about being suspended outside the norm, it is constantly subject to social forces seeking to resolve it, to eliminate its destabilizing ambiguity. Although, as we have seen, most of the liminal conditions in this book have not been overhauled, inhabiting liminal spaces means living with the perpetual threat of upheaval. Whether through illegalization or formalization, the ethnographies have shown that the processes of transitioning to clarity of status, when they occur, are deeply destabilizing. Of course, repression most evidently destroys homes, livelihoods, and community networks, but even when resolution comes in the form of regularization, the process of moving into the post-liminal condition is often alarming and disempowering. Indeed, the various regularization procedures unpacked in the case studies have been experienced by their targets as oppressive in their modalities, weakening their sense of autonomy and control. In response, many of the coping strategies and social systems developed in the liminal spaces have lived on in the post-liminal period. They have remained a set of dispositions enabling actors to make sense of their new conditions and evaluate which elements of informality are worth maintaining in their new reality and which may be worth returning to in full. However, as with all the informalities in this book, periods lived in liminality have not led to transformation: to the production of new institutions, identities, ways of thinking about the city. Even in the case of waste reclaimers whose practices could easily become core to a new approach to sustainable environmental management, their skills and practices remain denigrated, treated as ineluctably outside the city's needs and logics.

We can conclude, therefore, that the mechanisms of informality and its liminal variants in Rome conserve the imbalances of what Loic Wacquant has called the Centaur State (2012). The concept focuses on how deregulation – in our case, the legitimization of irregularities – at the top end of social hierarchies provides opportunities for extraction, while simultaneously effecting domination, constraint, and penalty at the bottom end. In order to survive, many of the disadvantaged actors living in protracted liminality must engage in neoliberal entrepreneurship of the self. They must brand themselves as both productive and deserving, enact self-surveillance and control, compete against others who are dispossessed, hide the poverty and precarity into which they are forced. These informalities in Rome have their origins in economic and political relations that predate neoliberal policies and that often run counter to neoliberal logics (such as Italy's many regulatory and fiscal obstacles to business). Nevertheless, they are ultimately unable to counteract the symbolic and practical violence of a neoliberal system that withdraws state protections and equal rights to services, and then sporadically seeks to reaffirm state supremacy through dramatic and often deeply disempowering interventions.

Recommendations

The multiple types of informal manoeuvres covered in this book – ranging from the voluntary, self-advancing varieties to the forced, survival-based ones – have been fostered by local institutions that have tended to prioritize short-term political interests over constructing transparent systems of resource allocation and management for the long term. Rome is a rentier city, perhaps even a colonial one in its extractive logics (Tocci, 2015), where power relations and vested interests have become crystallized over decades. Its political history is one in which social mobility and equality have rarely been a sustained policy focus beyond electoral promises. Frequent political obeisance to the demands of historical landowning classes and corporations, parastate and religious institutions, and the lobby power of particular professions have combined with decades of financial mismanagement. The city has repeatedly demonstrated great difficulty in planning spending for the long term, tending to maintain expensive stopgap practices rather than moving towards financial efficiency. Consequently, the many structural gaps in its service provision remain unaddressed. To build more public housing and enforce its fair distribution, develop environmentally sustainable waste infrastructure, establish progressive systems and locations for street trade, create safe accessible credit mechanisms for small-scale borrowers, would all require heavy investment in the present and for the future. The long-established preference for short-term outlays aiming to defuse residents' immediate frustrations and garner support at the next elections mean that the structural inadequacies upon which the inequalities studied in this book are based continue. Yet, as Causi (2021) has demonstrated in a close reading of the city's finances, the municipality does not lack the necessary funds to invest in socially equitable urban management. What is missing is a governance strategy for doing so.

Recent years have seen urban scholars and commentators become increasingly vocal in their critiques of the city's numerous governance dysfunctionalities and their direct effects on escalating social inequalities (Berdini & Nalbone, 2011; Causi, 2018; D'Albergo & Moini, 2015; De Lucia & Erbani, 2016; Erbani, 2013; Lelo et al., 2019; Tocci, 2020; Violante, 2008). Many of them have also advanced a wide range of insightful recommendations for developing a sustainable approach to governing the capital that goes beyond the (largely unsuccessful) focus on economic growth and consumption of the last three decades. In particular, a network of scholars has come together under the name Romaricercaroma to mobilize their data and analysis to offer concrete and achievable policy proposals for a more socially equitable future. It would be superfluous to repeat their extensive and complex suggestions for reforming crucial pillars of Rome's public management system (Romaricercaroma, 2021a, 2021b, 2021c, 2021d). Instead, it is worth adding a few caveats and integrations that spring directly from the case studies discussed here and the broader debates on urban informalities.

One common recommendation is that the city authorities valorize and take note of the knowledge and initiatives generated by Rome's vast galaxy of civil society and self-help movements. Indeed, there is a need for much deeper participatory governance strategies than currently exist. However, two risks must be avoided in this process. First, it is essential that these not be co-opted into a further neoliberal outsourcing of governance and social care to what is often a precarious and under-paid labour-force in the third sector. Grassroots work cannot serve to further absolve the state from its constitutionally mandated responsibility to create systems for guaranteeing basic services, welfare, and rights to all. Second, many of the most disadvantaged groups studied in this book do not participate in social movements and generally lack any direct voice in the governance consultations that do exist. At best, they are spoken for by NGOs that do not always convey their interests as they would. As so much of the literature on informal practices around the world shows, it is only when informal actors' own knowledge and priorities are brought into policy planning that long-term inclusion and empowerment can be achieved. Rome needs to learn from the wealth of successful initiatives in other continents that engage "informals" in developing micro-credit provisions for at-risk-businesses, for upgrading informal housing in ways that work for its residents, for integrating waste reclaimers in environmental management systems, for making the streets a place of fair and safe employment.

As Romaricercaroma (2021c) underlines, the city has a wealth of resources that are currently under-exploited. Rome could make some first steps towards housing justice, for example, by raising taxes on land use, empty property, and tourist accommodation. It could invest funds on recovering the approximately 16% of public property that is currently unused, as well as creating incentives for the social use of abandoned private buildings. Similar recovery of unoccupied facilities and spaces could be employed for waste regeneration and vending locations for street traders. More generally, the city needs to remove the multitude of bureaucratic obstacles that make collective initiatives logistically difficult and that obstruct the efficient mapping of needs and the development of appropriate social infrastructures (Romaricercaroma, 2021d). This requires a paradigm shift that moves away from the current prioritization of private wellbeing to that of the collective good; that places policies of protection for the socially weak and the redistribution of resources at the centre of its agenda beyond mere slogans.

Many of the recommendations currently emerging – while well conceived and necessary – appear based on the assumption that if the policies are activated by future city administrations, their good intentions will naturally trickle down to the actions of individual front-line bureaucrats. As we have seen, though, informal practices have built up over time and have become entrenched methods of getting things done. Moreover, procedural manoeuvres and selective implementations often serve to protect vested interests. The temporal slowness and discretional behaviours that have become the norm in many public services are unlikely to be easily uprooted: they require a concerted policy of their own. I would argue that a restructuring of rules and processes needs to be accompanied by strict deadlines for responding to users and allocating services. These need to be supported by systematic training and awareness-raising campaigns that inform public officials of the structural inequalities that bureaucratic informalities generate. As we saw in the survey, there appears to be little awareness among Romans that the bending of rules may solve problems in the short term but aggravates the inaccessibility of services to all – especially those who need them most – in the long term. If we want to resolve the feelings of legal alienation identified in our data, Rome's public institutions need to move towards the systematic creation of a *representative* bureaucracy (Gouldner, 1954). The values and goals espoused by policy-planners need to be shared and implemented by functionaries at all institutional levels and this citizen-centred ethos needs to be clearly communicated to service users. Only then can the frustrations conveyed in our survey gradually begin to retreat.

The accessibility of core rights and services cannot be left only to good intentions. There needs to be effective sanctioning of public service entities when they do not resolve obstacles to fair, speedy, and transparent provision. As various chapters have shown, the judiciary has stepped in numerous times to investigate officials who have broken the law or abused their power. However, there also need to be mechanisms that enable residents to make complaints about inadequate services and ensure that these will not simply be ignored. Italy arguably needs to expand its institutional frameworks to create an independent body for investigating and sanctioning local government dis-services, along the lines of the UK's Local Government and Social Care Ombudsman. Moreover, it is now technically possible to initiate class action lawsuits against public service providers in Italy. This legislative reform is still very recent (introduced with Legge 12 aprile 2019, n. 31 and in effect since November 2020), making it too early to assess its potential versatility as a tool for improving public sector accountability. In any case, it is important that urban justice movements in Italy begin to make more creative use of the law to demand greater protections and rights. An example of critical legal engineering initiated in Berlin (Kusiak, 2021; see also Vasudevan, 2021) provides an excellent illustration of how legal technologies can be harnessed not to navigate around socially unjust rules, but to force radical policy change for the long run.

References

Altrock, U. (2016). Conceptualising informality: Some thoughts on the way towards generalization. In C. McFarlane & M. Waibel (eds), *Urban informalities: Reflections on the formal and informal* (pp. 171–193). Routledge. https://doi.org/10.4324/9781315548814.

Bayat, A. (2004). Globalization and the politics of the informals in the Global South. In A. Roy & N. AlSayyad (eds), *Urban informality: Transnational perspectives from the Middle East, Latin America, and South Asia*, pp. 64–80. Lexington Books.

Berdini, P., & Nalbone, D. (2011). *Le mani sulla città: Da Veltroni ad Alemanno storia di una capitale in vendita*. Alegre.

Causi M. (2018). *SOS Roma: La crisi della capitale. Da dove viene, come uscirne*. Armando Editore.

Causi, M. (2021). Il bilancio del Comune di Roma e la città. *Romaricercaroma*. www.ricercaroma.it/wp-content/uploads/2021/03/Causi_bilancio-comunale-e-citta%CC%80.pdf.

Chiodelli, F., & Moroni, S. (2014). The complex nexus between informality and the law: Reconsidering unauthorised settlements in light of the concept of nomotropism. *Geoforum*, 51, 161–169. https://doi.org/10.1016/j.geoforum.2013.11.004.

D'Albergo, E., & Moini, G. (2015). *Il regime dell'Urbe: Politica, economia e potere a Roma*. Carocci.

De Lucia, V., & Erbani, F. (2016). *Roma disfatta: Perché la capitale non è più una città e cosa fare per ridarle una dimensione pubblica*. Castelvecchi.

Erbani, F. (2013). *Roma: Il tramonto della città pubblica*. Editori Laterza.

Gillespie, T. (2017). From quiet to bold encroachment: Contesting dispossession in Accra's informal sector. *Urban Geography*, 38(7), 974–992. https://doi.org/10.1080/02723638.2016.1191792.

Gouldner, A. W. (1954). *Patterns of industrial bureaucracy.* Free Press.
Kusiak, J. (2021). Trespassing on the law: Critical legal engineering as a strategy for action research. *Area.* doi:10.1111/area.12700.
Lelo, K., Monni, S., & Tomassi, F. (2019). *Le mappe della disuguaglianza: Una geografia sociale metropolitana.* Donzelli.
Romaricercaroma. (2021a). *Un manifesto per Roma. Governo: spazi di democrazia e trasformazioni istituzionali.* www.ricercaroma.it/wp-content/uploads/2021/06/Roma-Ricerca-Roma-Governo.-Spazi-di-democrazia-e-trasformazioni-istituzionali.pdf.
Romaricercaroma. (2021b). Abitare di qualità a Roma. Per un rilancio dell'azione "pubblica". www.ricercaroma.it/wp-content/uploads/2021/02/Roma-Ricerca-Roma-Abitare-1-2.pdf.
Romaricercaroma. (2021c). Un manifesto per Roma. Il diritto a una città giusta. Percorsi per uscire dalla crisi del valore. www.ricercaroma.it/wp-content/uploads/2021/04/Roma-Ricerca-Roma-Il-diritto-a-una-citta%CC%80-giusta.pdf.
Romaricercaroma. (2021d). Un manifesto per Roma. Welfare, sanità e politiche sociali a Roma. Rilanciare gli investimenti e liberare il potenziale di innovazione delle reti sociali. www.ricercaroma.it/wp-content/uploads/2021/04/Roma-Ricerca-Roma-Welfare-sanita%CC%80-e-politiche-sociali-1-1.pdf.
Robinson, J. (2005). *Ordinary cities.* Routledge. doi:10.4324/9780203506554.
Tocci, W. (2015). *Non si piange su una città colonial: Note sulla politica romana.* goWare.
Tocci, W. (2020). *Roma come se: Alla ricerca del futuro per la capitale.* Donzelli.
Tucker, J. L., & Devlin, R. T. (2019). Uncertainty and the governance of street vending: A critical comparison across the North/South divide. *International Journal of Urban and Regional Research*, 43(3), 460–475. doi:10.1111/1468-2427.12792.
Vasudevan, A. (2021). Between illegality and insurgency: Notes on the history of urban informality in the Global North. [Conference presentation]. Houses of Cards? The Rules and Institutions of Housing Illegality in Western Countries. Cambridge University. Online, 19–21 April. [Video]. Youtube. https://youtu.be/UXKhgujsoqE.
Violante, A. (2008). *La metropoli spezzata: Sviluppo urbano di una città mediterranea.* Francoangeli.
Wacquant, L. (2012). Three steps to a historical anthropology of actually existing neoliberalism. *Social Anthropology*, 20(1), 66–79. doi:10.1111/j.1469-8676.2011.00189.x.

Index

Page numbers in **bold** refer to figures, page numbers in *italic* refer to tables.

FSC
www.fsc.org
MIX
Papier | Fördert
gute Waldnutzung
FSC® C083411

Kolibri 360 GmbH
Ferdinand-Jühlke-Straße 7
99095 Erfurt, Deutschland
produktsicherheit@kolibri360.de